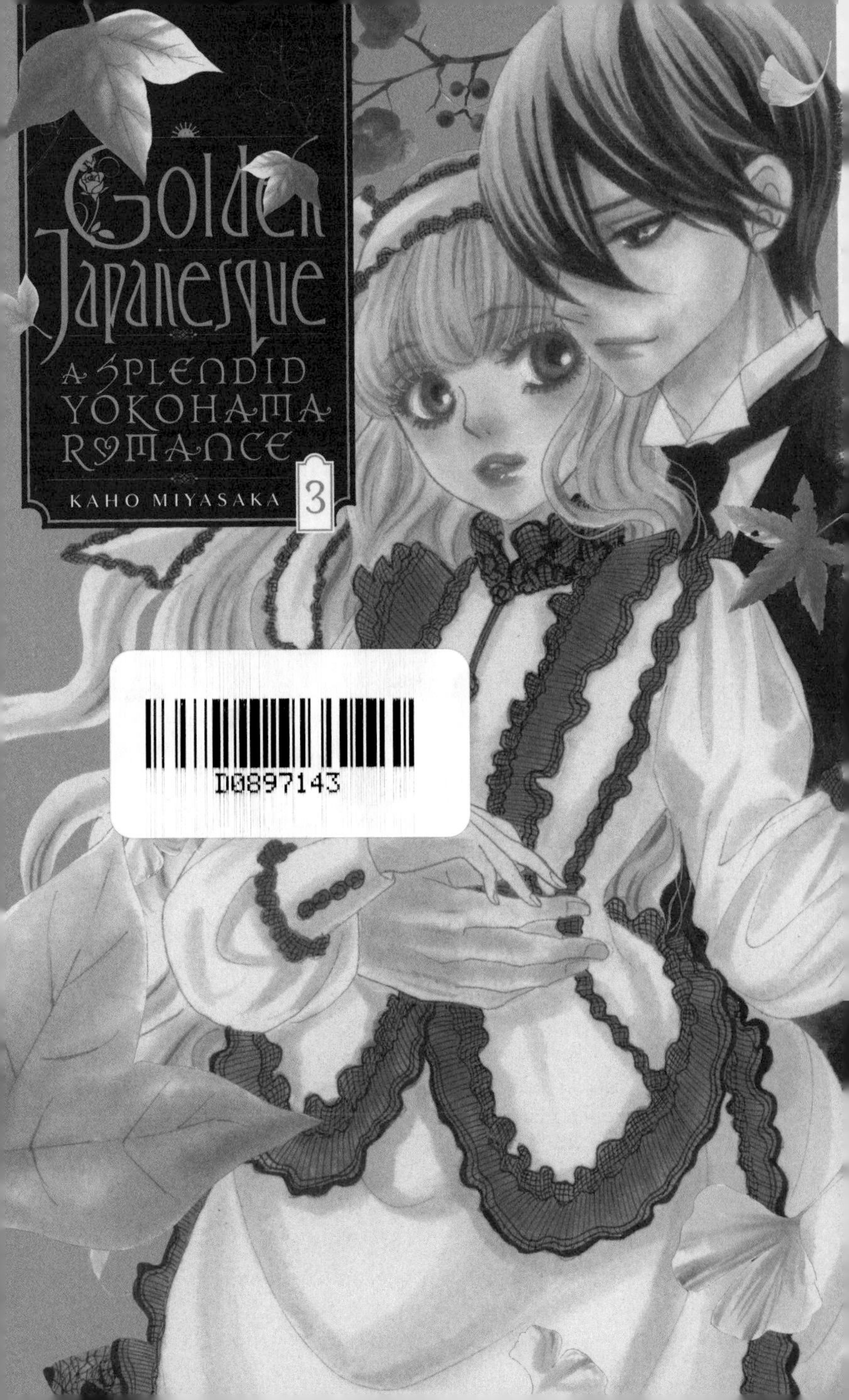
Golden Japanesque
A Splendid Yokohama Romance
Kaho Miyasaka
3

Golden Japanesque
A SPLENDID YOKOHAMA ROMANCE

3

Contents

Story

◆ The port town of Yokohama, during the Meiji era—
Maria inherited blond hair and blue eyes from her
father, and her mother strictly trained her to hide
them so she wouldn't be the target of discrimination.

◆ One day, she met Rintarou, the son of the
distinguished family that employed her mother.
Although Maria hated him at first, every time they met,
she found herself more and more drawn to him.

◆ At a party given by the Mayuzumis, Yuriko,
a young lady from a respectable family, insulted Maria
and her mother. However, Maria objected in grand style,
then left the party with Rintarou. The very next day,
Rintarou invited her out on a date...!!

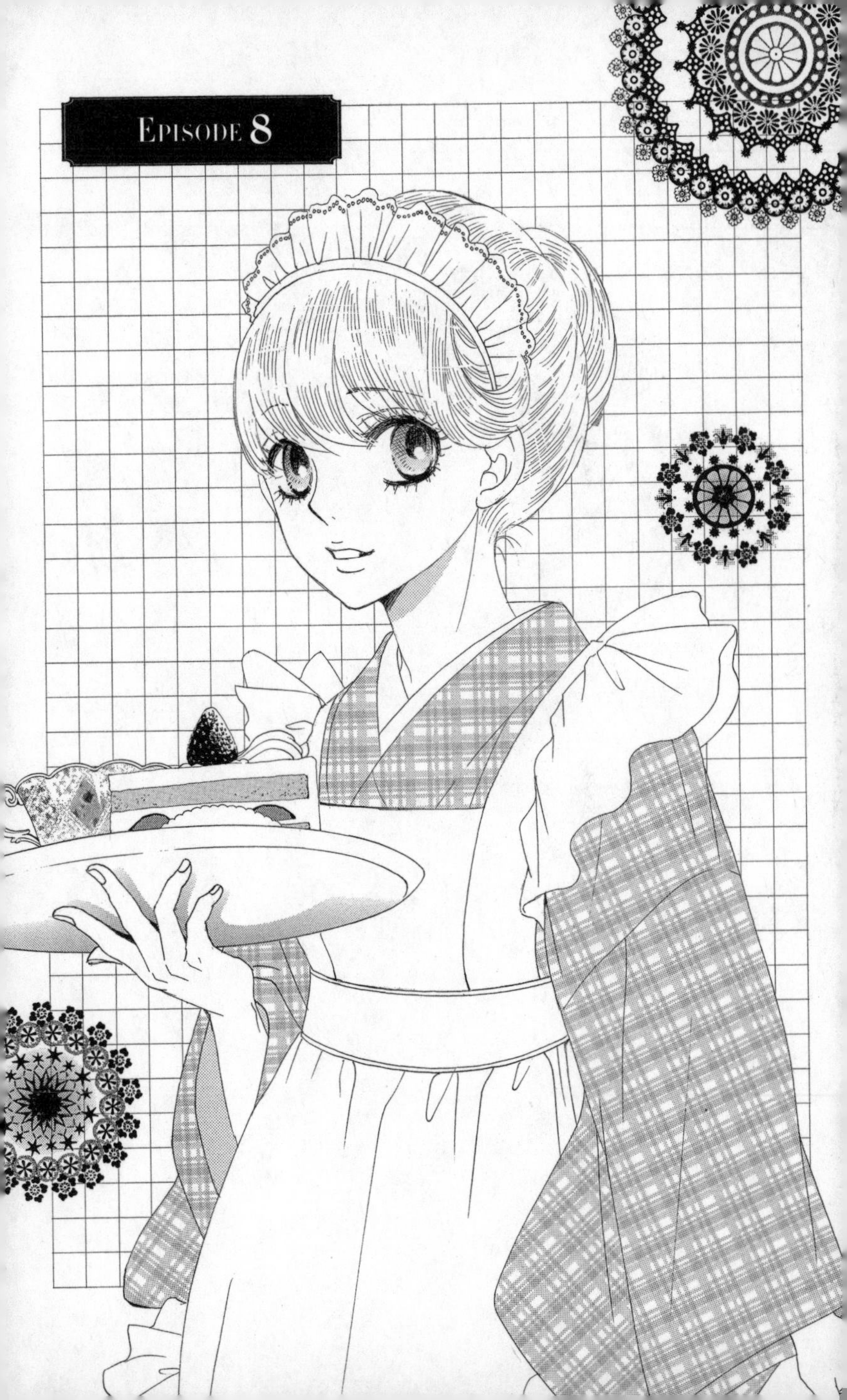
EPISODE 8

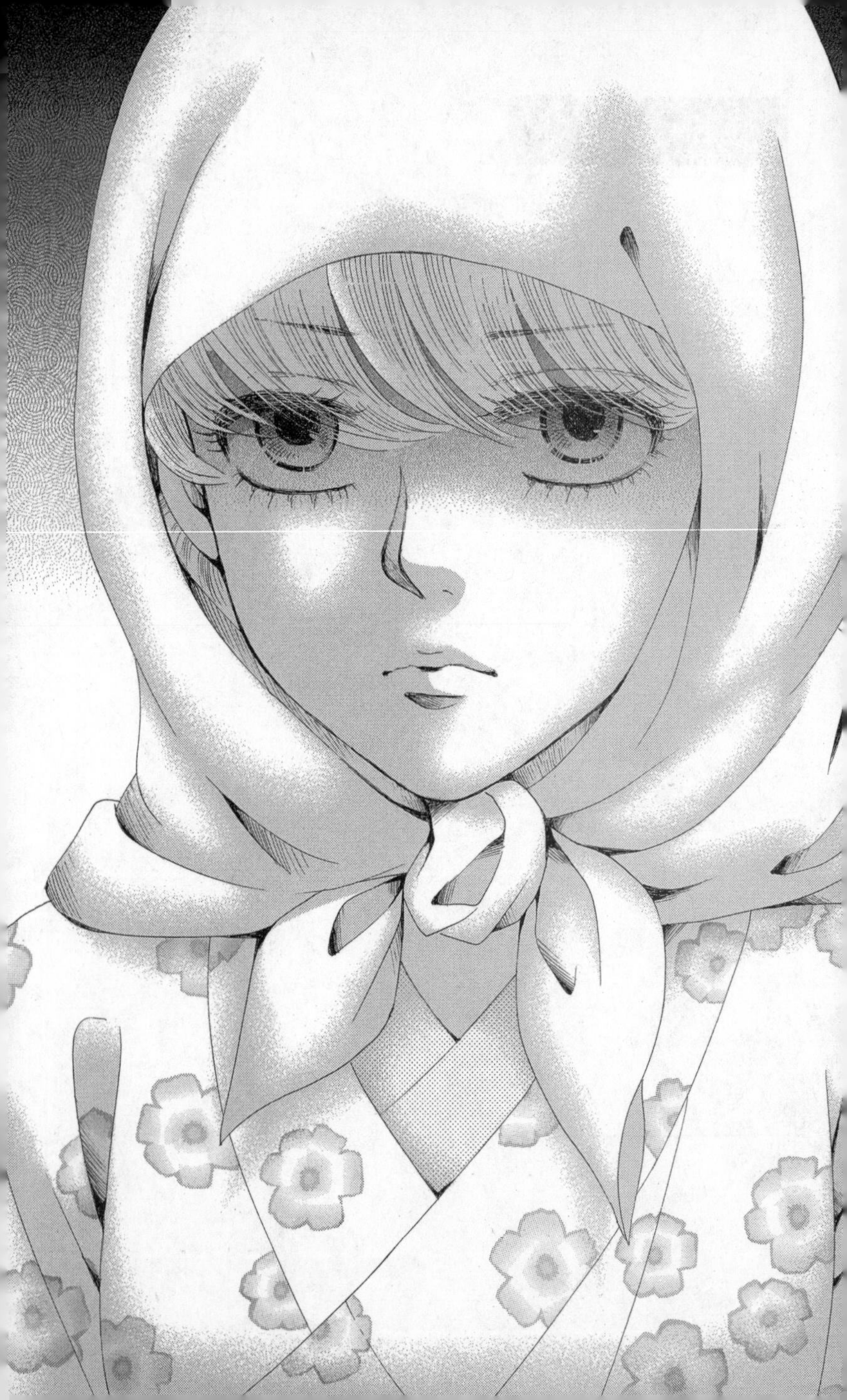

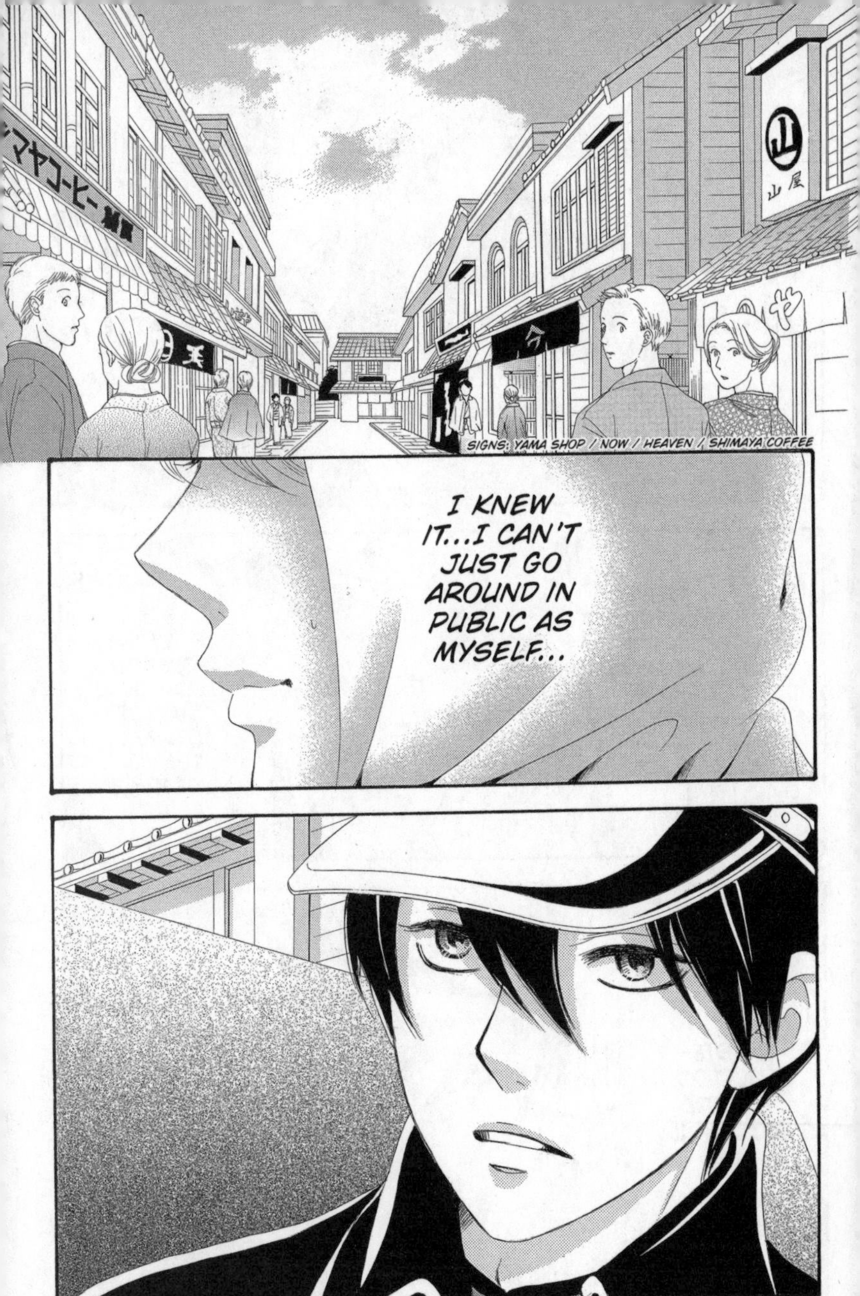
SIGNS: YAMA SHOP / NOW / HEAVEN / SHIMAYA COFFEE
I KNEW IT...I CAN'T JUST GO AROUND IN PUBLIC AS MYSELF...

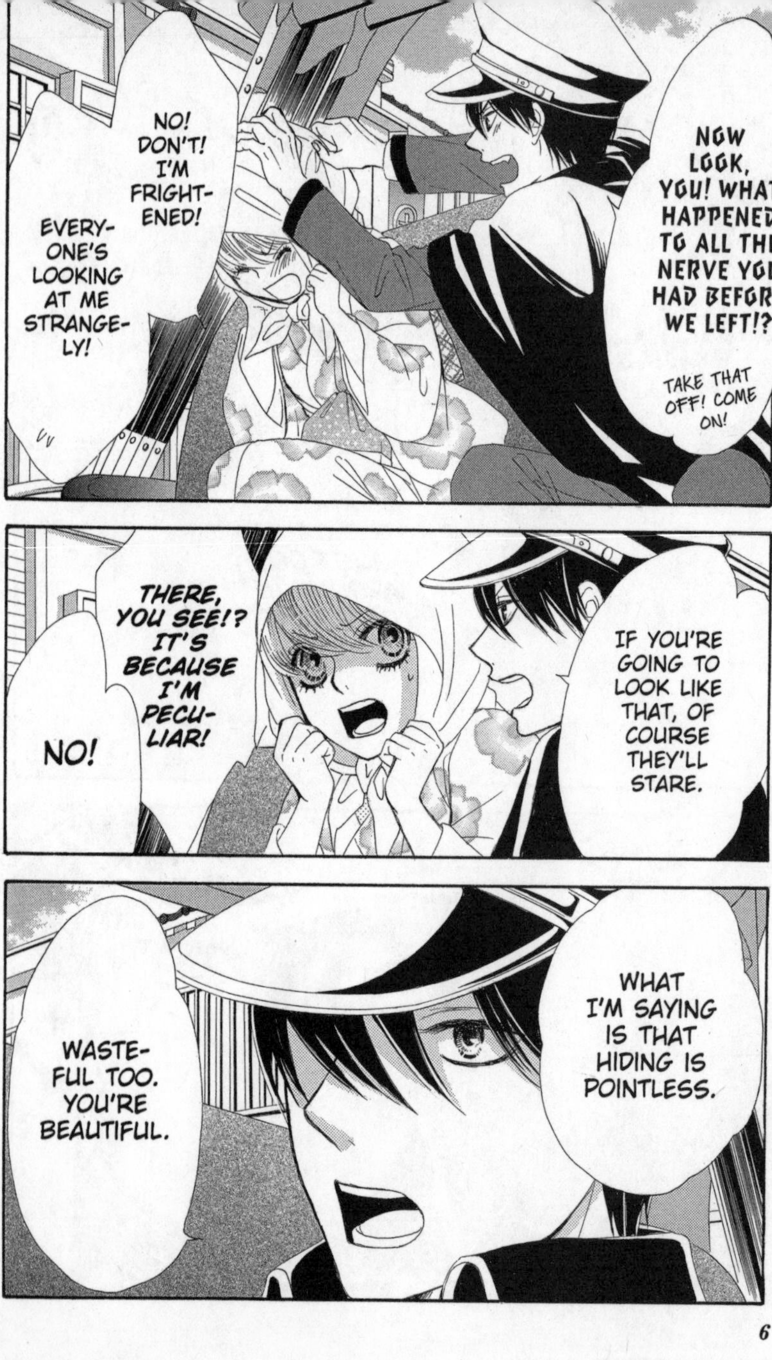
NOW LOOK, YOU! WHAT HAPPENED TO ALL THE NERVE YOU HAD BEFORE WE LEFT!?
TAKE THAT OFF! COME ON!
NO! DON'T! I'M FRIGHTENED!
EVERYONE'S LOOKING AT ME STRANGELY!
IF YOU'RE GOING TO LOOK LIKE THAT, OF COURSE THEY'LL STARE.
THERE, YOU SEE!? IT'S BECAUSE I'M PECULIAR!
NO!
WHAT I'M SAYING IS THAT HIDING IS POINTLESS.
WASTEFUL TOO. YOU'RE BEAUTIFUL.

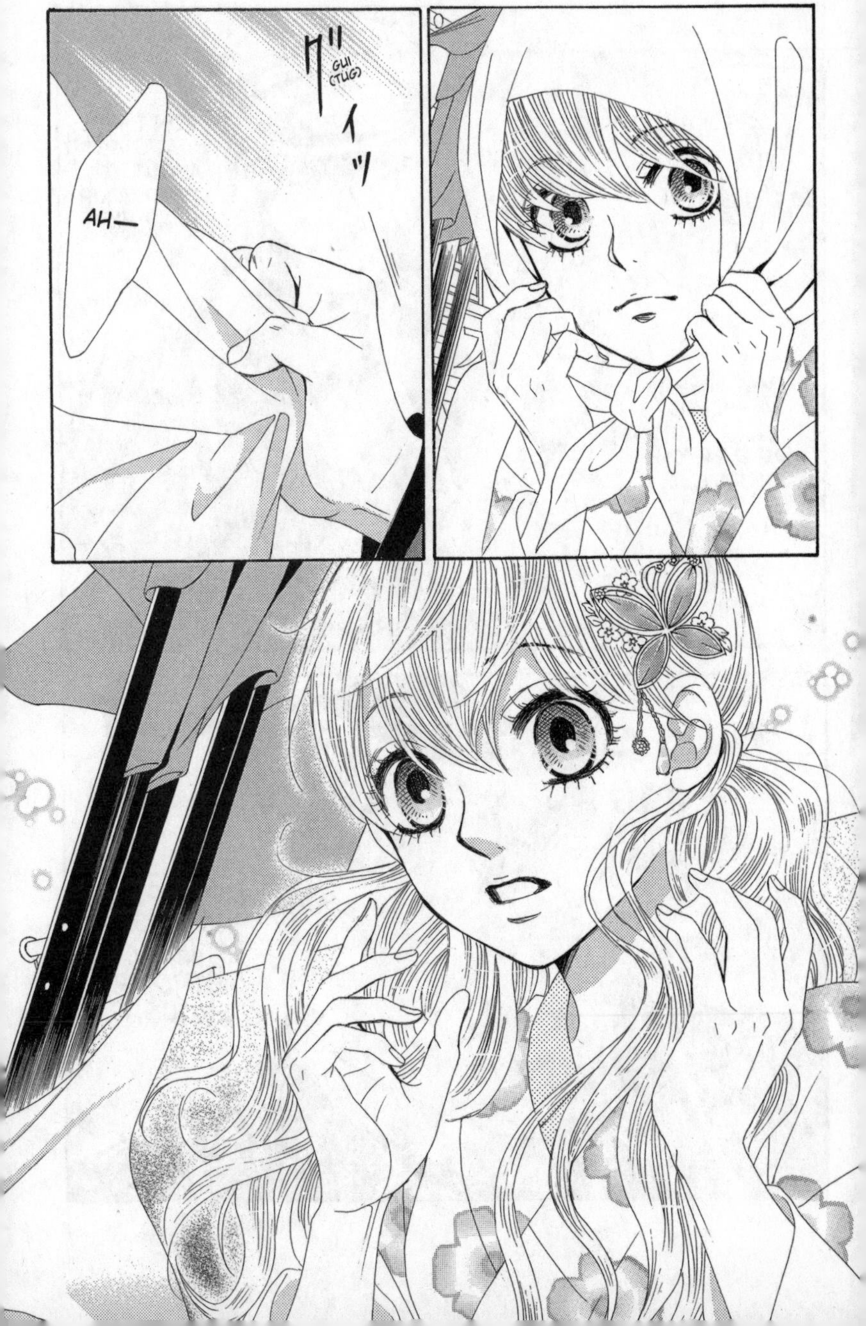
グイッ
GUI (TUG)
AH—

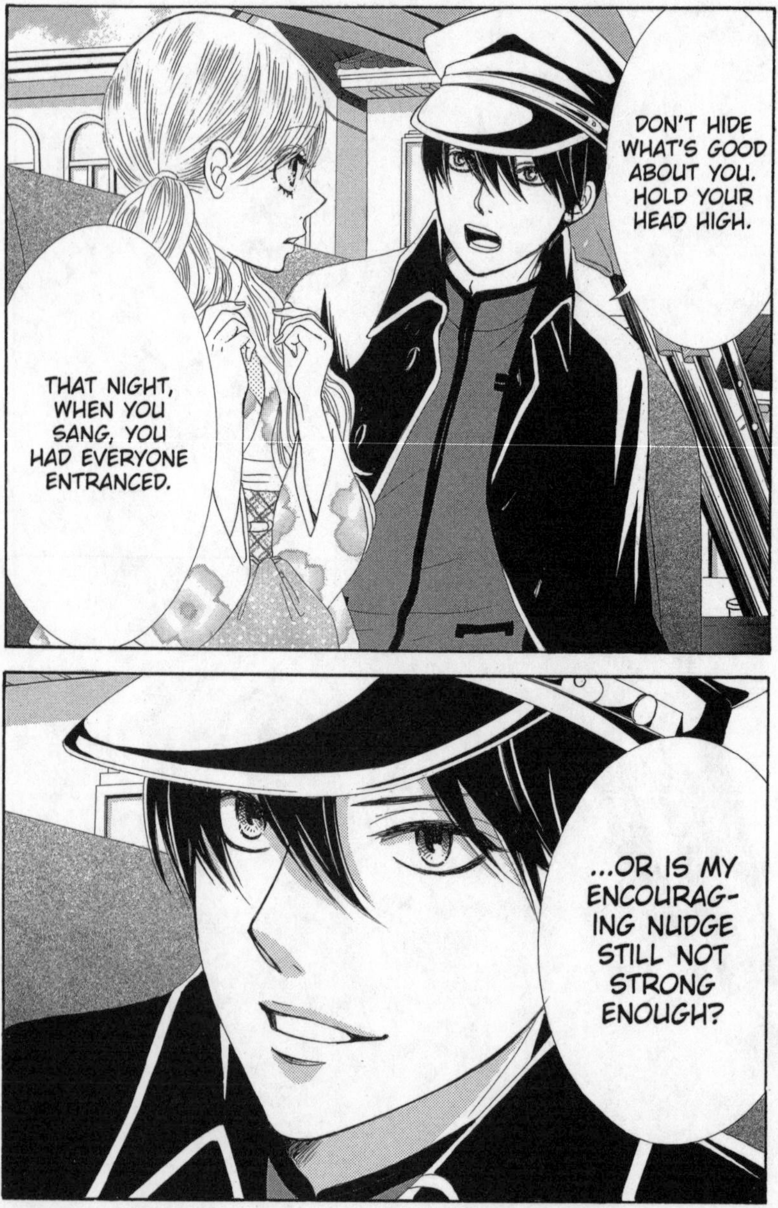
DON'T HIDE WHAT'S GOOD ABOUT YOU. HOLD YOUR HEAD HIGH.
THAT NIGHT, WHEN YOU SANG, YOU HAD EVERYONE ENTRANCED.
...OR IS MY ENCOURAG-ING NUDGE STILL NOT STRONG ENOUGH?

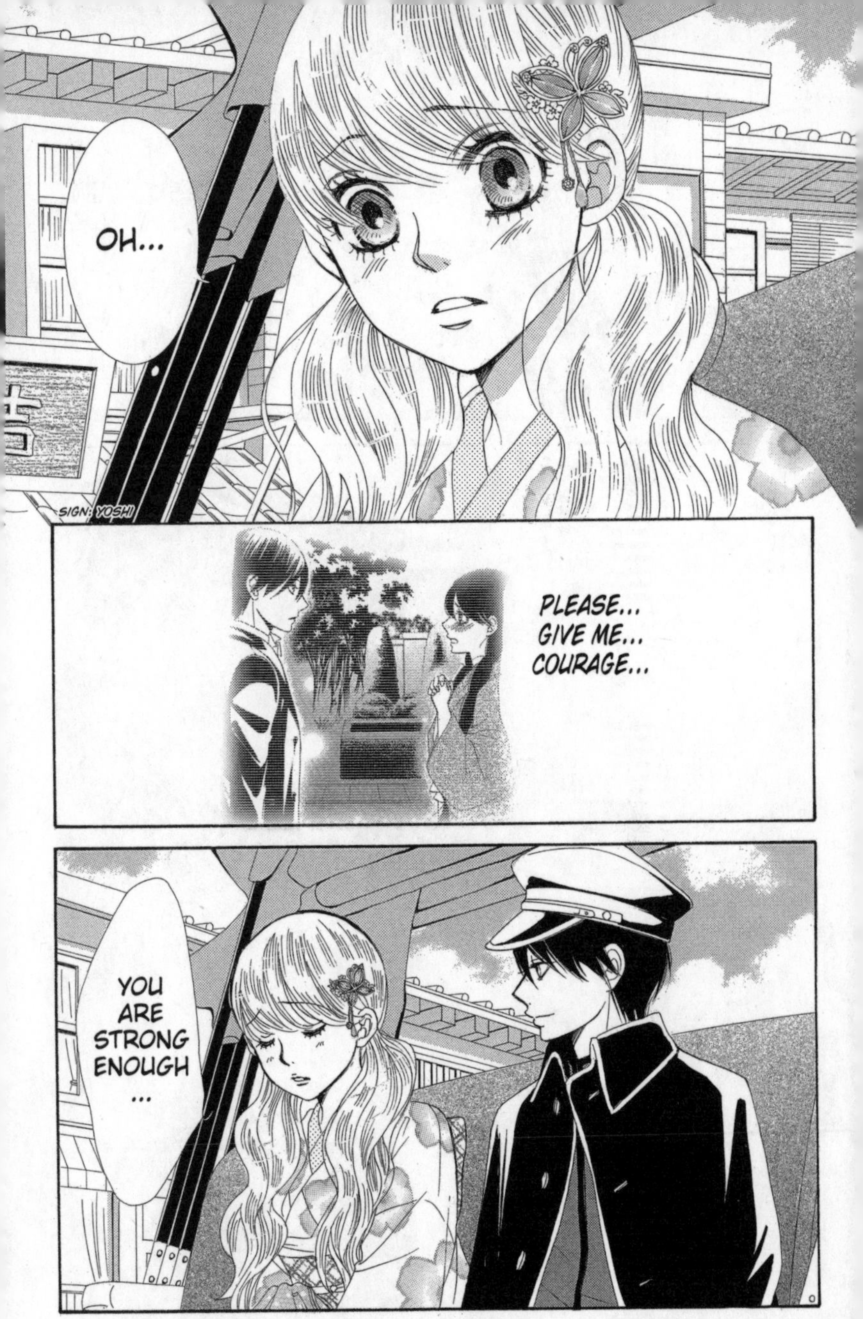
OH...
SIGN: YOSHI
PLEASE... GIVE ME... COURAGE...
YOU ARE STRONG ENOUGH ...

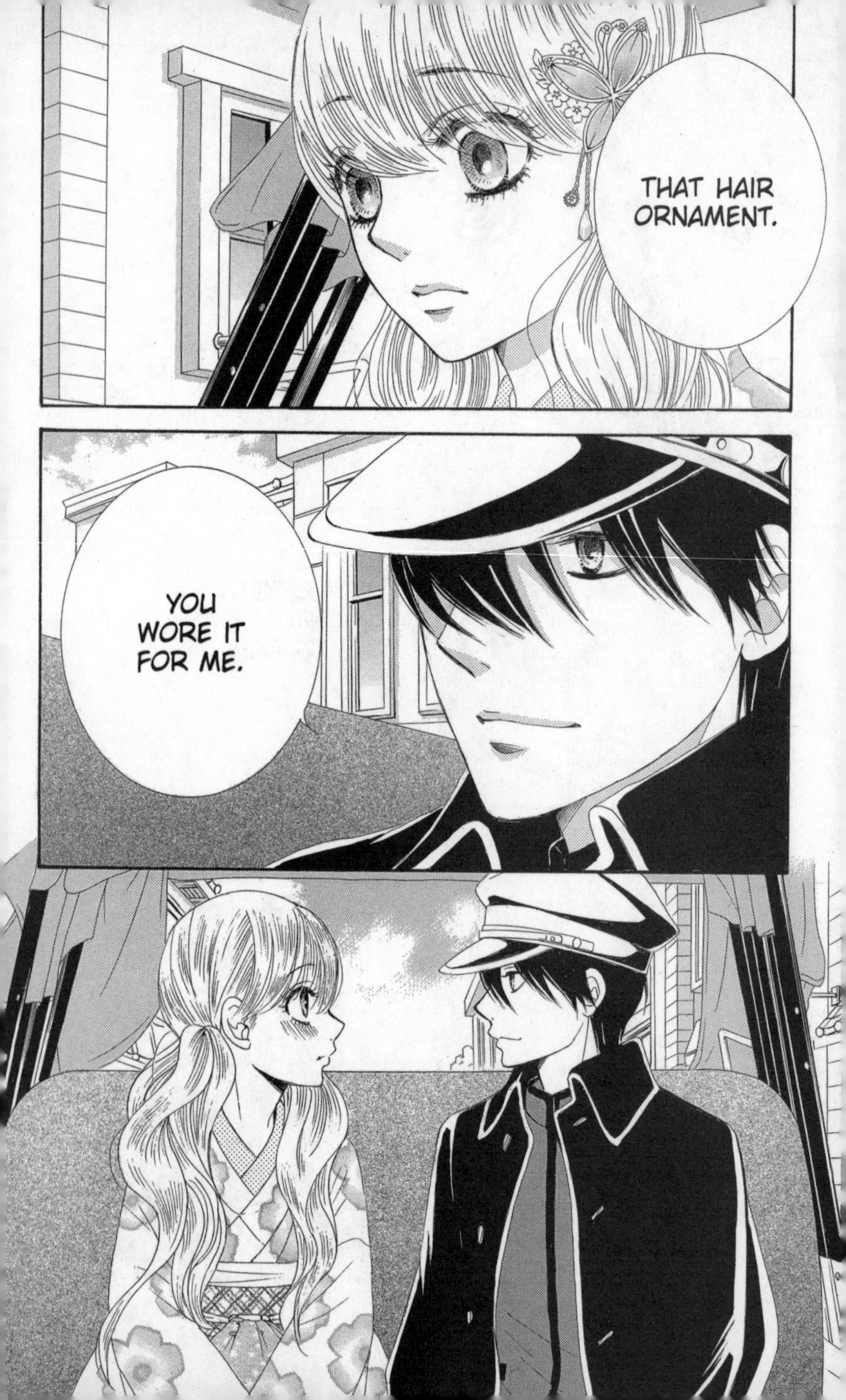
THAT HAIR ORNAMENT.
YOU WORE IT FOR ME.

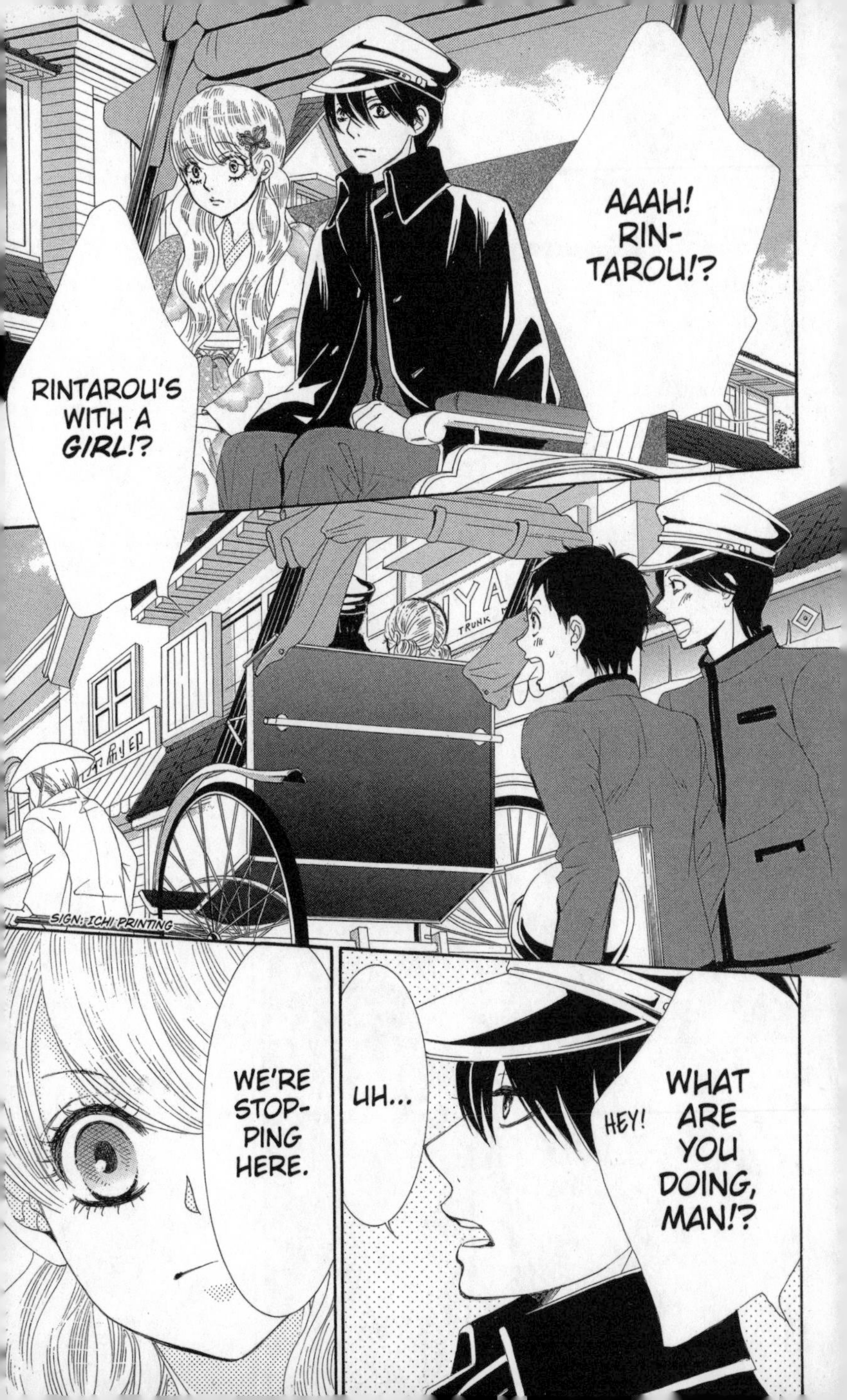
AAAH! RIN-TAROU!?
RINTAROU'S WITH A GIRL!?
TRUNK
SIGN: ICHI PRINTING
HEY!
WHAT ARE YOU DOING, MAN!?
UH...
WE'RE STOP-PING HERE.

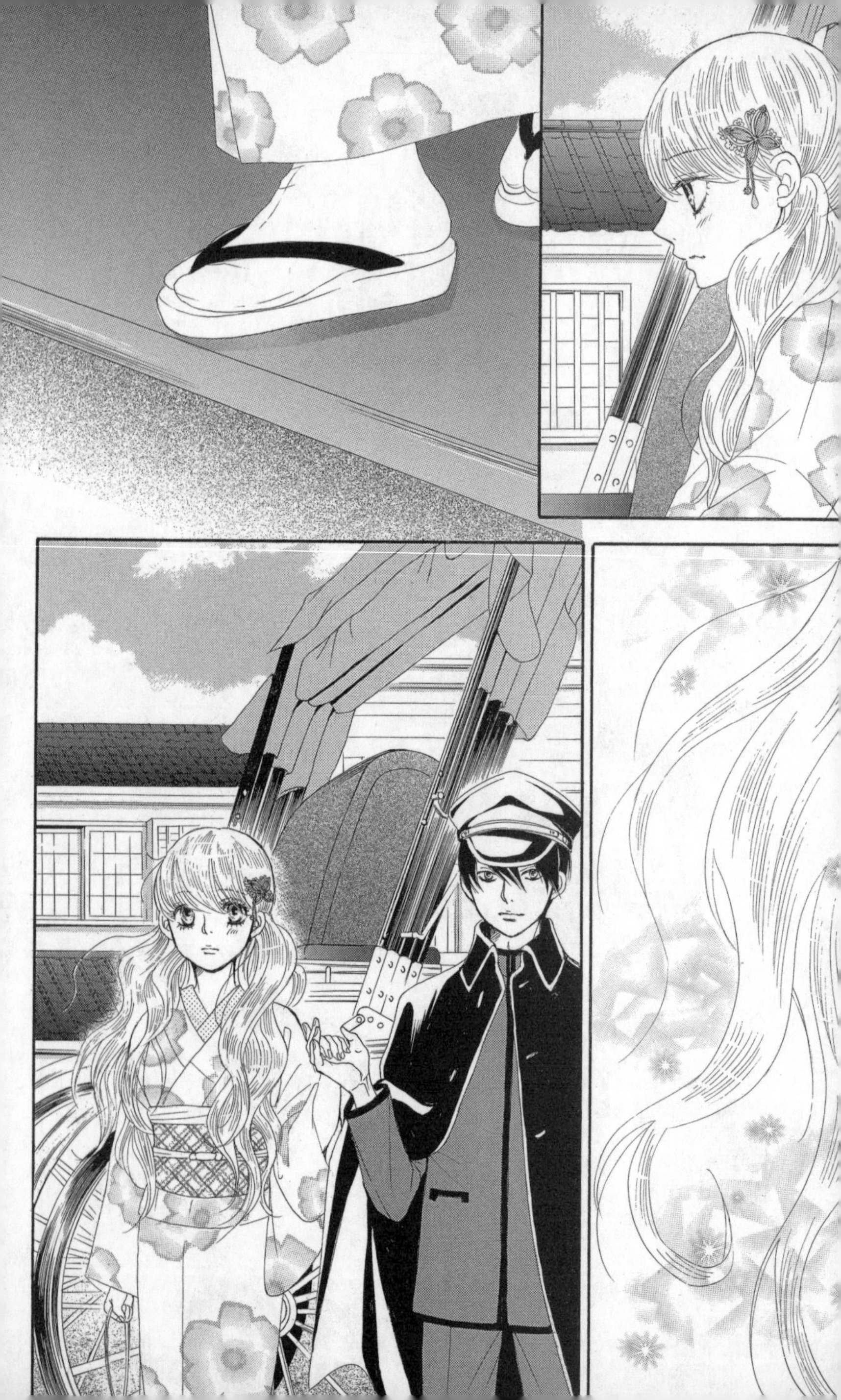

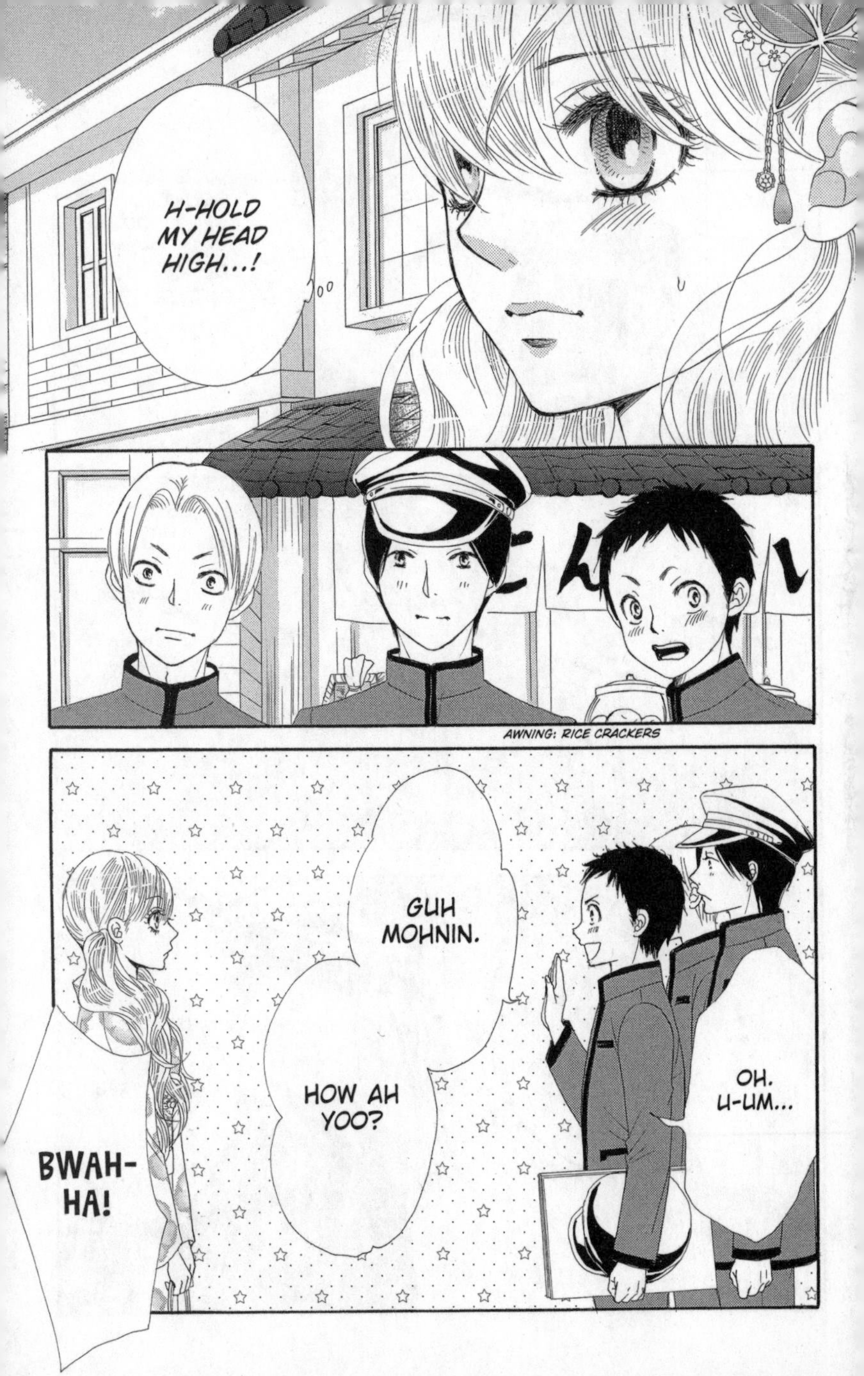
H-HOLD MY HEAD HIGH...!
AWNING: RICE CRACKERS
GUH MOHNIN.
HOW AH YOO?
OH. U-UM...
BWAH-HA!

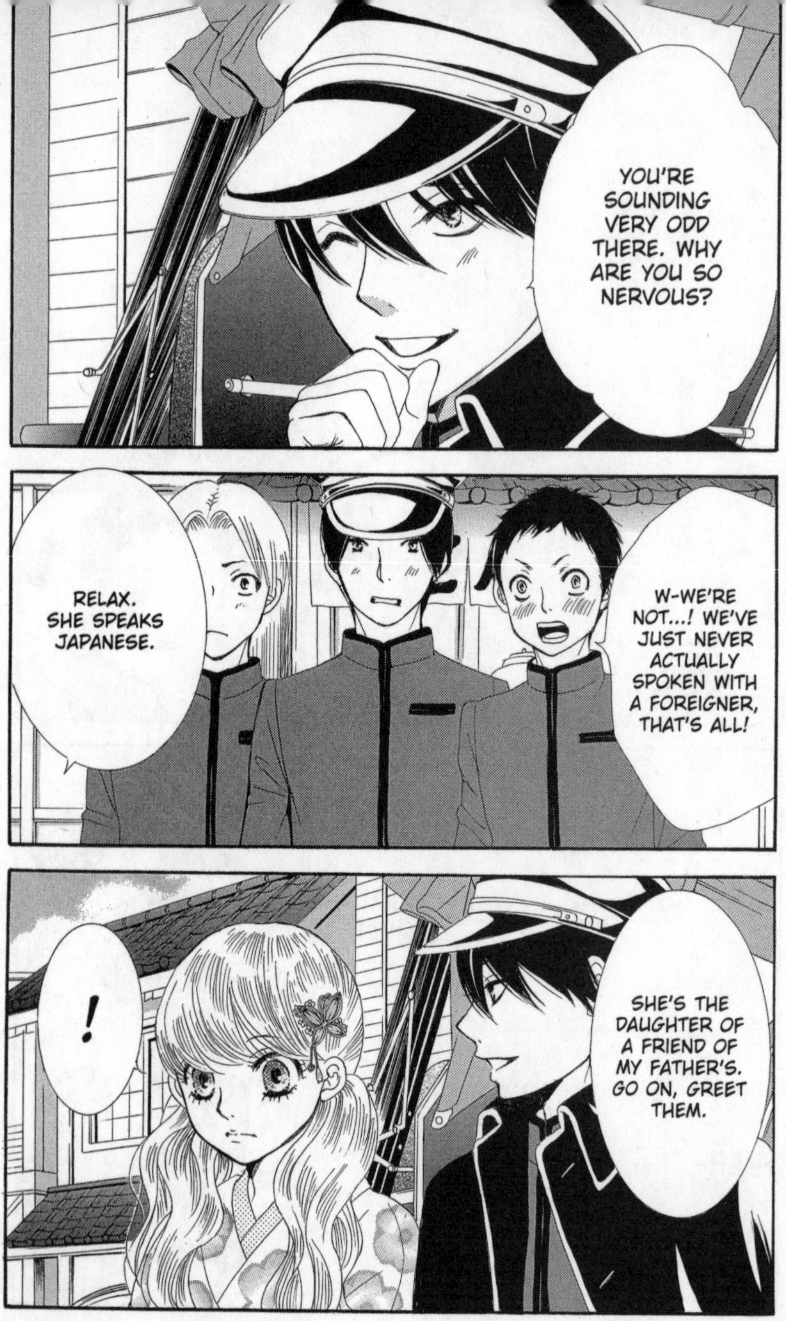
YOU'RE SOUNDING VERY ODD THERE. WHY ARE YOU SO NERVOUS?
W-WE'RE NOT...! WE'VE JUST NEVER ACTUALLY SPOKEN WITH A FOREIGNER, THAT'S ALL!
RELAX. SHE SPEAKS JAPANESE.
SHE'S THE DAUGHTER OF A FRIEND OF MY FATHER'S. GO ON, GREET THEM.
!

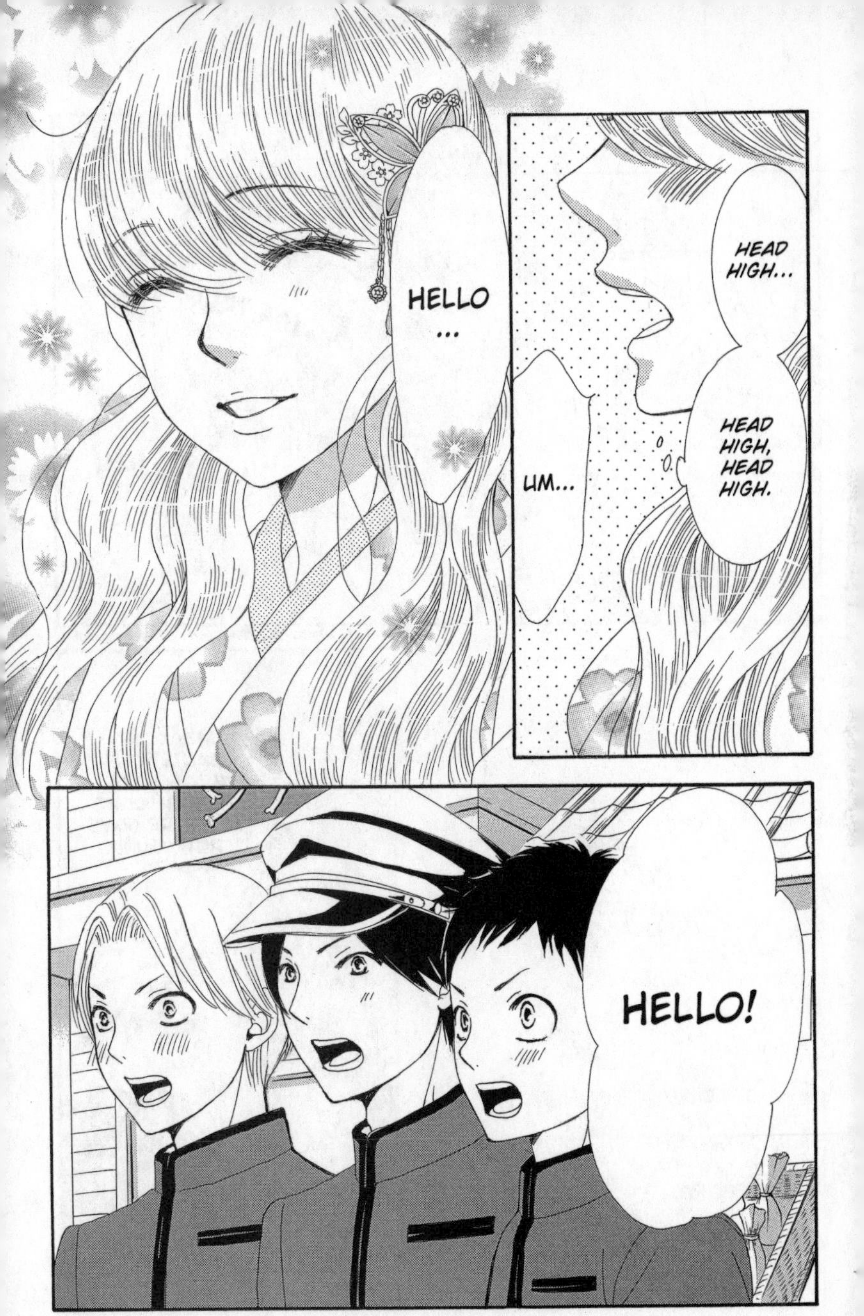
HEAD HIGH...
HEAD HIGH, HEAD HIGH.
UM...
HELLO ...
HELLO!

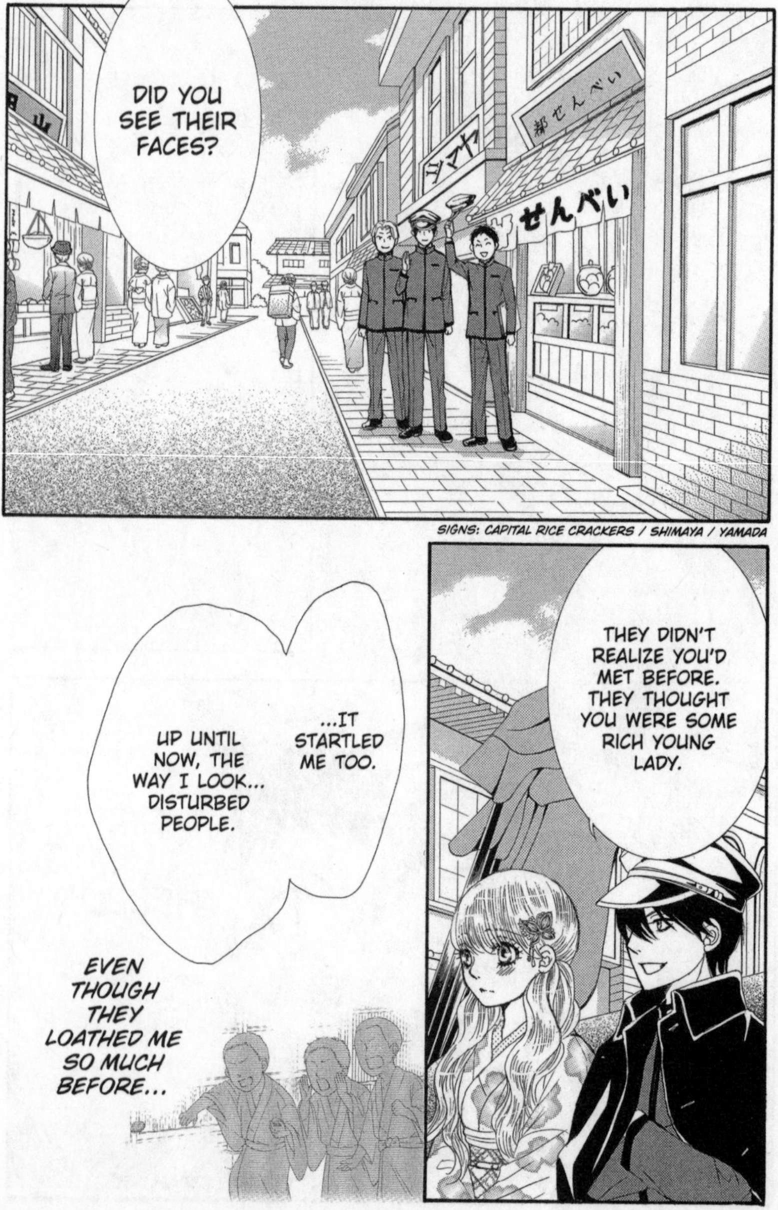
DID YOU SEE THEIR FACES?
都せんべい
シマヤ
せんべい
SIGNS: CAPITAL RICE CRACKERS / SHIMAYA / YAMADA
THEY DIDN'T REALIZE YOU'D MET BEFORE. THEY THOUGHT YOU WERE SOME RICH YOUNG LADY.
...IT STARTLED ME TOO.
UP UNTIL NOW, THE WAY I LOOK... DISTURBED PEOPLE.
EVEN THOUGH THEY LOATHED ME SO MUCH BEFORE...

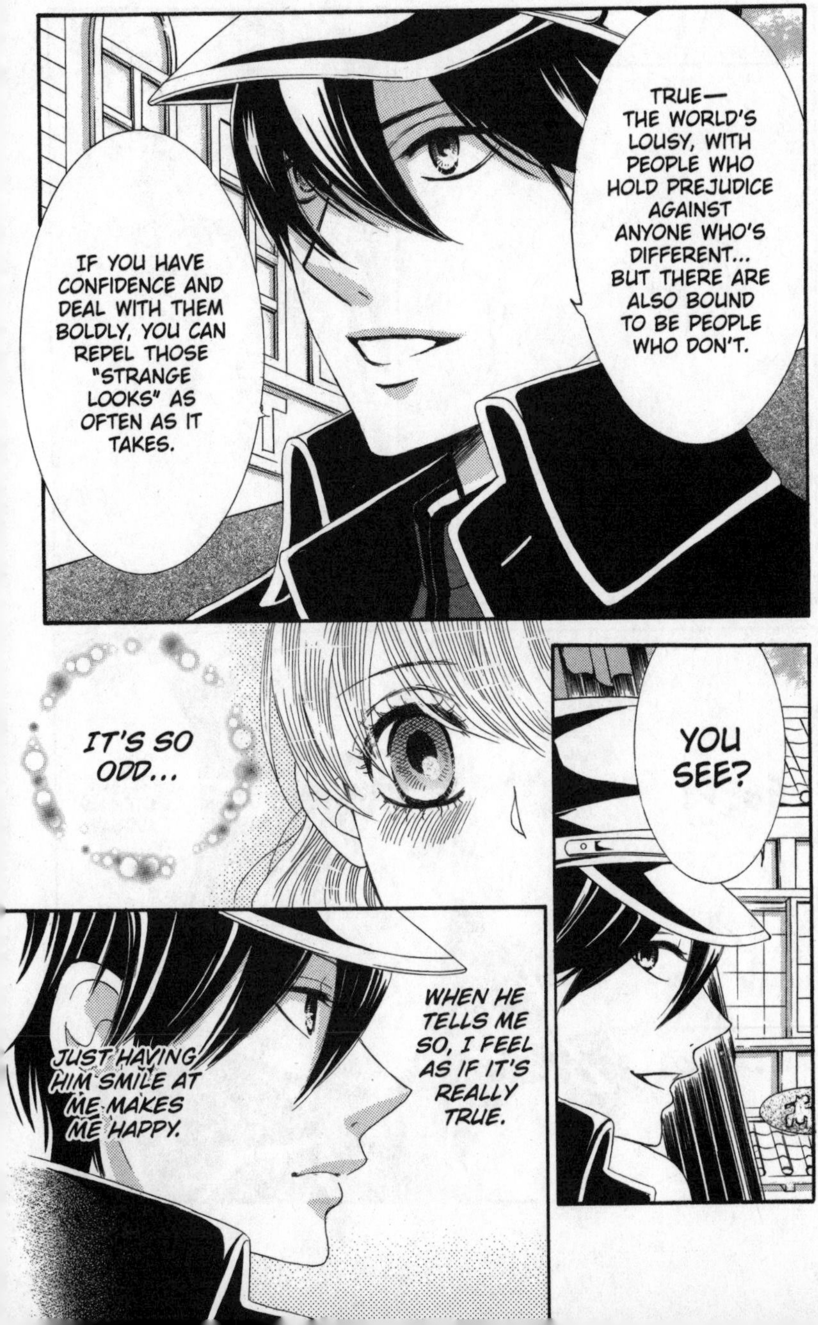
TRUE— THE WORLD'S LOUSY, WITH PEOPLE WHO HOLD PREJUDICE AGAINST ANYONE WHO'S DIFFERENT... BUT THERE ARE ALSO BOUND TO BE PEOPLE WHO DON'T.
IF YOU HAVE CONFIDENCE AND DEAL WITH THEM BOLDLY, YOU CAN REPEL THOSE "STRANGE LOOKS" AS OFTEN AS IT TAKES.
YOU SEE?
IT'S SO ODD...
WHEN HE TELLS ME SO, I FEEL AS IF IT'S REALLY TRUE.
JUST HAVING HIM SMILE AT ME MAKES ME HAPPY.

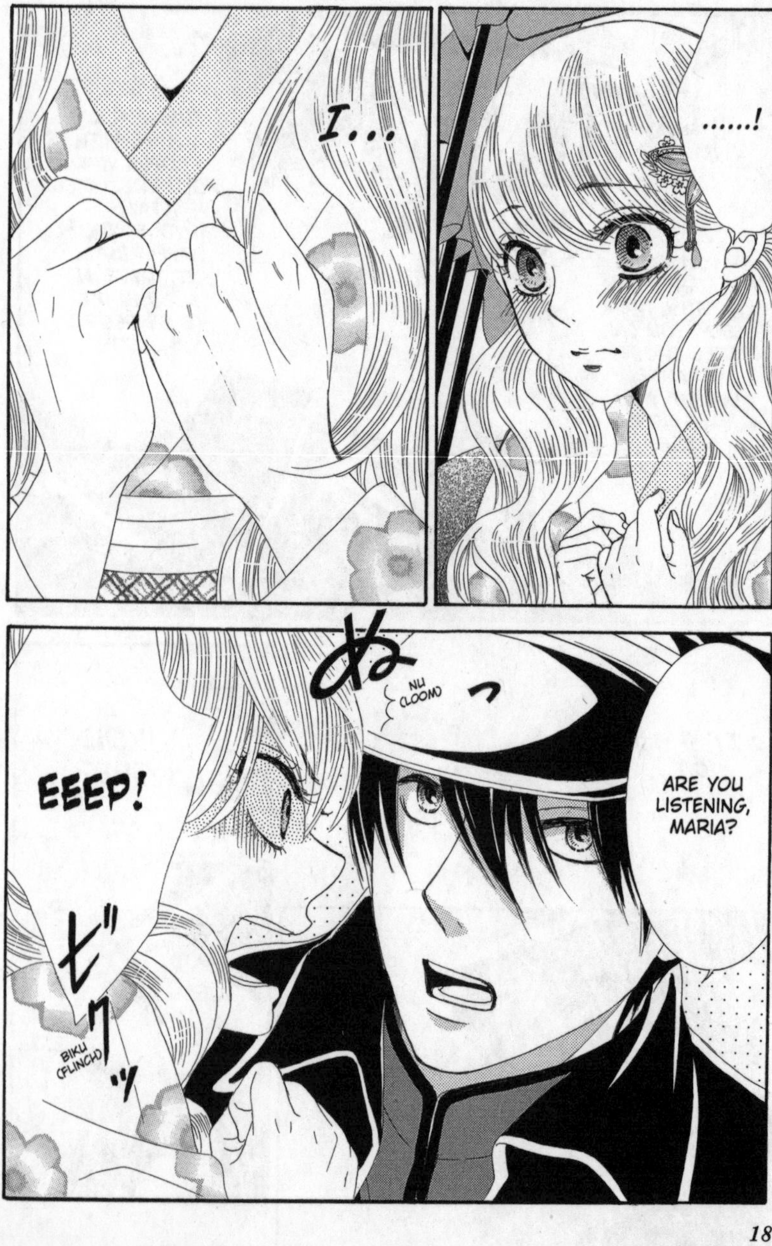
......!
I...
ぬっ
NU (LOOM)
ARE YOU LISTENING, MARIA?
EEEP!
ビクッ
BIKU (FLINCH)

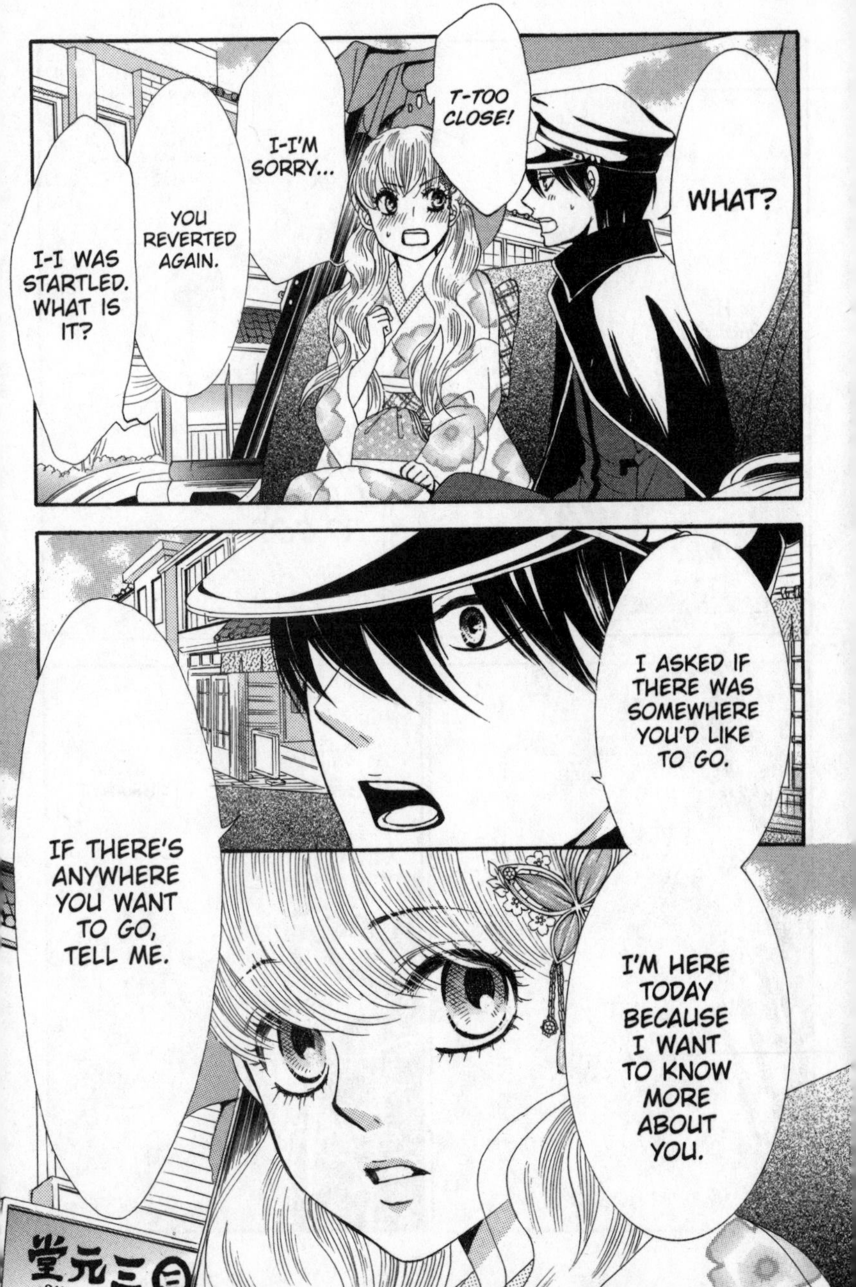
WHAT?
T-TOO CLOSE!
I-I'M SORRY...
YOU REVERTED AGAIN.
I-I WAS STARTLED. WHAT IS IT?
I ASKED IF THERE WAS SOMEWHERE YOU'D LIKE TO GO.
IF THERE'S ANYWHERE YOU WANT TO GO, TELL ME.
I'M HERE TODAY BECAUSE I WANT TO KNOW MORE ABOUT YOU.
堂元三
SANGEN-DOU

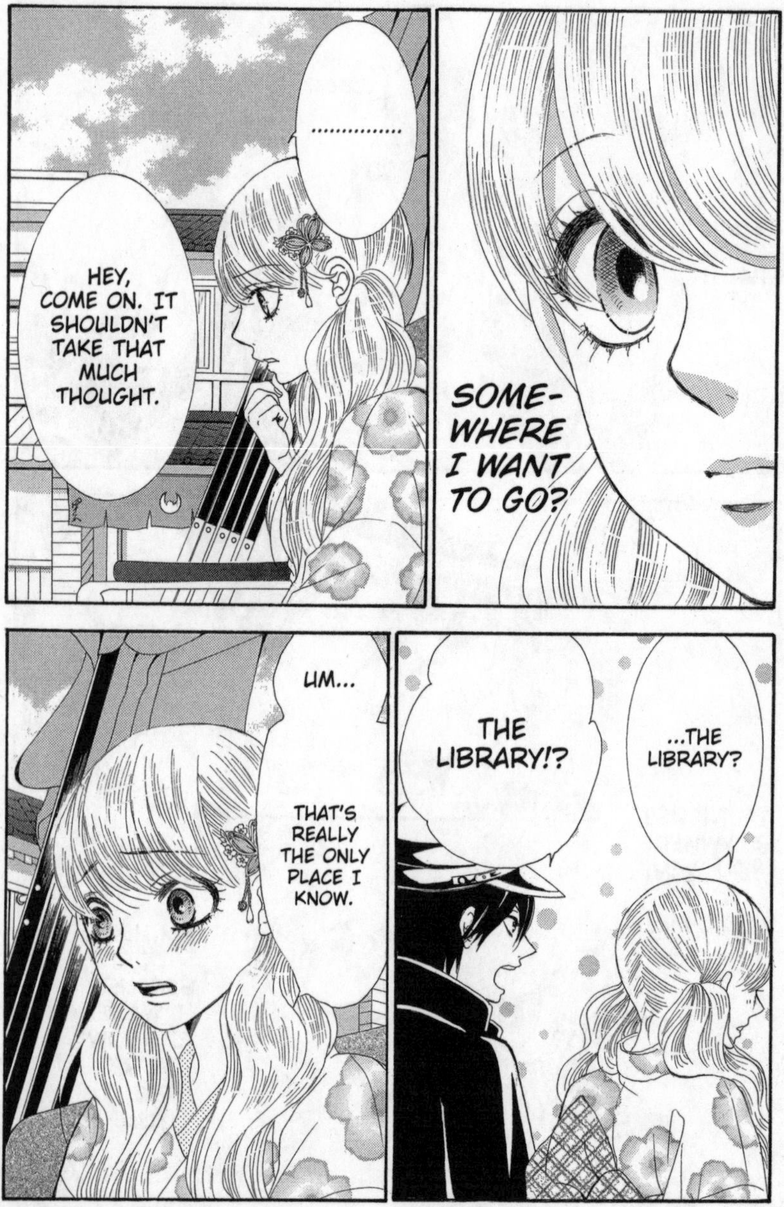
SOMEWHERE I WANT TO GO?
....
HEY, COME ON. IT SHOULDN'T TAKE THAT MUCH THOUGHT.
...THE LIBRARY?
THE LIBRARY!?
UM...
THAT'S REALLY THE ONLY PLACE I KNOW.

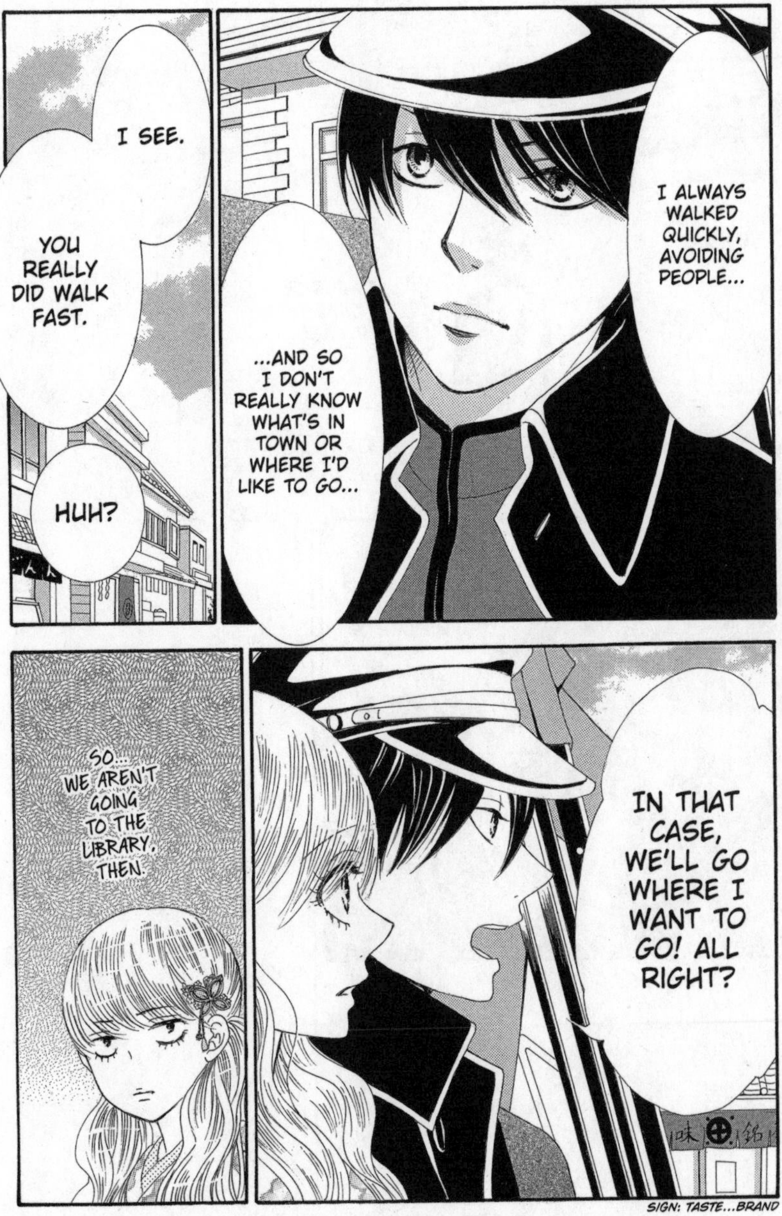
I ALWAYS WALKED QUICKLY, AVOIDING PEOPLE...
...AND SO I DON'T REALLY KNOW WHAT'S IN TOWN OR WHERE I'D LIKE TO GO...
I SEE.
YOU REALLY DID WALK FAST.
HUH?
IN THAT CASE, WE'LL GO WHERE I WANT TO GO! ALL RIGHT?
SO... WE AREN'T GOING TO THE LIBRARY, THEN.

SIGN: TASTE...BRAND

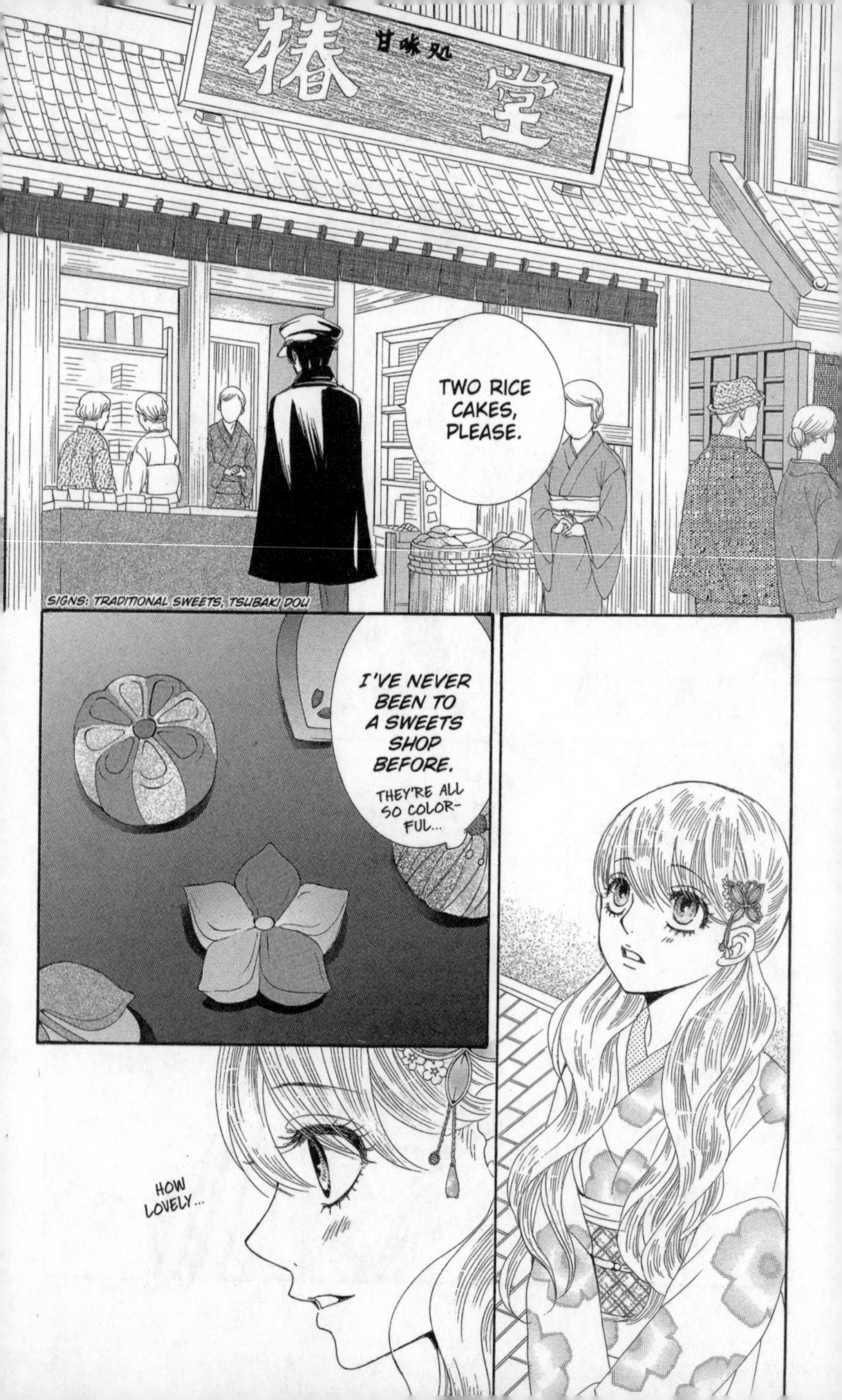
椿堂
甘味処
TWO RICE CAKES, PLEASE.
SIGNS: TRADITIONAL SWEETS, TSUBAKI DOU
I'VE NEVER BEEN TO A SWEETS SHOP BEFORE.
THEY'RE ALL SO COLOR-FUL...
HOW LOVELY...

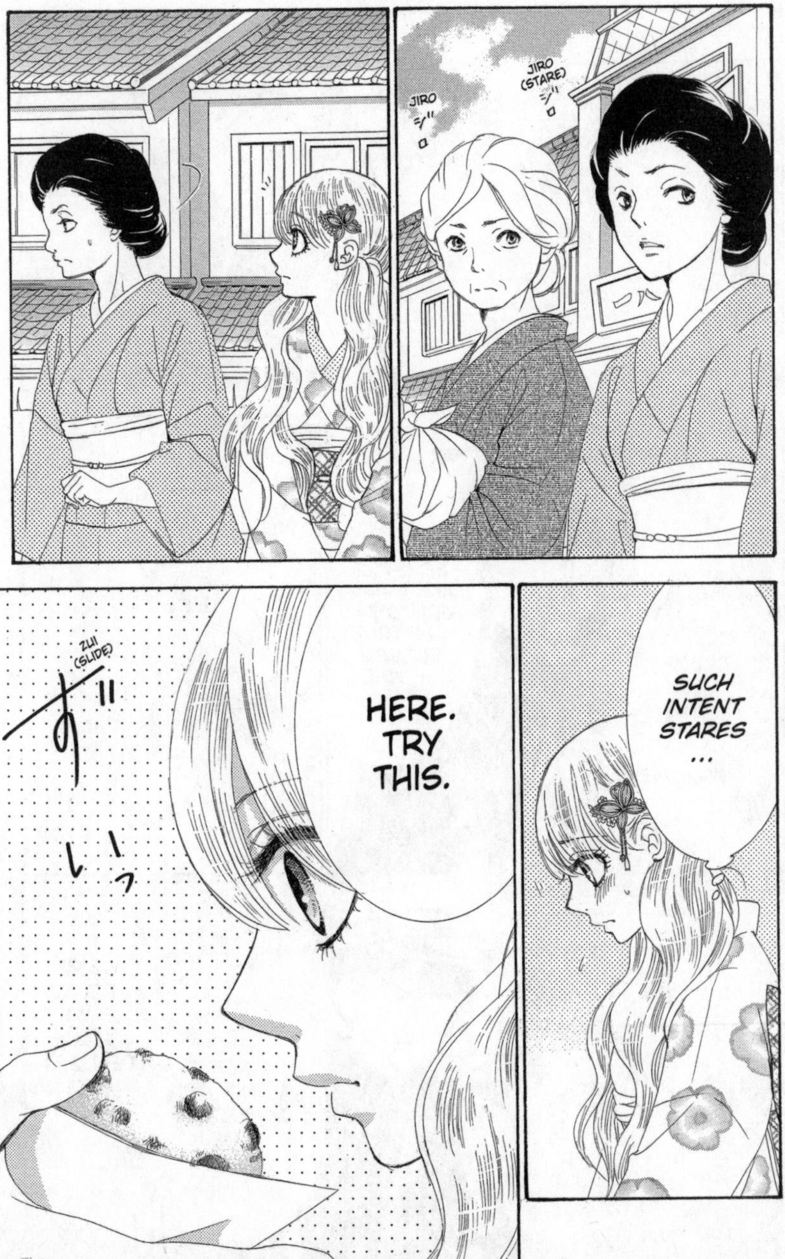
JIRO (STARE)
JIRO
SUCH INTENT STARES ...
HERE. TRY THIS.
ZUI (SLIDE)

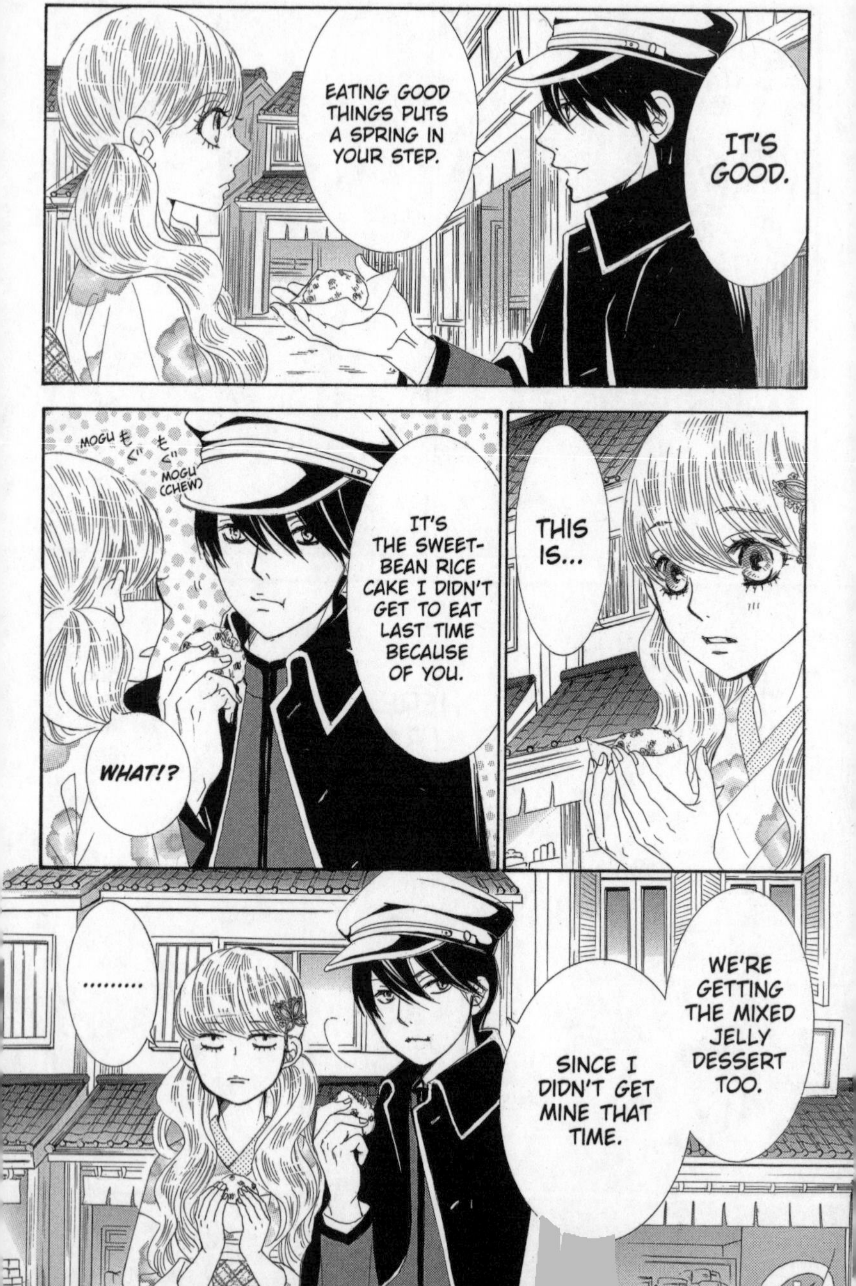
IT'S GOOD.
EATING GOOD THINGS PUTS A SPRING IN YOUR STEP.
THIS IS...
IT'S THE SWEET-BEAN RICE CAKE I DIDN'T GET TO EAT LAST TIME BECAUSE OF YOU.
MOGU もぐ MOGU もぐ (CHEW)
WHAT!?
WE'RE GETTING THE MIXED JELLY DESSERT TOO.
SINCE I DIDN'T GET MINE THAT TIME.
....

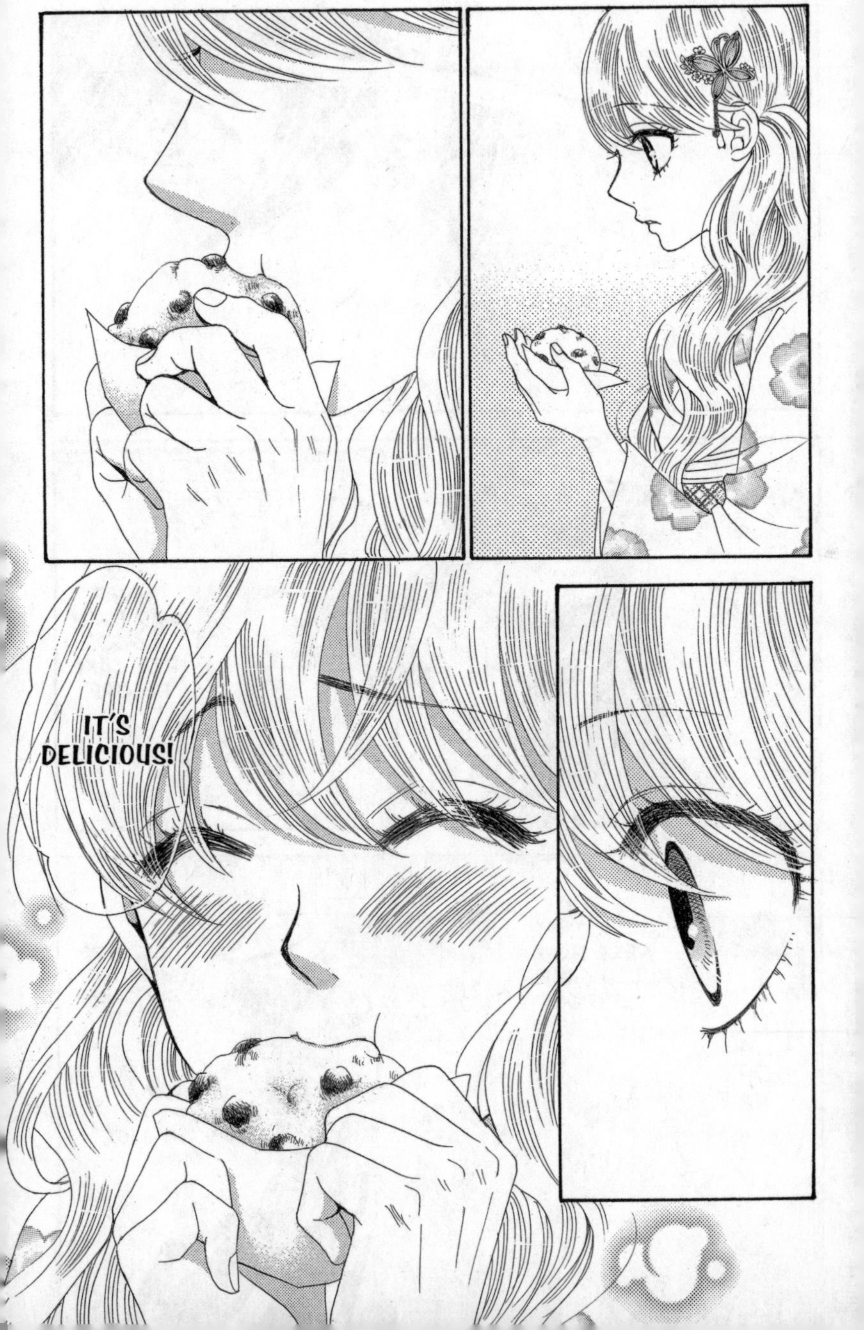
IT'S DELICIOUS!

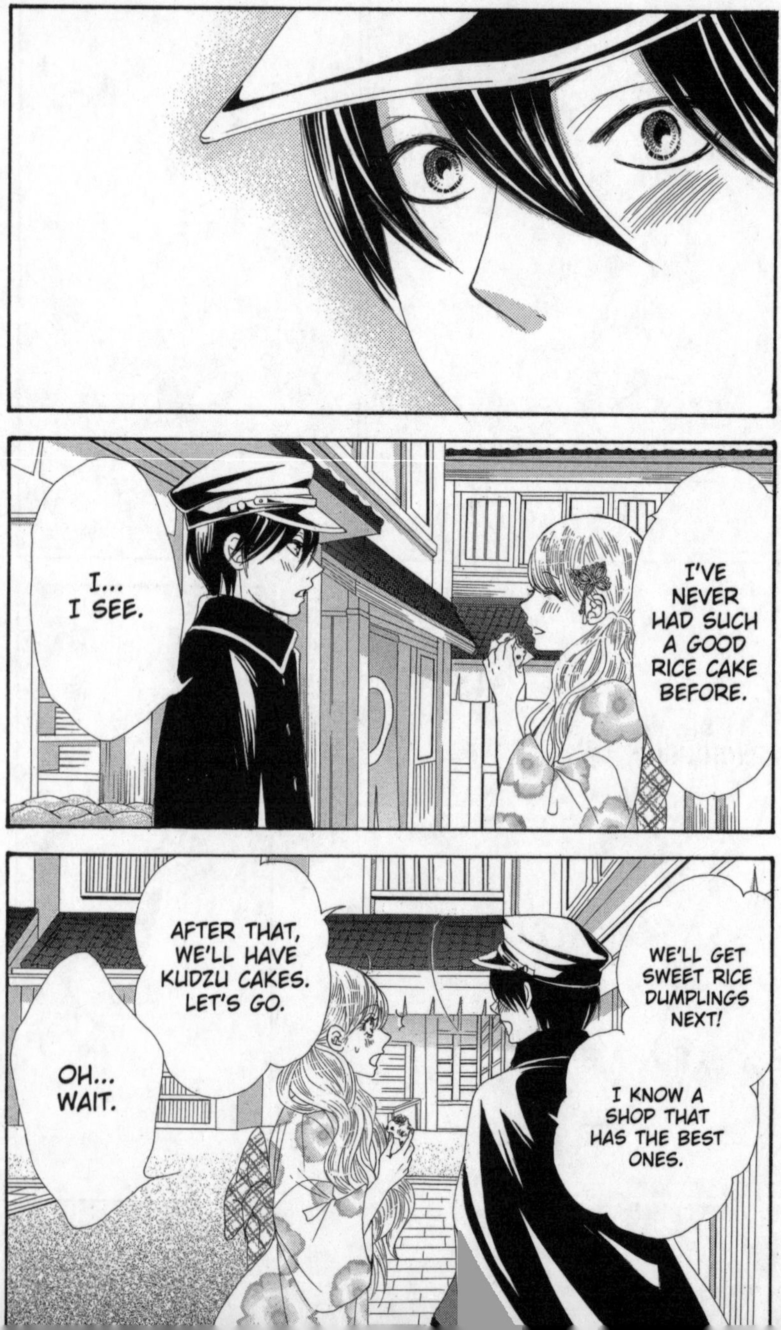
I'VE NEVER HAD SUCH A GOOD RICE CAKE BEFORE.
I... I SEE.
WE'LL GET SWEET RICE DUMPLINGS NEXT!
I KNOW A SHOP THAT HAS THE BEST ONES.
AFTER THAT, WE'LL HAVE KUDZU CAKES. LET'S GO.
OH... WAIT.

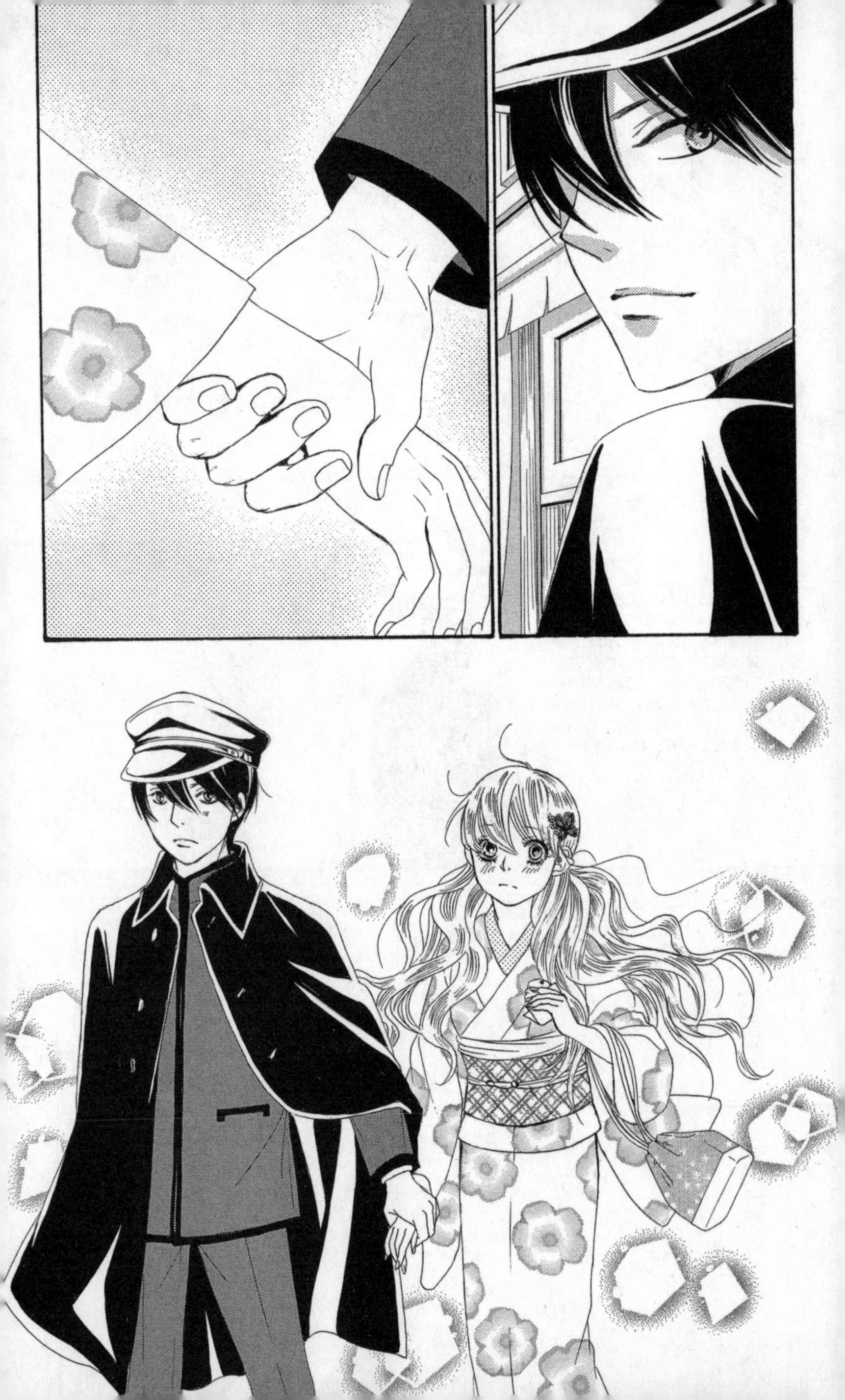

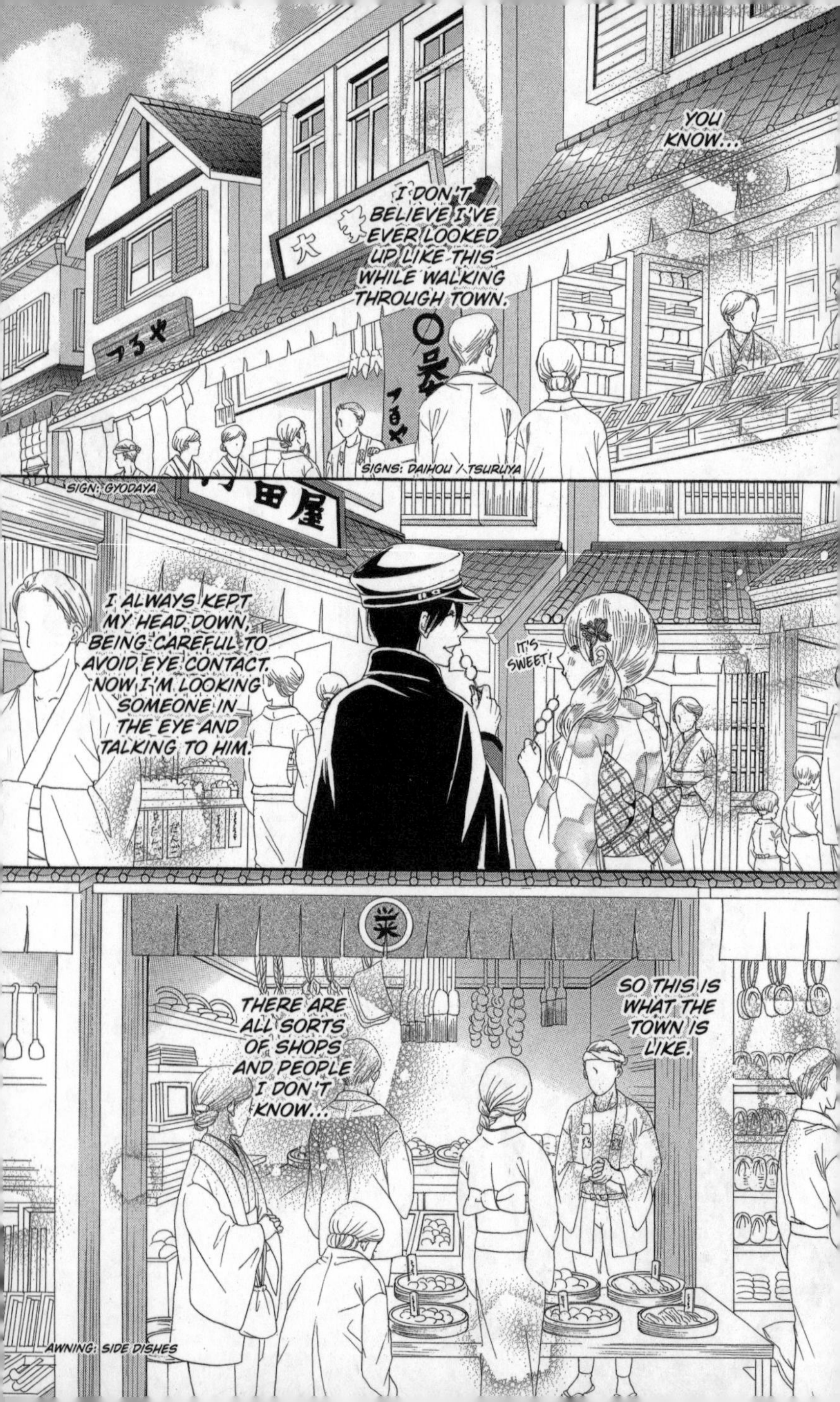
YOU KNOW...
I DON'T BELIEVE I'VE EVER LOOKED UP LIKE THIS WHILE WALKING THROUGH TOWN.
SIGNS: DAIHOU / TSURUYA
SIGN: GYODAYA
IT'S SWEET!
I ALWAYS KEPT MY HEAD DOWN, BEING CAREFUL TO AVOID EYE CONTACT. NOW I'M LOOKING SOMEONE IN THE EYE AND TALKING TO HIM.
SO THIS IS WHAT THE TOWN IS LIKE.
THERE ARE ALL SORTS OF SHOPS AND PEOPLE I DON'T KNOW...
AWNING: SIDE DISHES

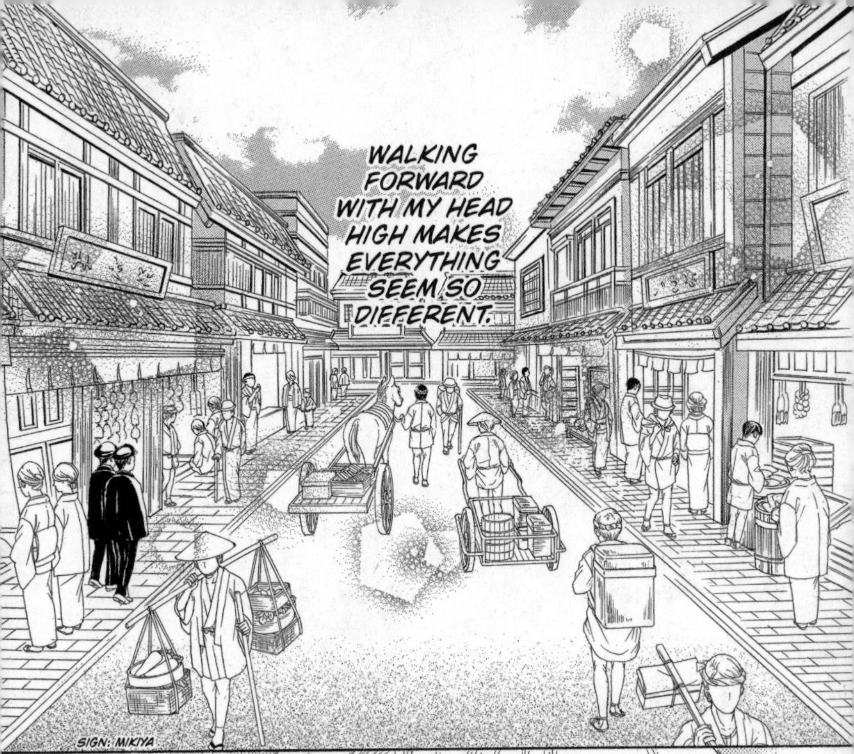
WALKING FORWARD WITH MY HEAD HIGH MAKES EVERYTHING SEEM SO DIFFERENT.
SIGN: MIKIYA
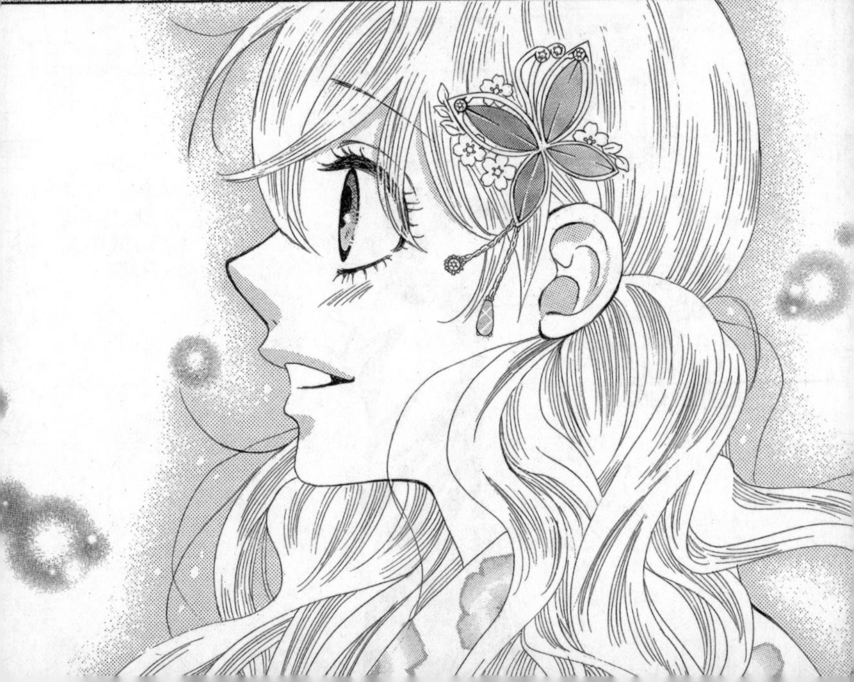

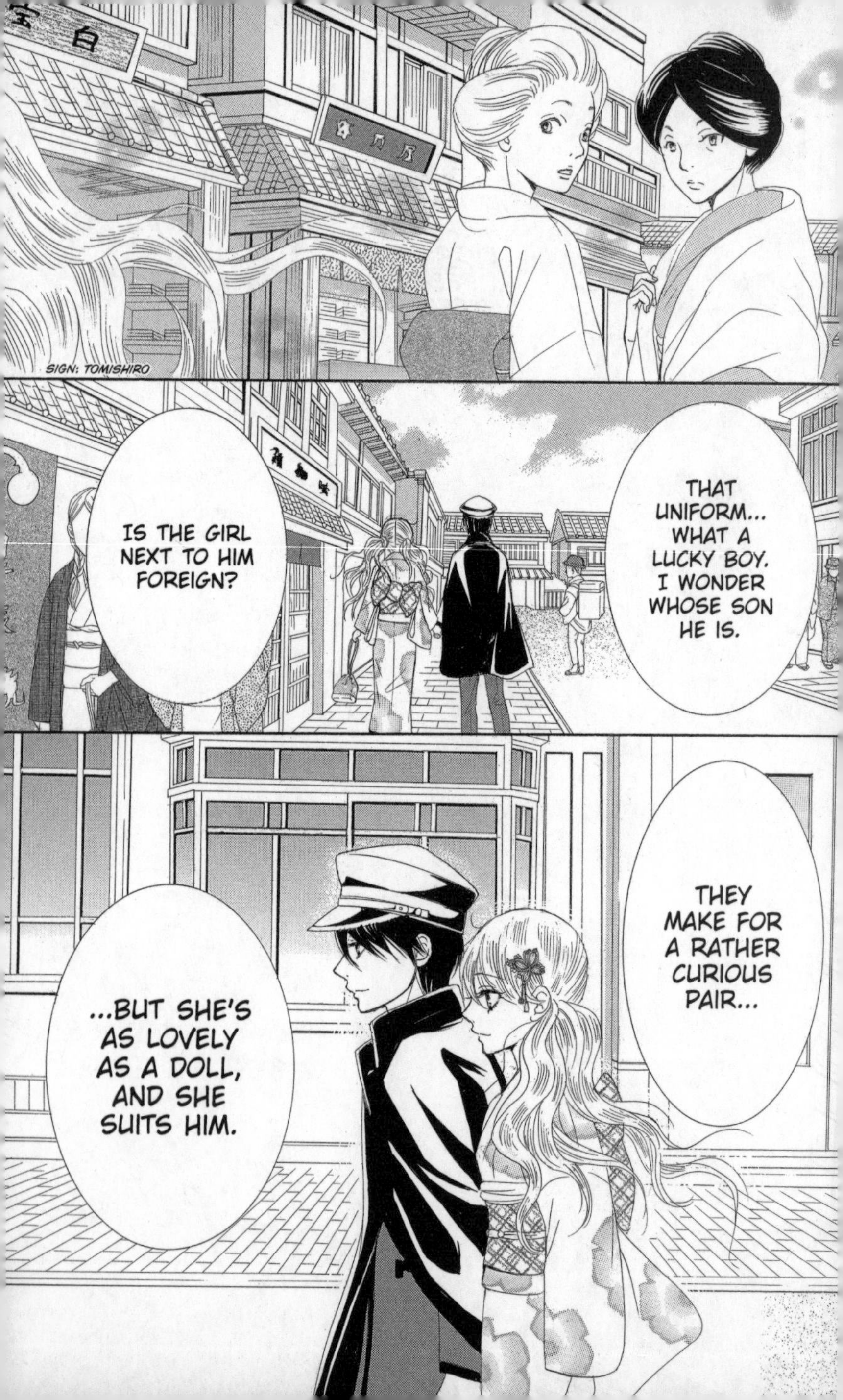
SIGN: TOMISHIRO
THAT UNIFORM... WHAT A LUCKY BOY. I WONDER WHOSE SON HE IS.
IS THE GIRL NEXT TO HIM FOREIGN?
THEY MAKE FOR A RATHER CURIOUS PAIR...
...BUT SHE'S AS LOVELY AS A DOLL, AND SHE SUITS HIM.

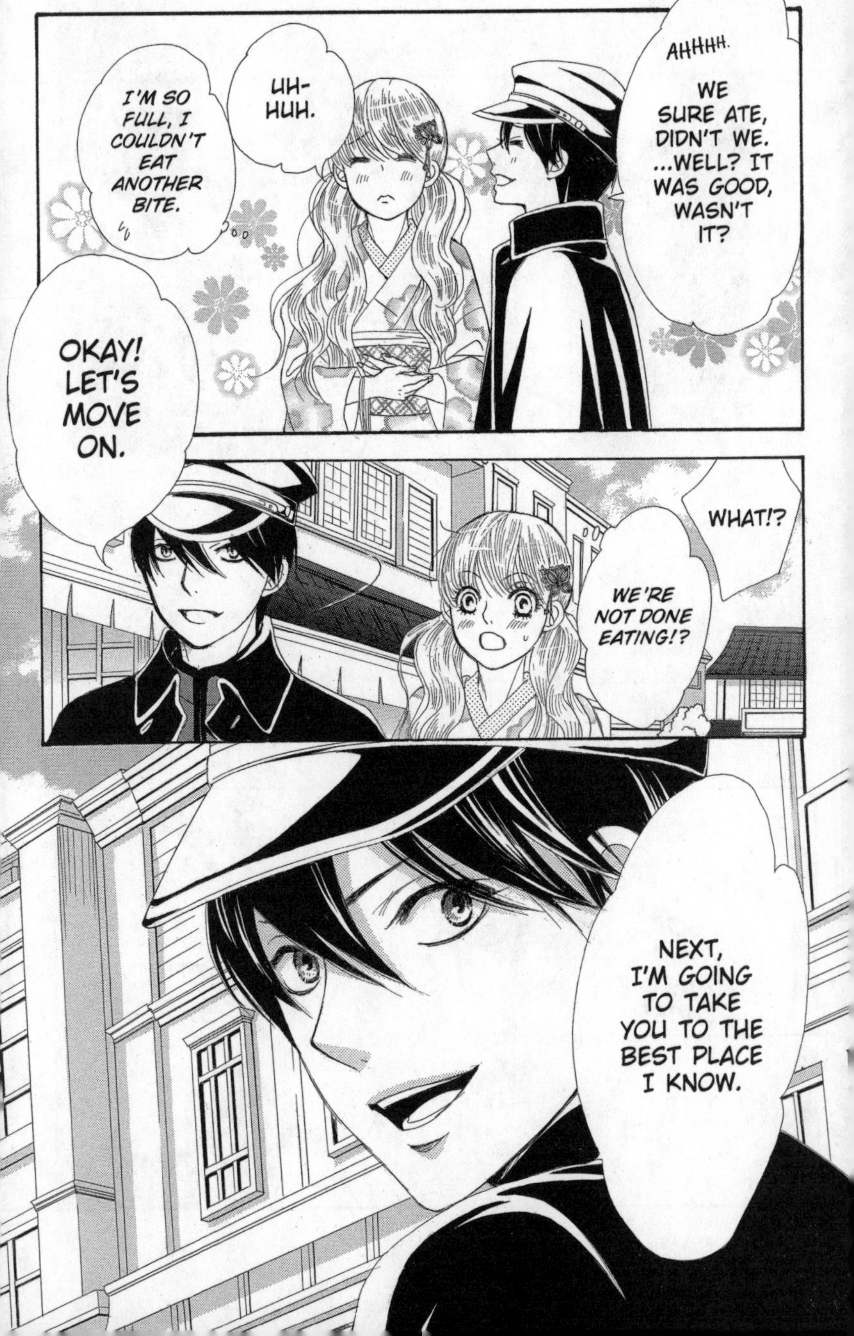
AHHHH.
WE SURE ATE, DIDN'T WE. ...WELL? IT WAS GOOD, WASN'T IT?
UH-HUH.
I'M SO FULL, I COULDN'T EAT ANOTHER BITE.
OKAY! LET'S MOVE ON.
WHAT!?
WE'RE NOT DONE EATING!?
NEXT, I'M GOING TO TAKE YOU TO THE BEST PLACE I KNOW.

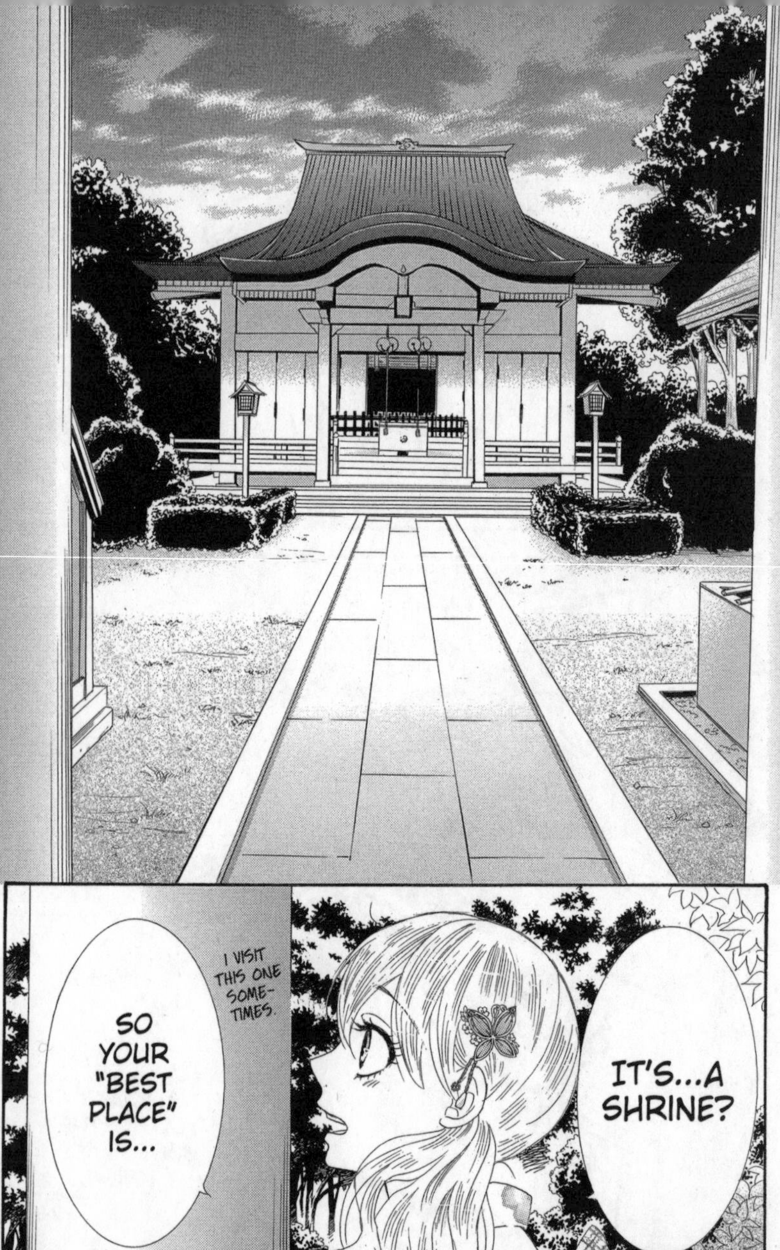
IT'S...A SHRINE?
I VISIT THIS ONE SOME-TIMES.
SO YOUR "BEST PLACE" IS...

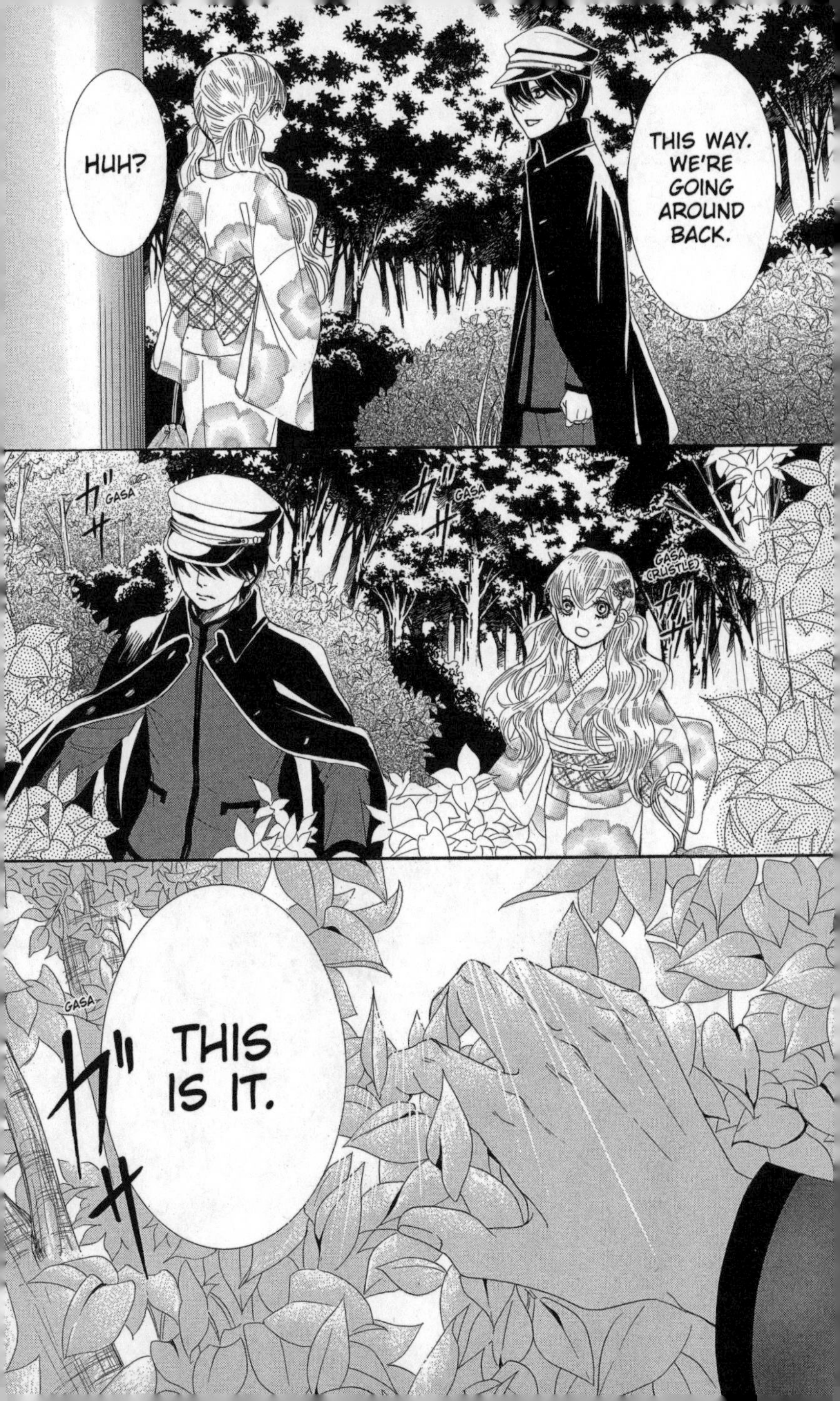

THIS WAY. WE'RE GOING AROUND BACK.
HUH?
GASA (RUSTLE)
GASA
GASA
THIS IS IT.
GASA

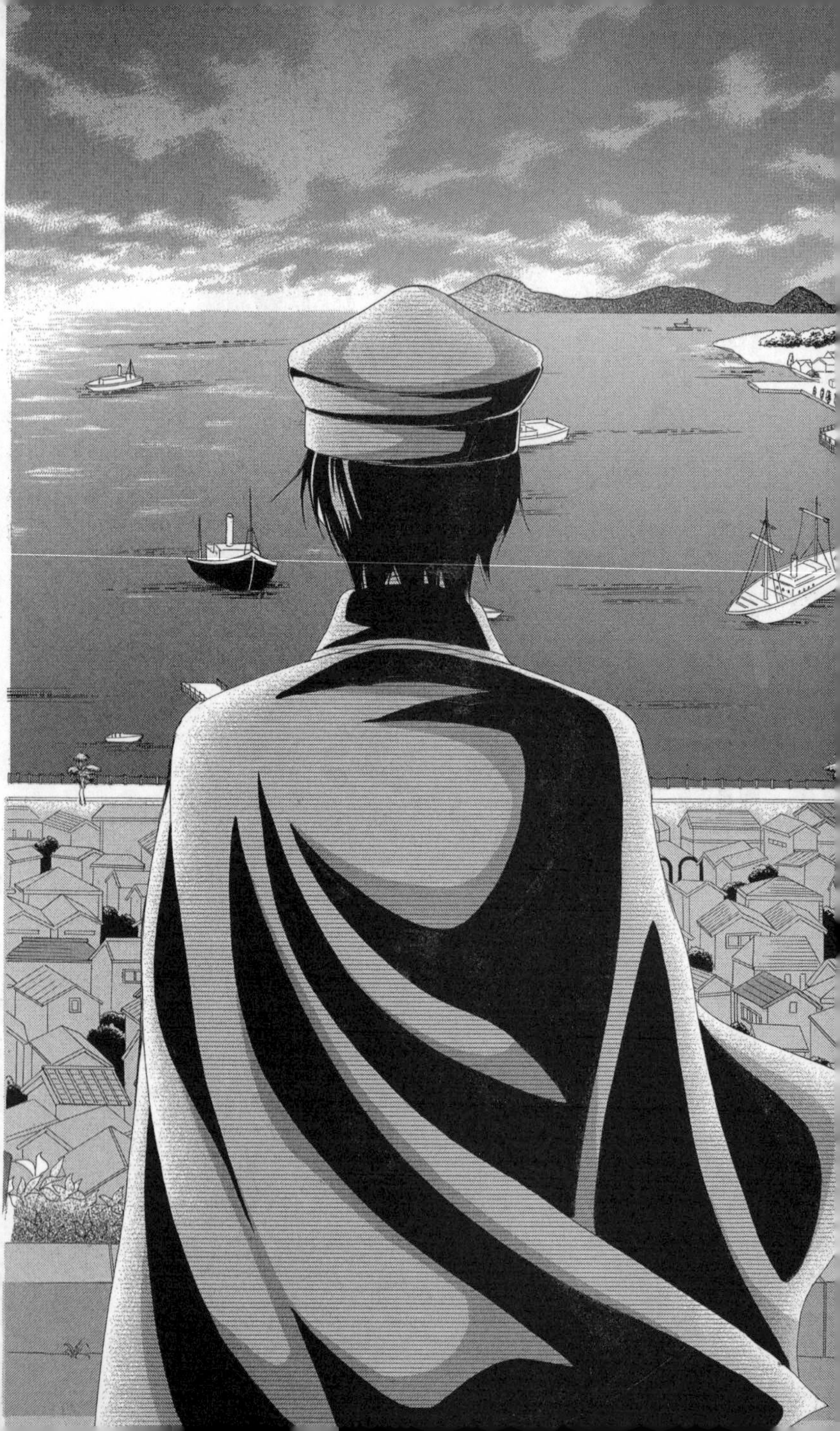

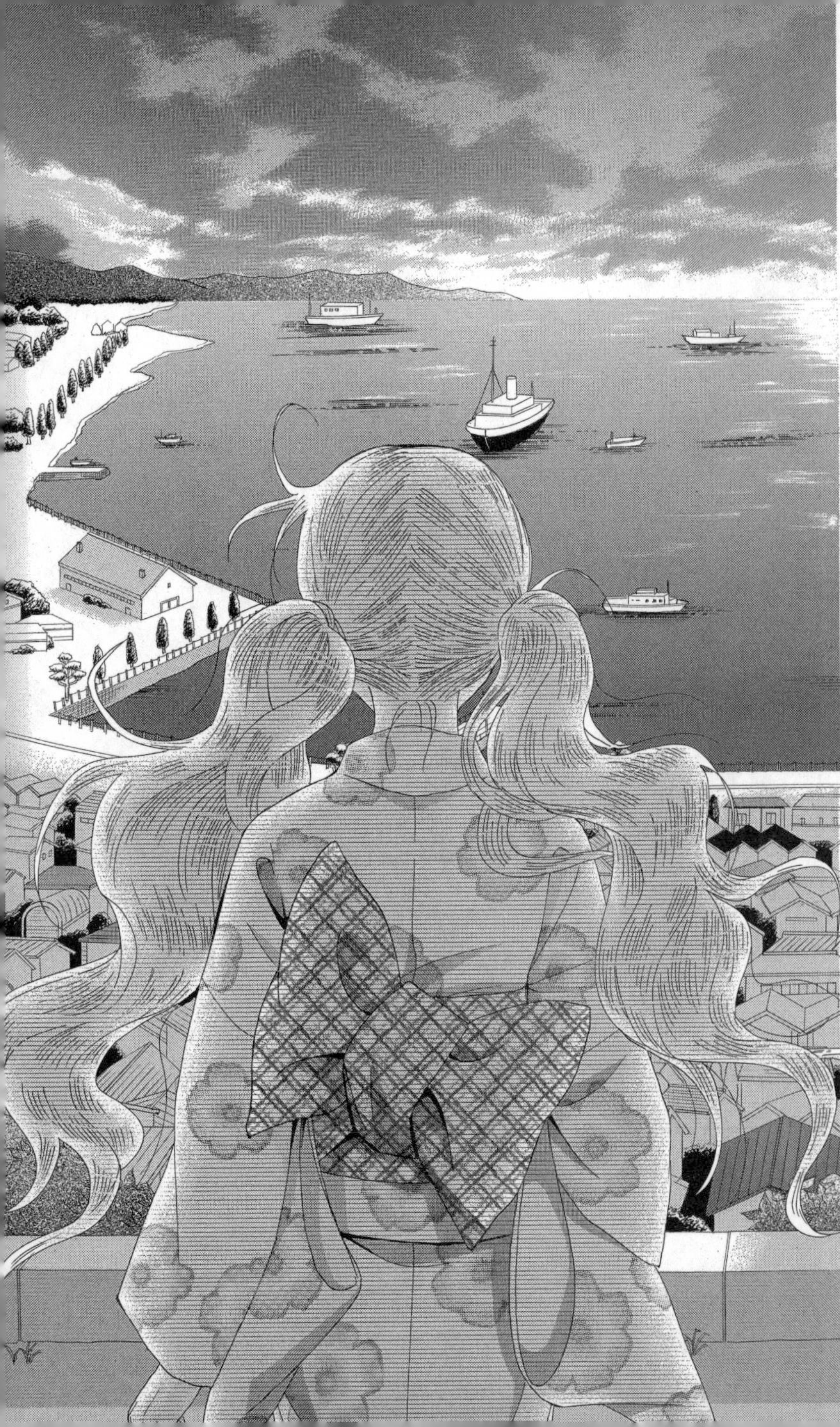

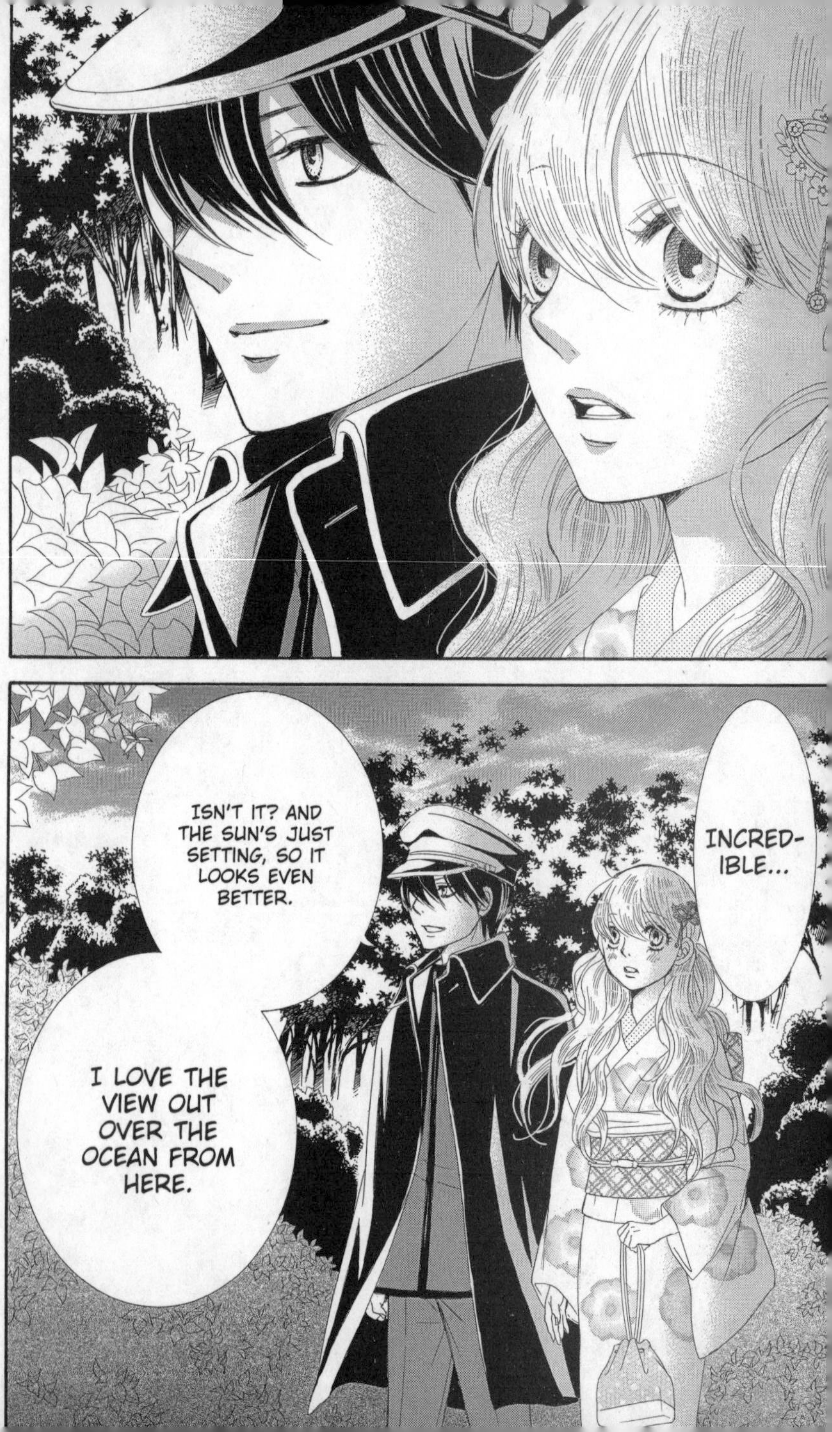
INCREDIBLE...
ISN'T IT? AND THE SUN'S JUST SETTING, SO IT LOOKS EVEN BETTER.
I LOVE THE VIEW OUT OVER THE OCEAN FROM HERE.

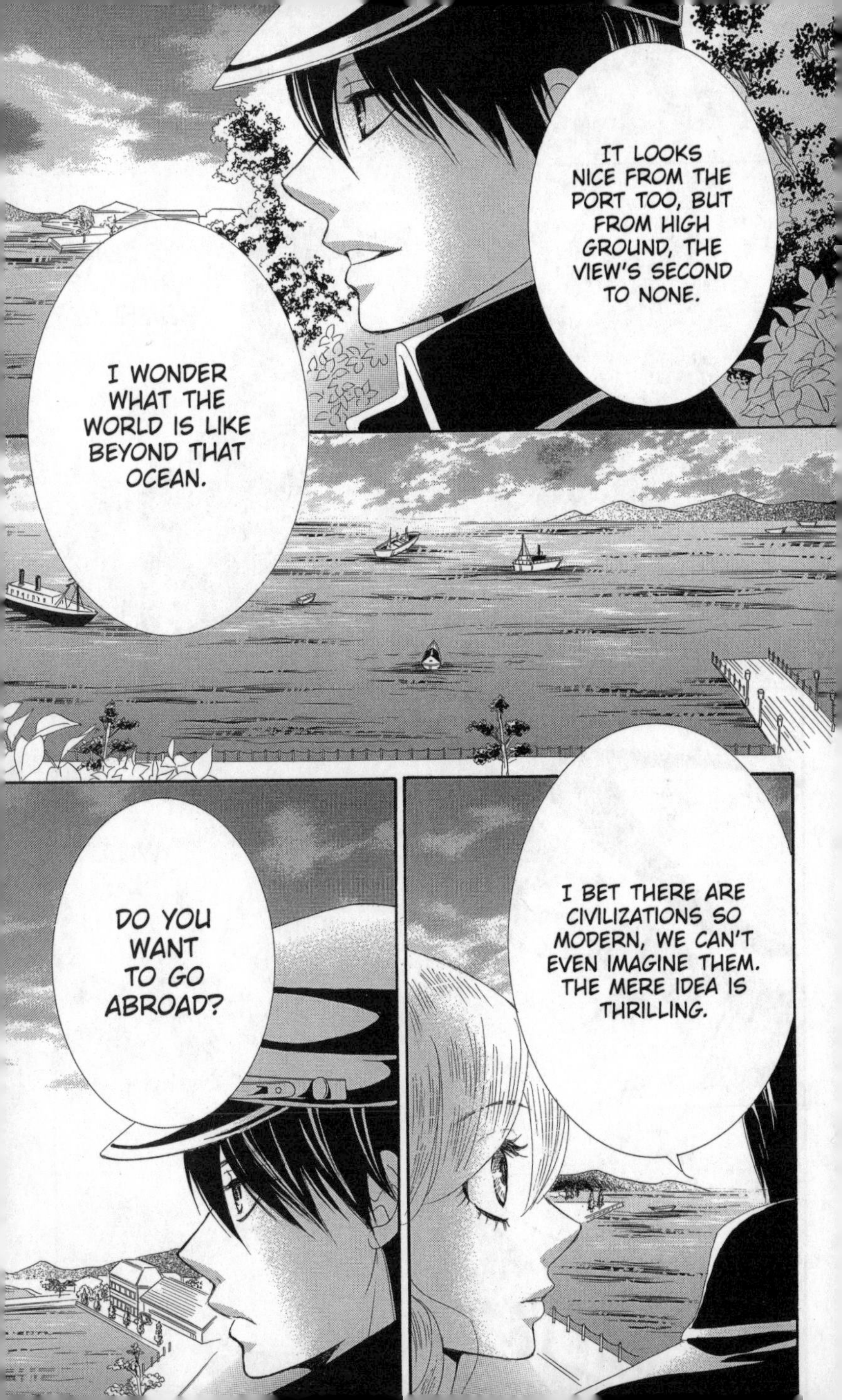
IT LOOKS NICE FROM THE PORT TOO, BUT FROM HIGH GROUND, THE VIEW'S SECOND TO NONE.
I WONDER WHAT THE WORLD IS LIKE BEYOND THAT OCEAN.
I BET THERE ARE CIVILIZATIONS SO MODERN, WE CAN'T EVEN IMAGINE THEM. THE MERE IDEA IS THRILLING.
DO YOU WANT TO GO ABROAD?

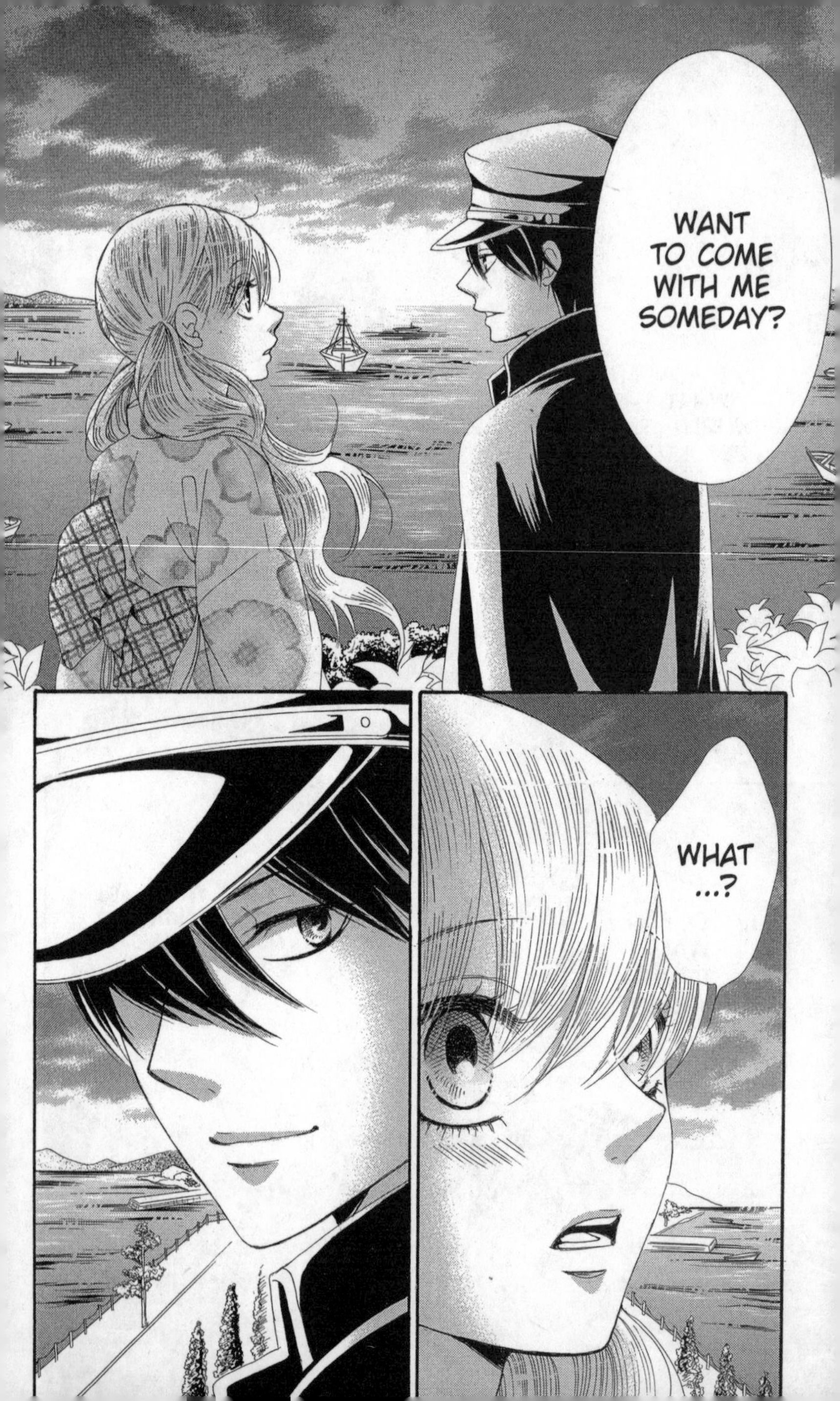
WANT TO COME WITH ME SOMEDAY?
WHAT ...?

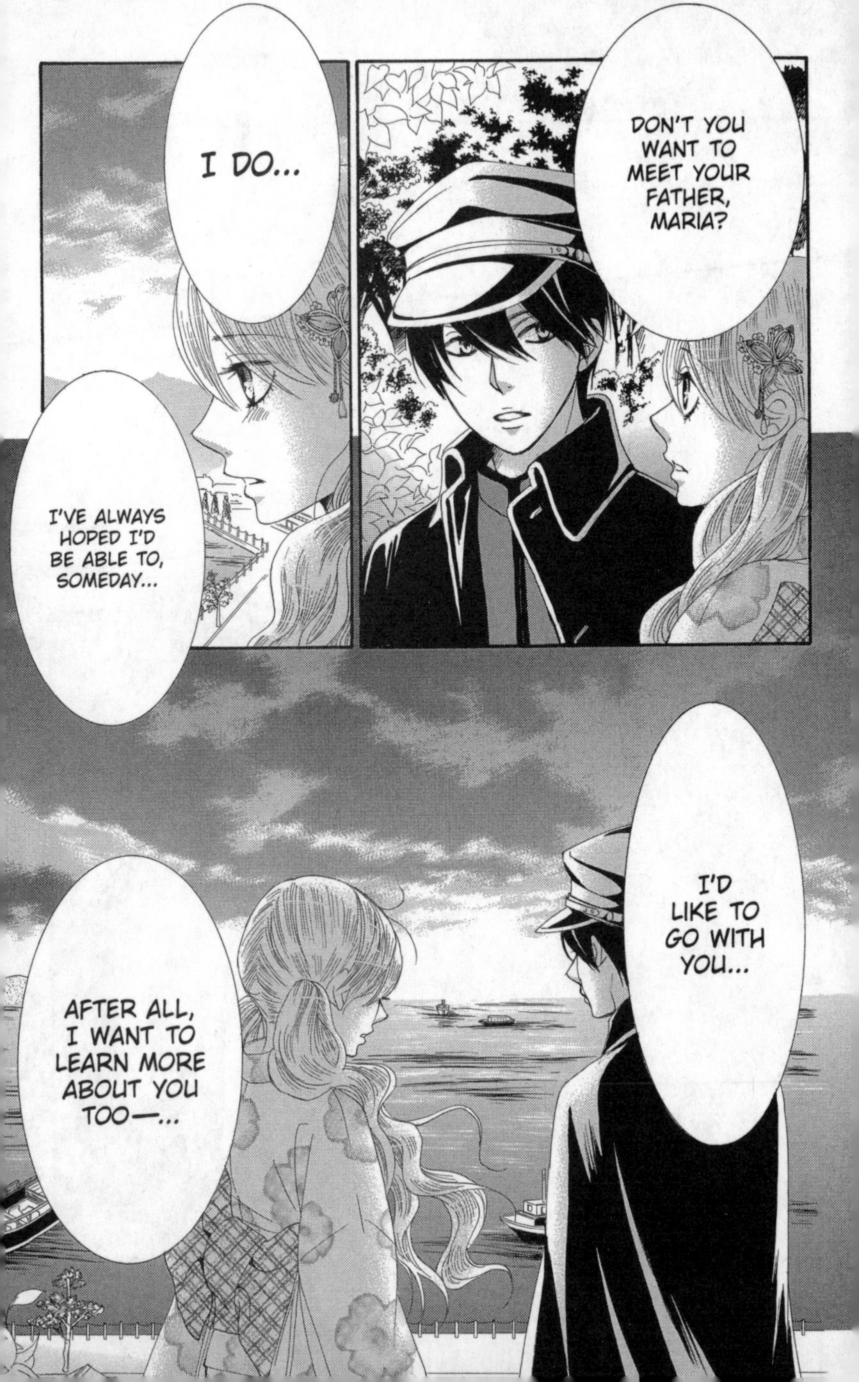
DON'T YOU WANT TO MEET YOUR FATHER, MARIA?
I DO...
I'VE ALWAYS HOPED I'D BE ABLE TO, SOMEDAY...
I'D LIKE TO GO WITH YOU...
AFTER ALL, I WANT TO LEARN MORE ABOUT YOU TOO—...

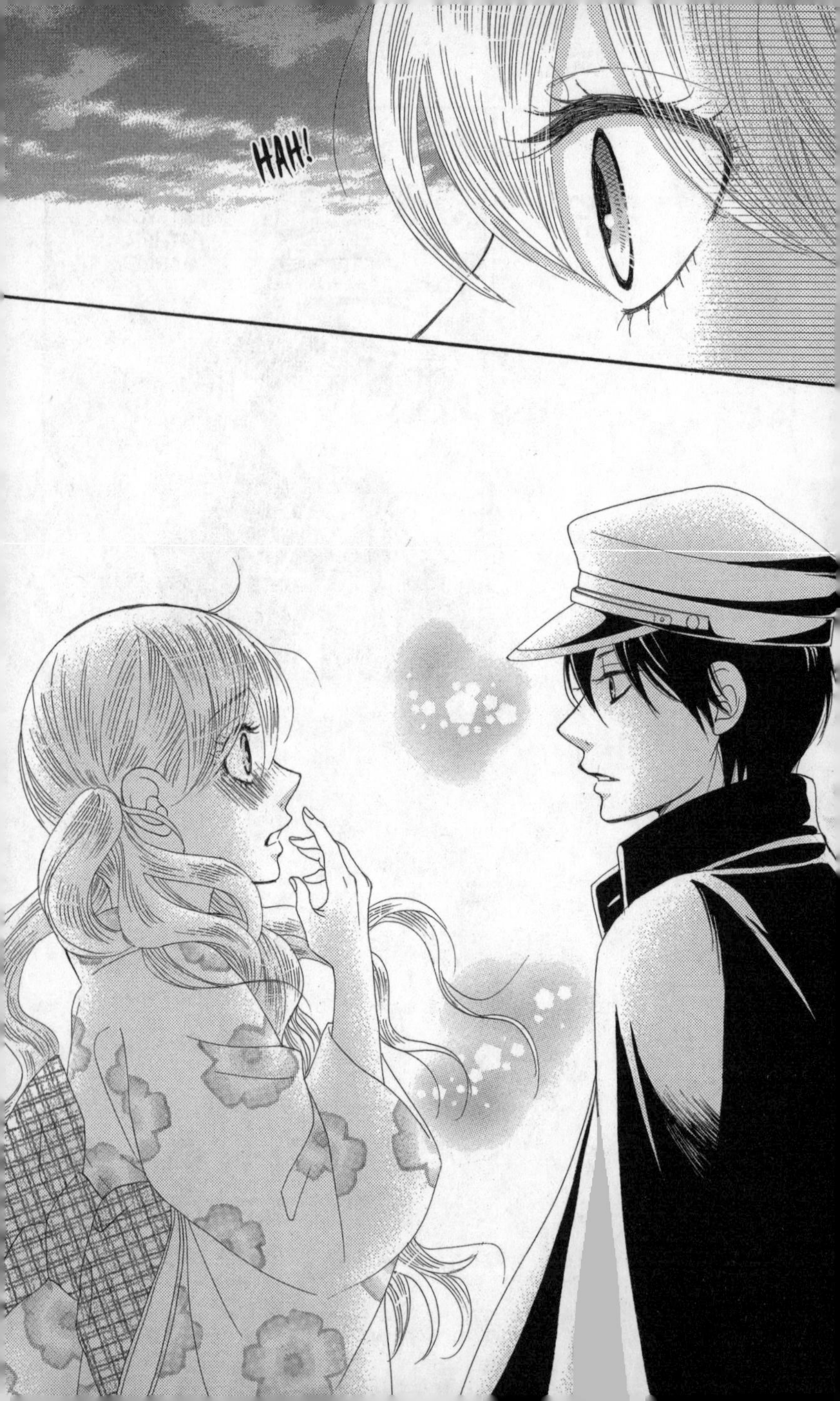
HAH!

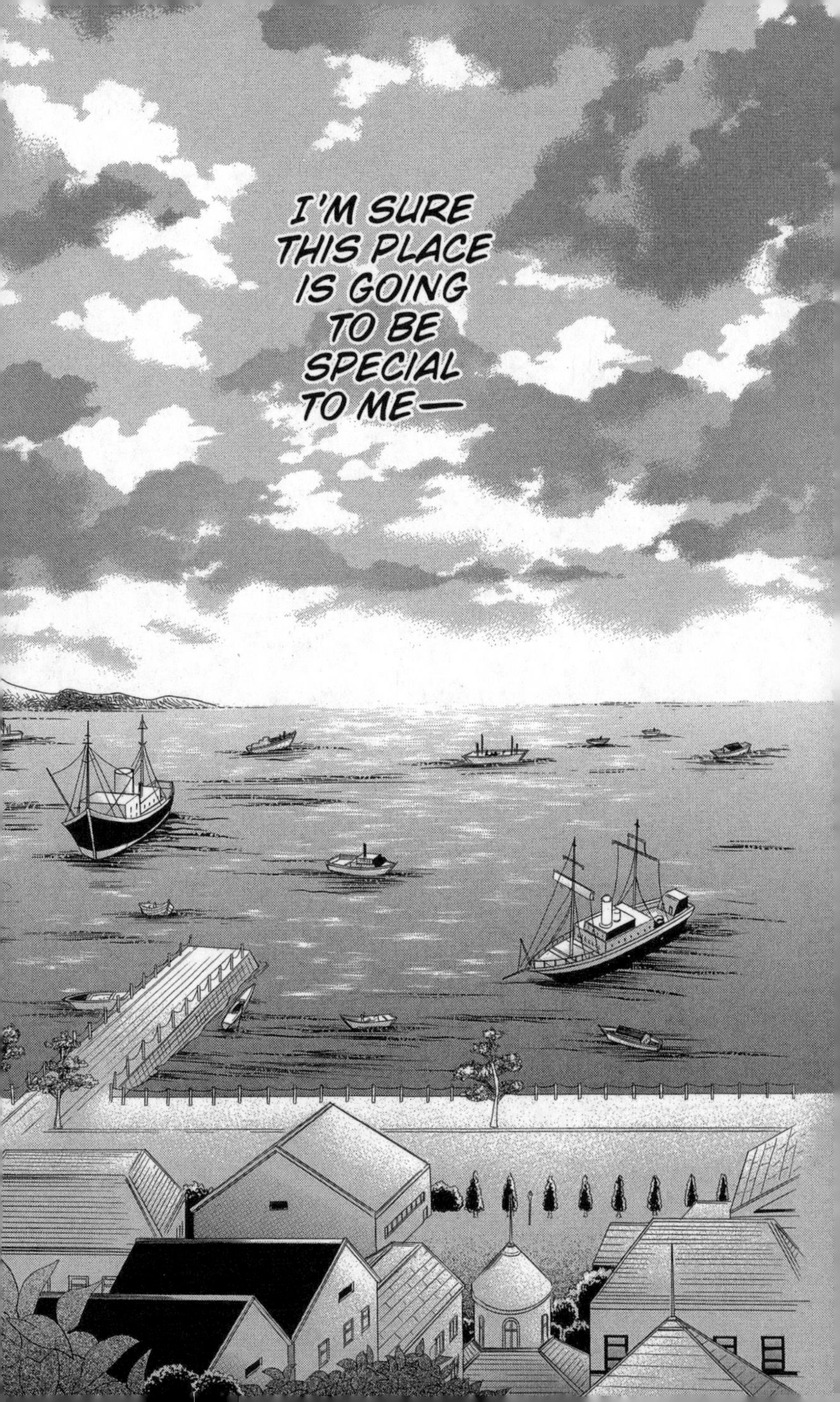
I'M SURE THIS PLACE IS GOING TO BE SPECIAL TO ME—

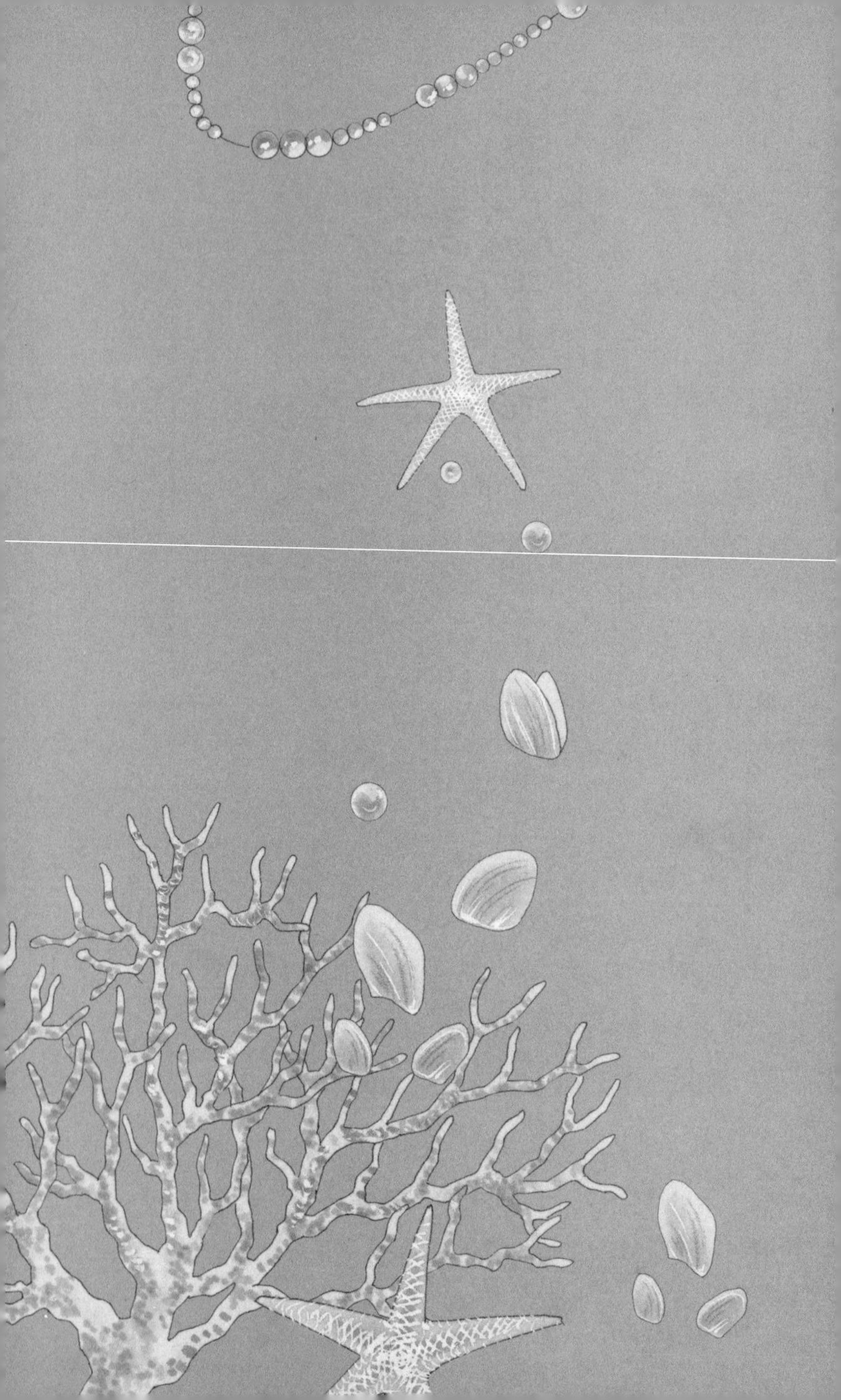

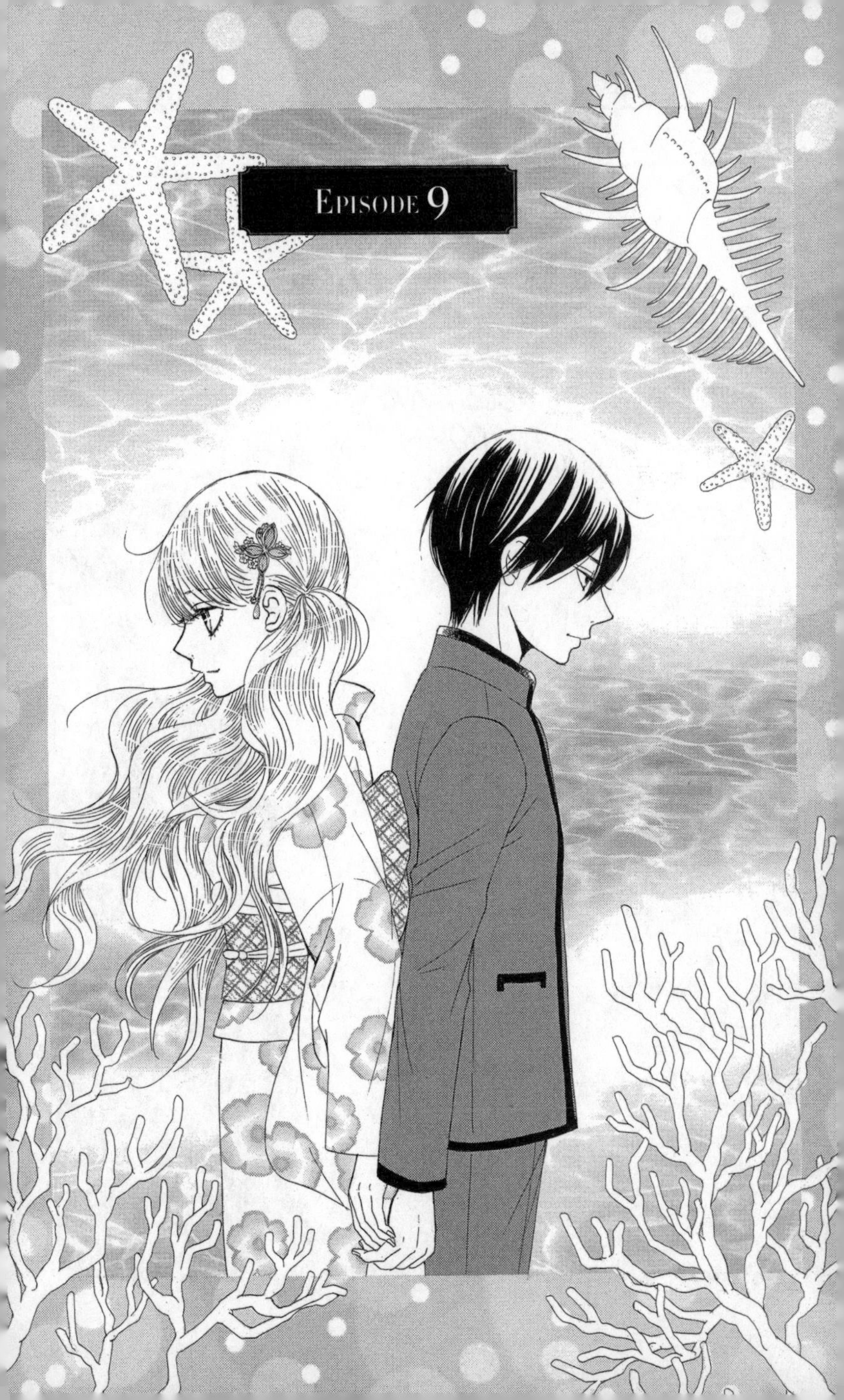
EPISODE 9

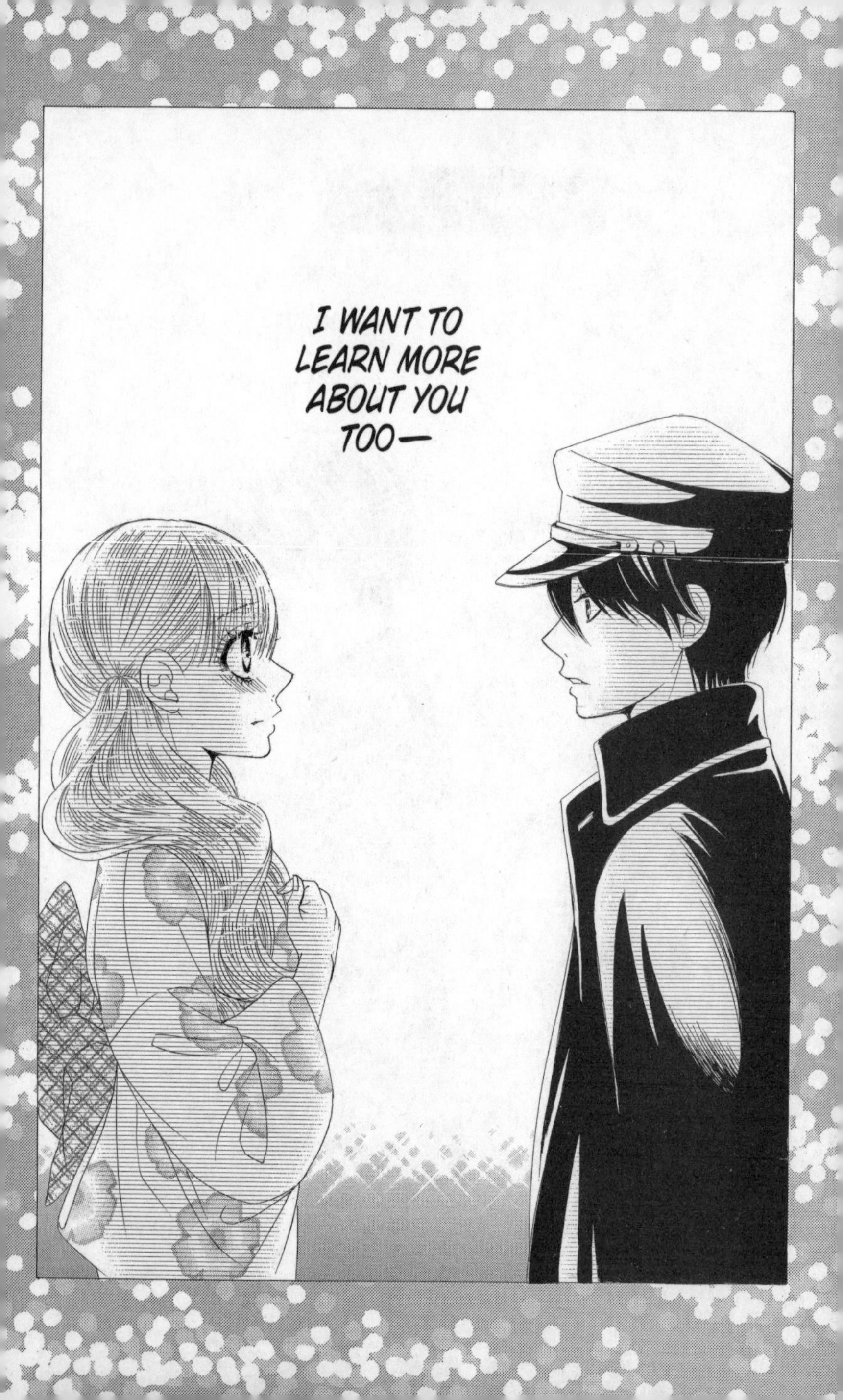
I WANT TO LEARN MORE ABOUT YOU TOO—

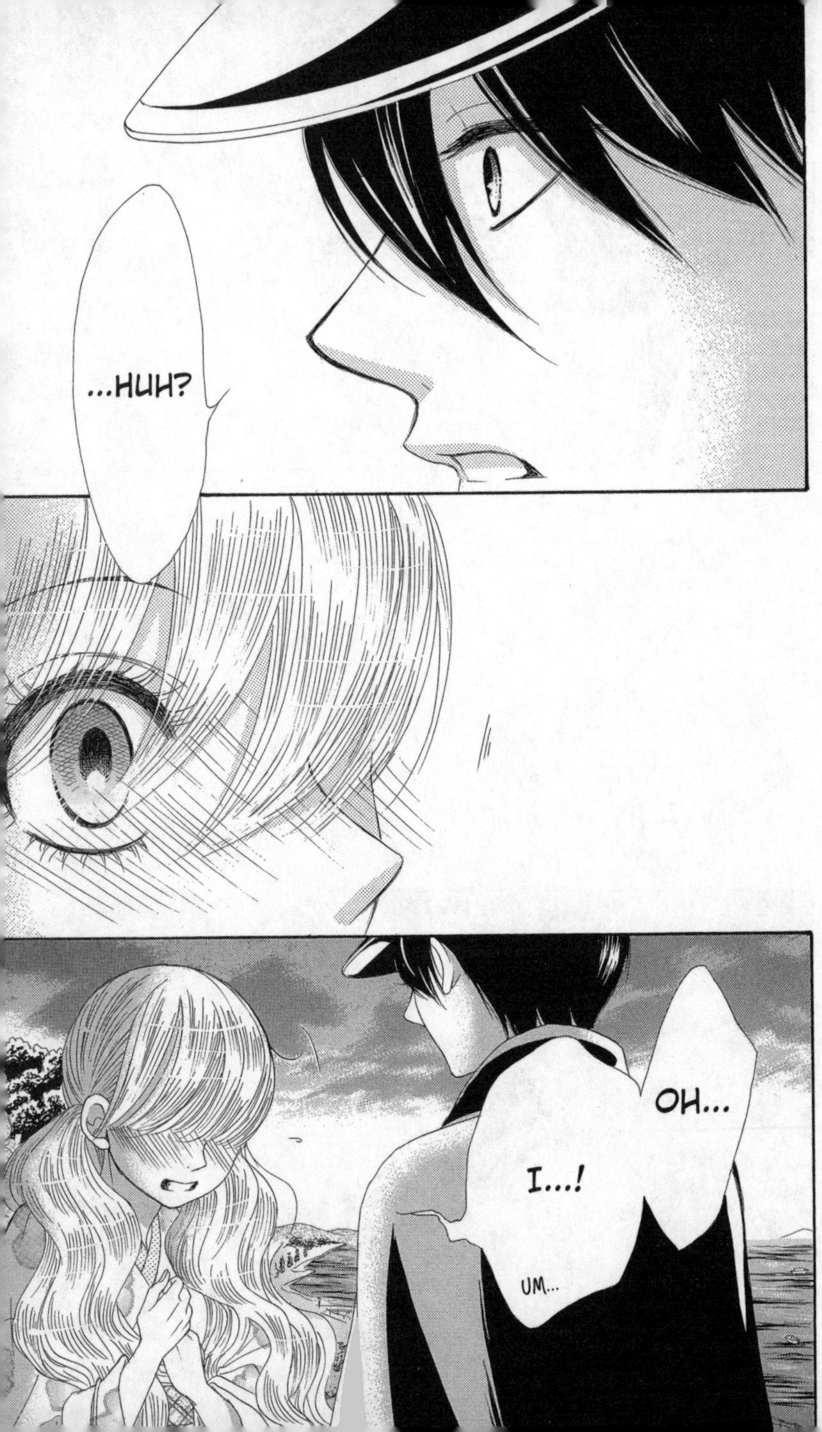
...HUH?
OH...
I...!
UM...

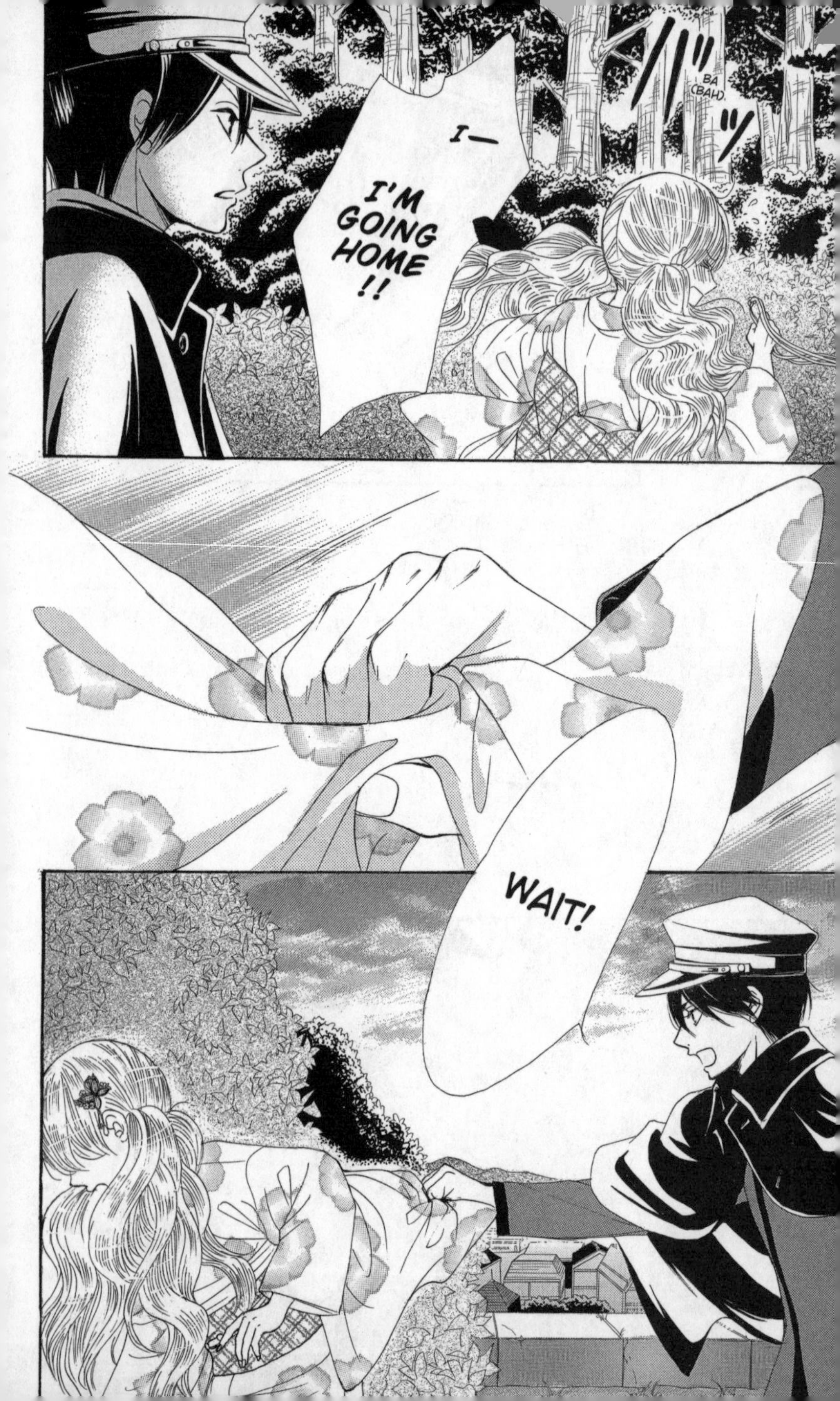
BA (BAH)
I—
I'M GOING HOME!!
WAIT!

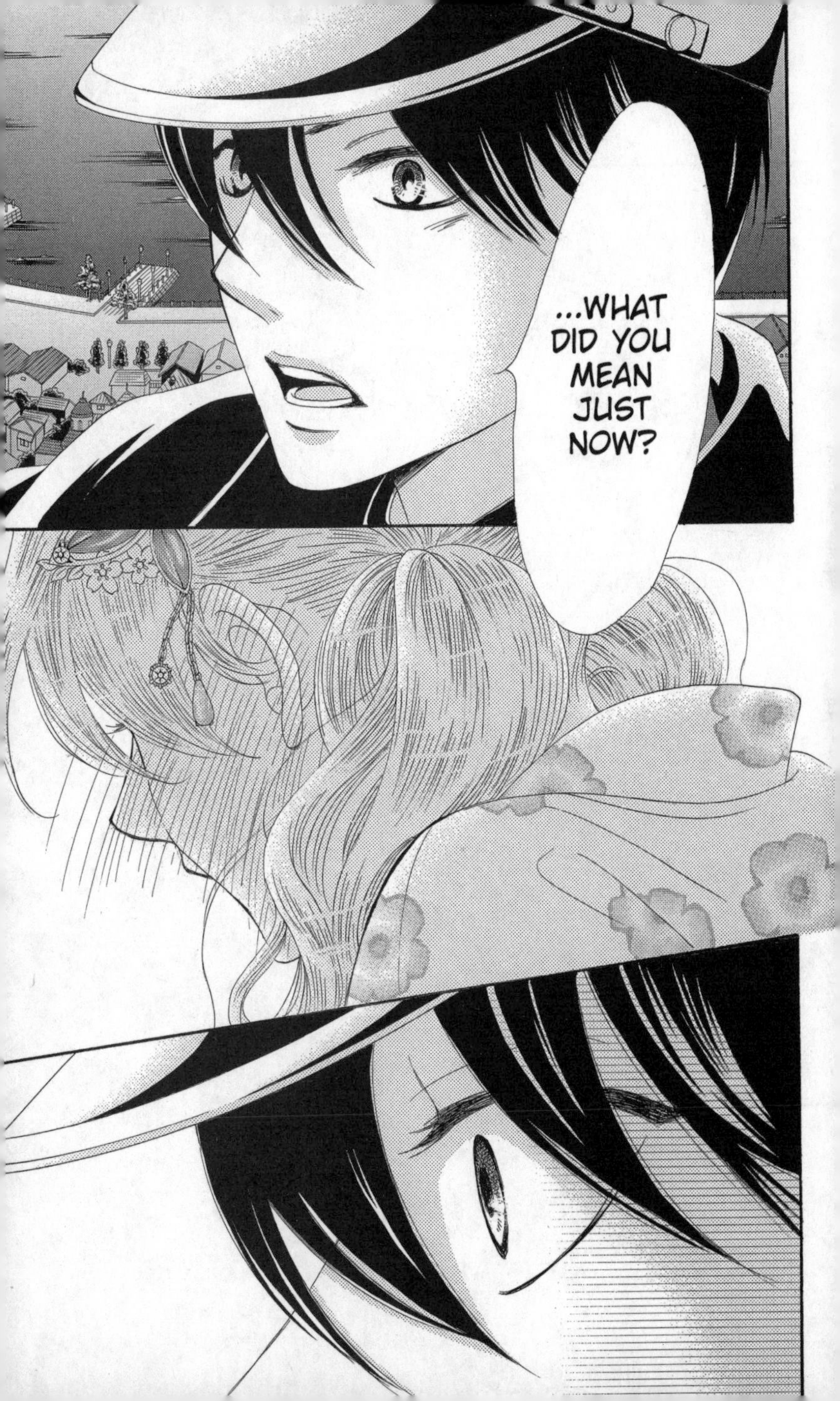
...WHAT DID YOU MEAN JUST NOW?

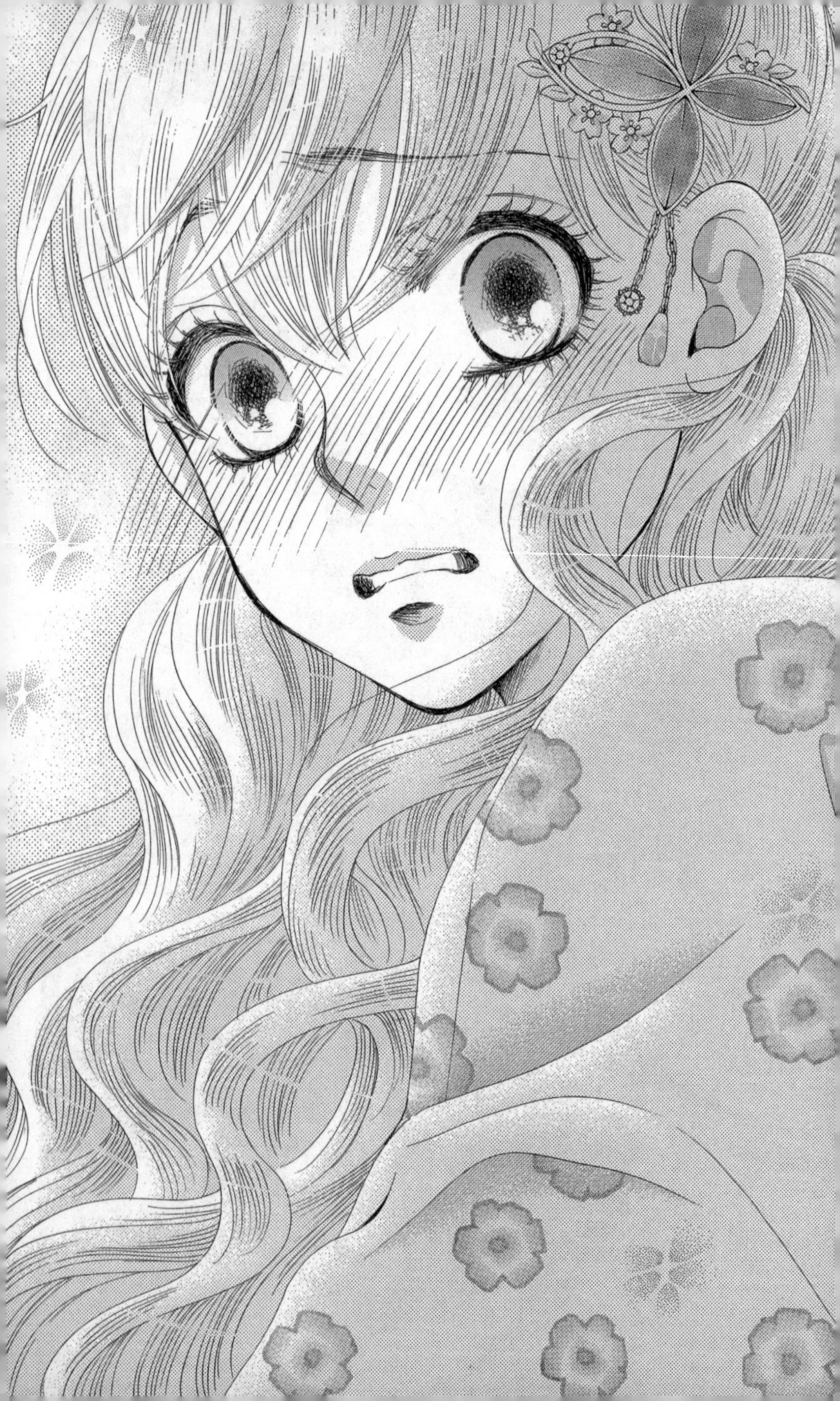

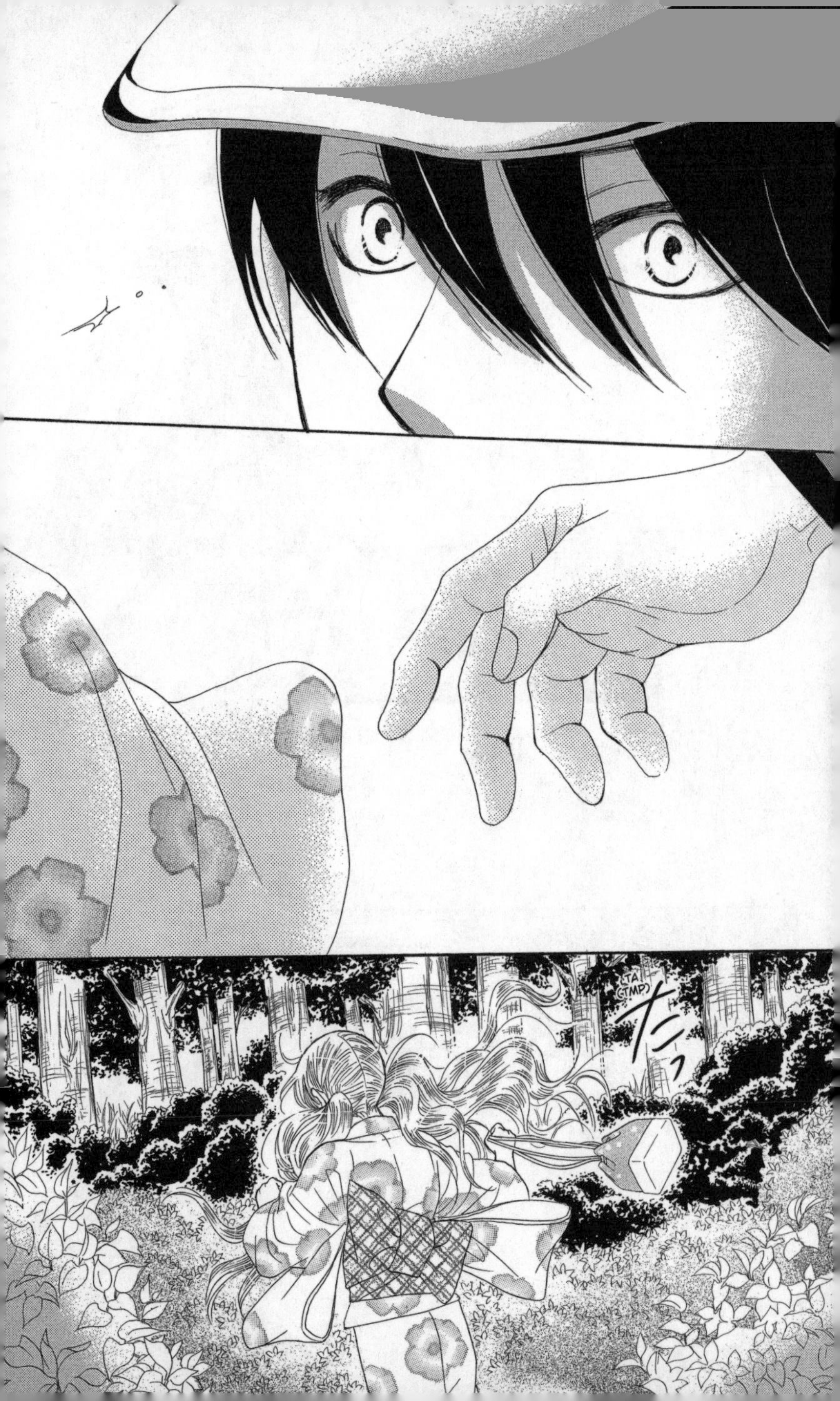
TA (TMP)
タッ

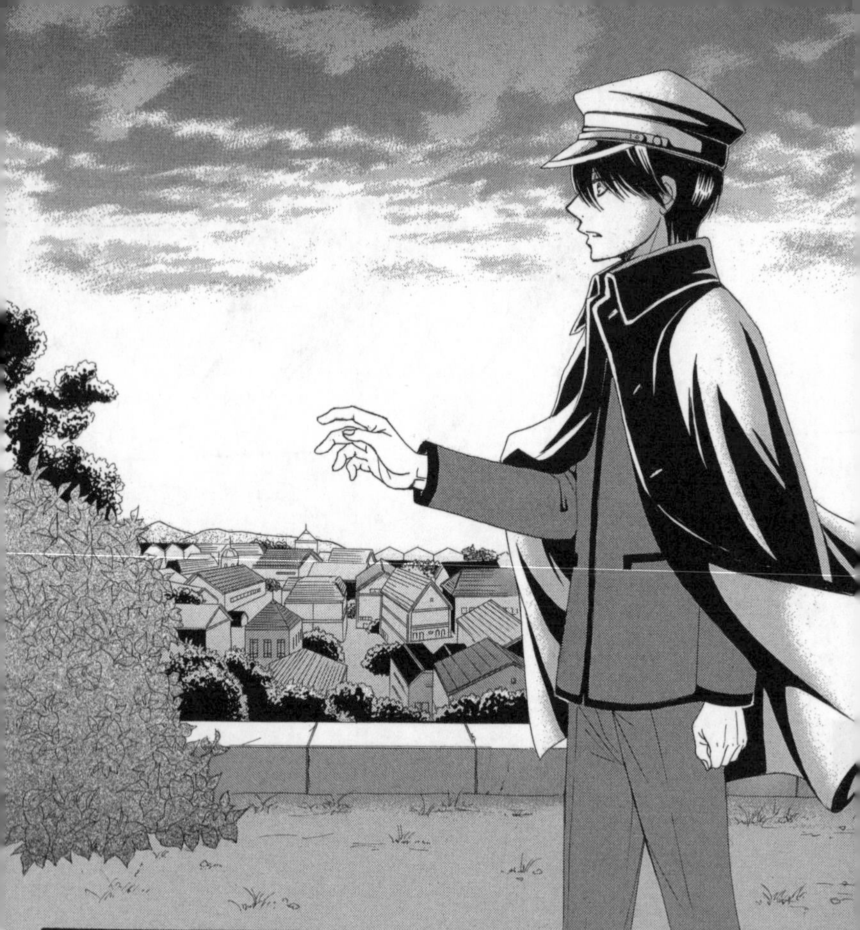
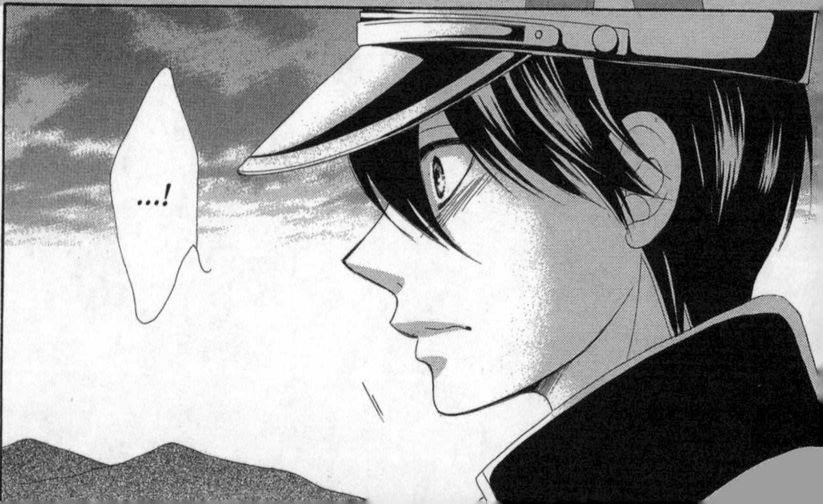
...!

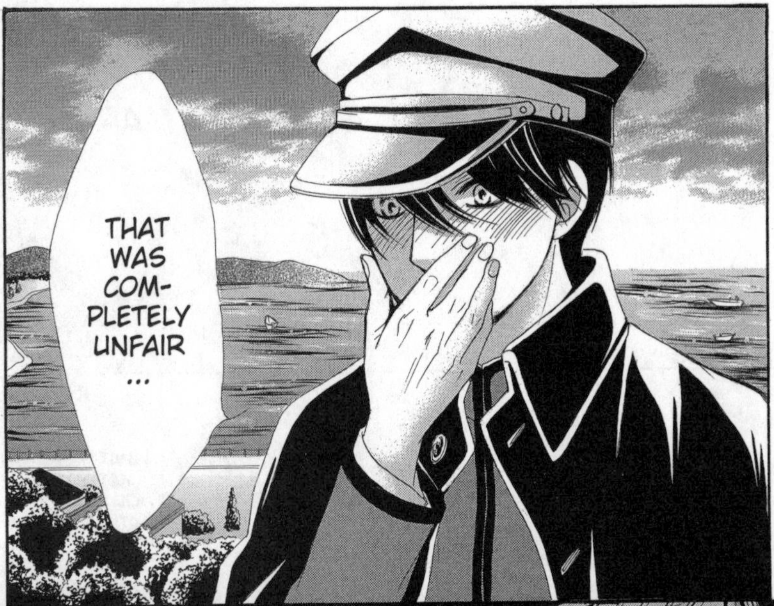
THAT WAS COM-PLETELY UNFAIR ...

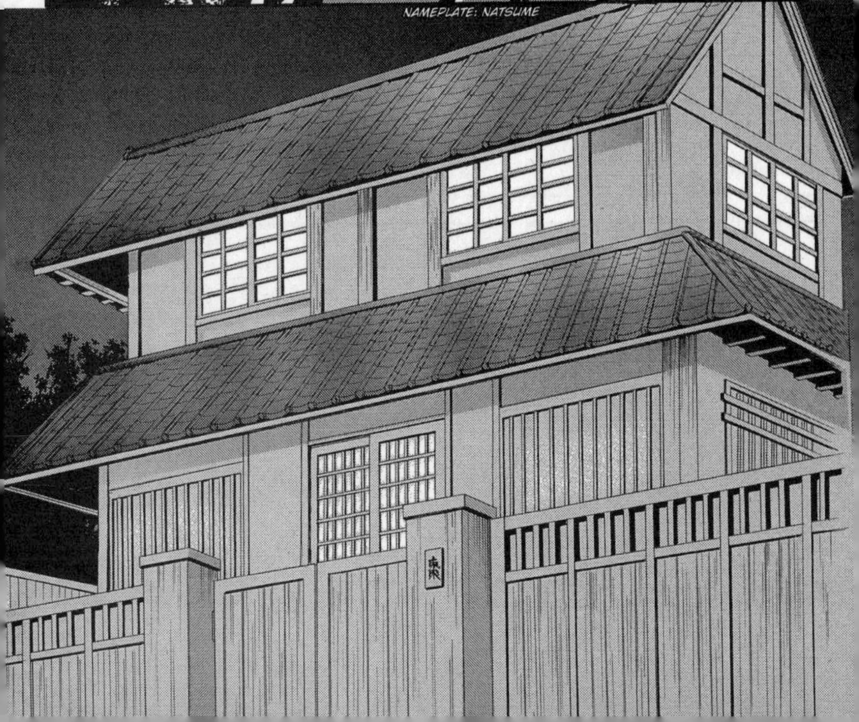
NAMEPLATE: NATSUME

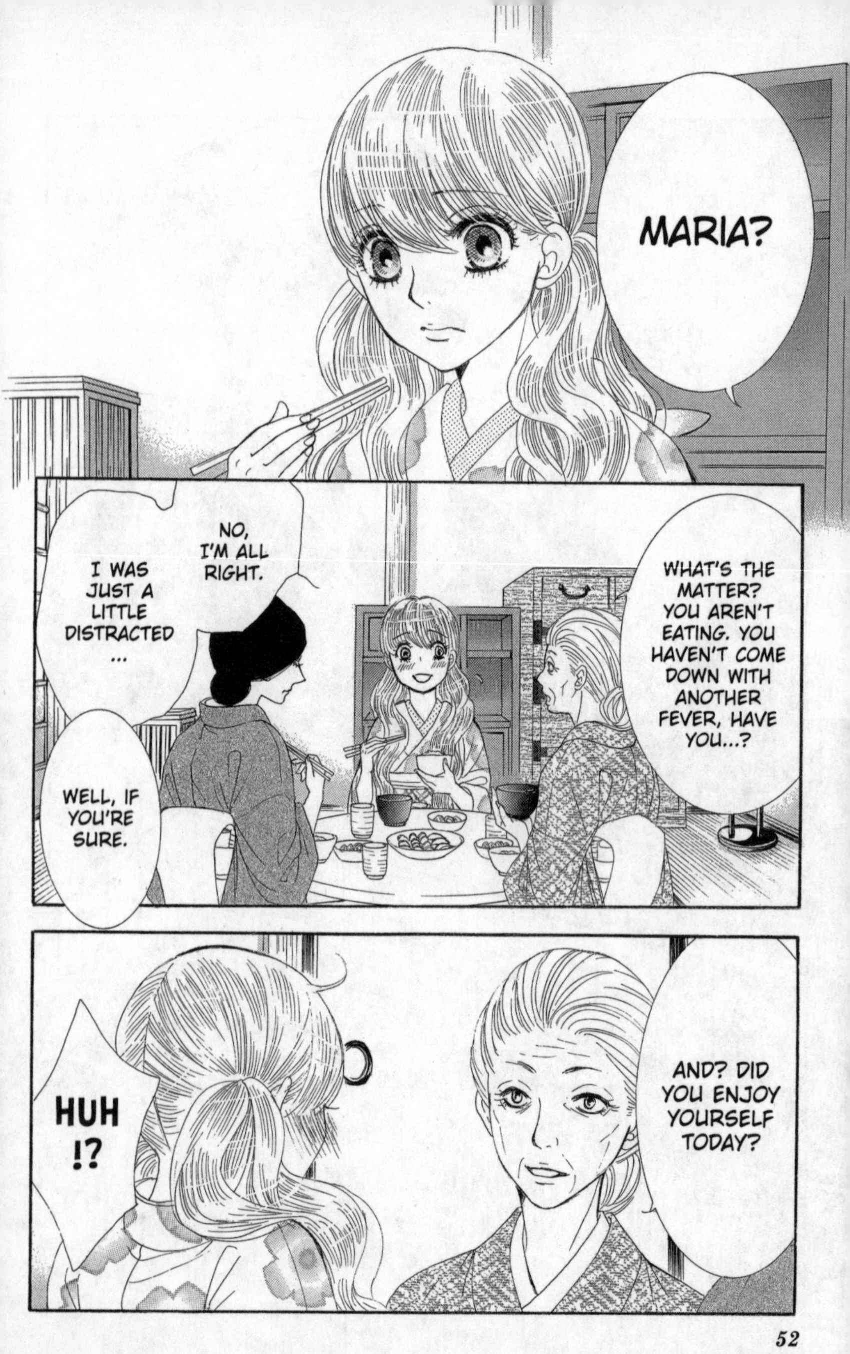
MARIA?
WHAT'S THE MATTER? YOU AREN'T EATING. YOU HAVEN'T COME DOWN WITH ANOTHER FEVER, HAVE YOU...?
NO, I'M ALL RIGHT.
I WAS JUST A LITTLE DISTRACTED ...
WELL, IF YOU'RE SURE.
AND? DID YOU ENJOY YOURSELF TODAY?
HUH !?

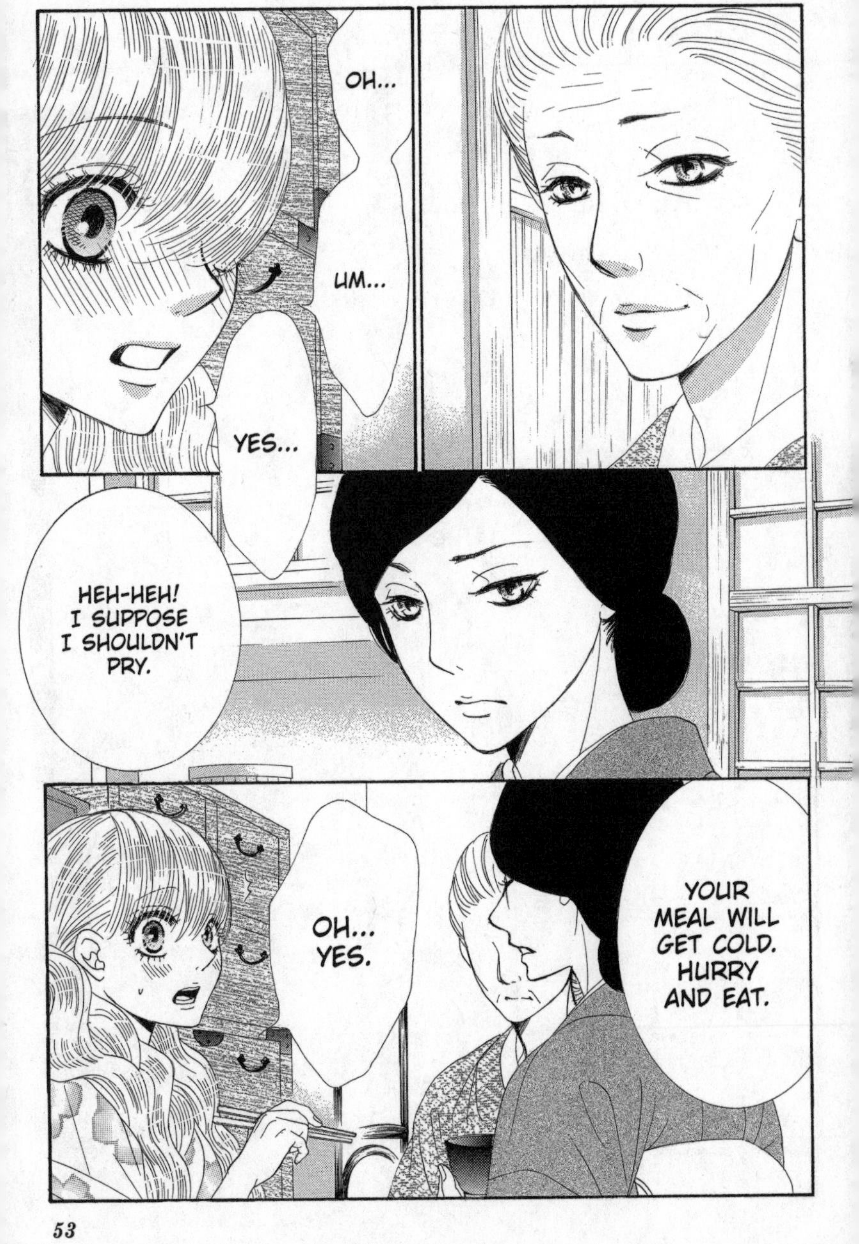
OH...
UM...
YES...
HEH-HEH! I SUPPOSE I SHOULDN'T PRY.
YOUR MEAL WILL GET COLD. HURRY AND EAT.
OH... YES.

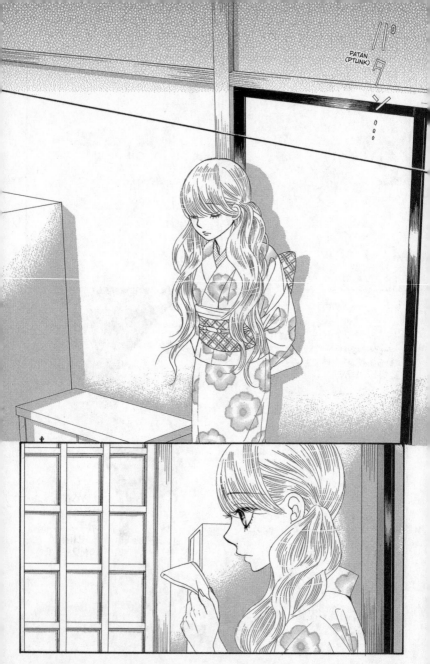

PATAN
(PTUNK)

54

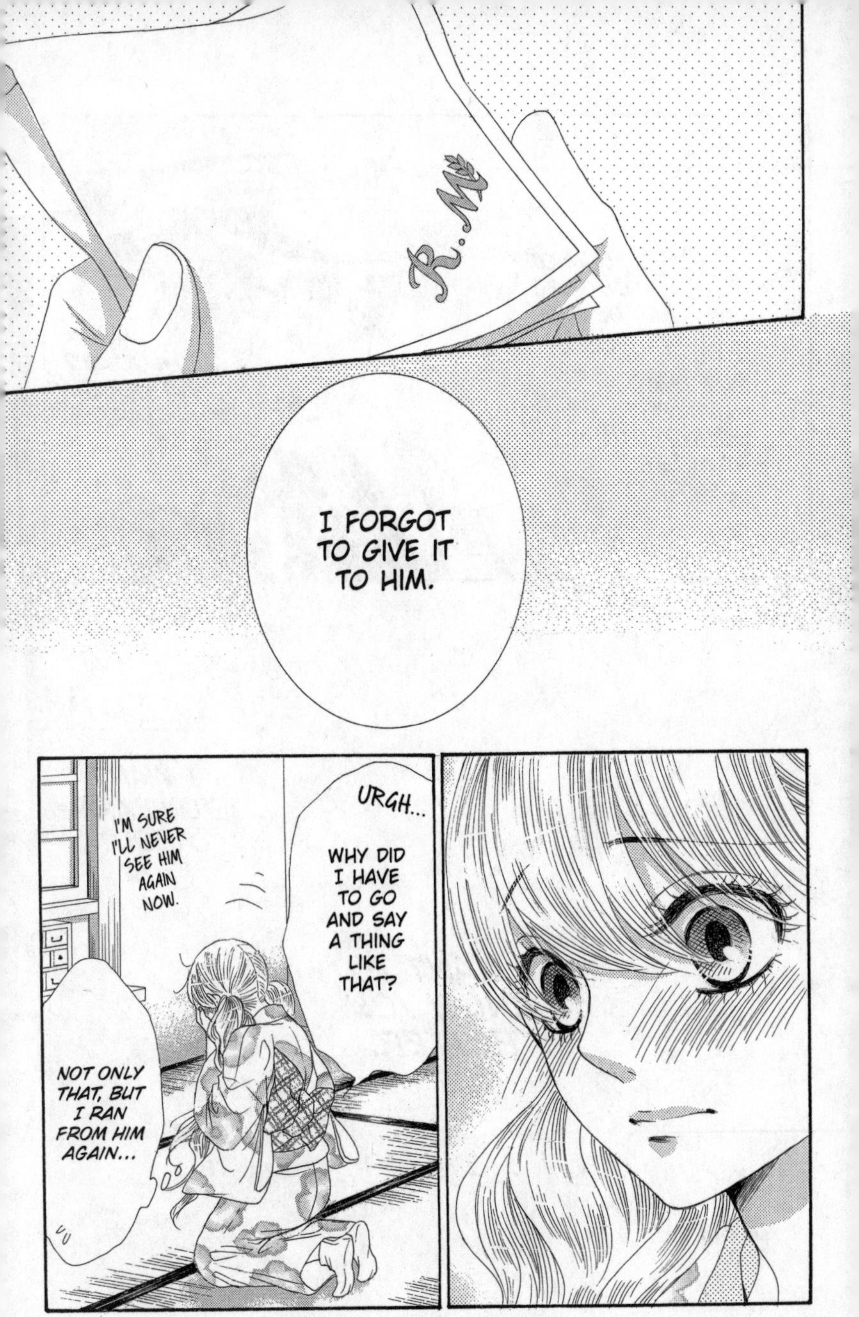
R.M
I FORGOT TO GIVE IT TO HIM.
URGH...
WHY DID I HAVE TO GO AND SAY A THING LIKE THAT?
I'M SURE I'LL NEVER SEE HIM AGAIN NOW.
NOT ONLY THAT, BUT I RAN FROM HIM AGAIN...

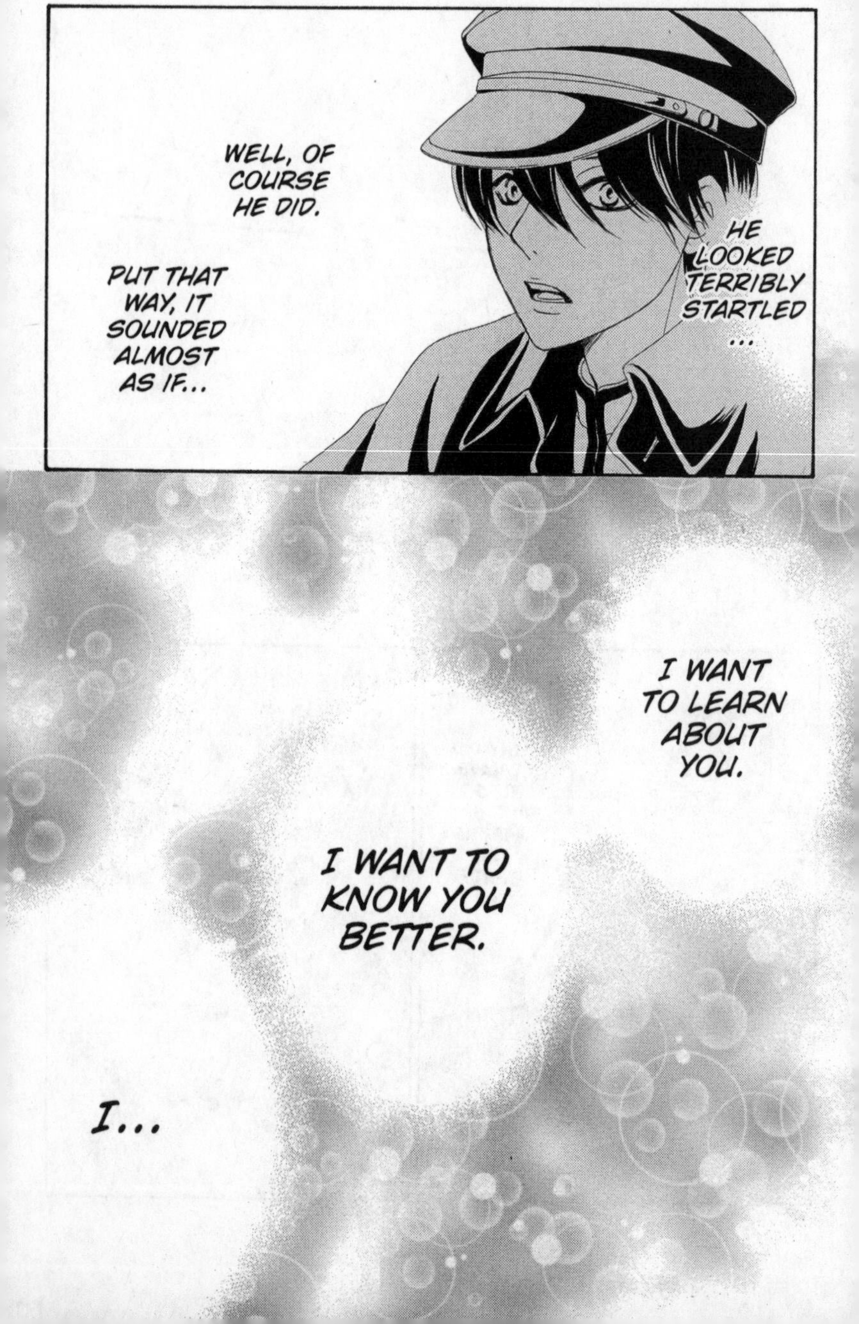
HE LOOKED TERRIBLY STARTLED...
WELL, OF COURSE HE DID.
PUT THAT WAY, IT SOUNDED ALMOST AS IF...
I WANT TO LEARN ABOUT YOU.
I WANT TO KNOW YOU BETTER.
I...

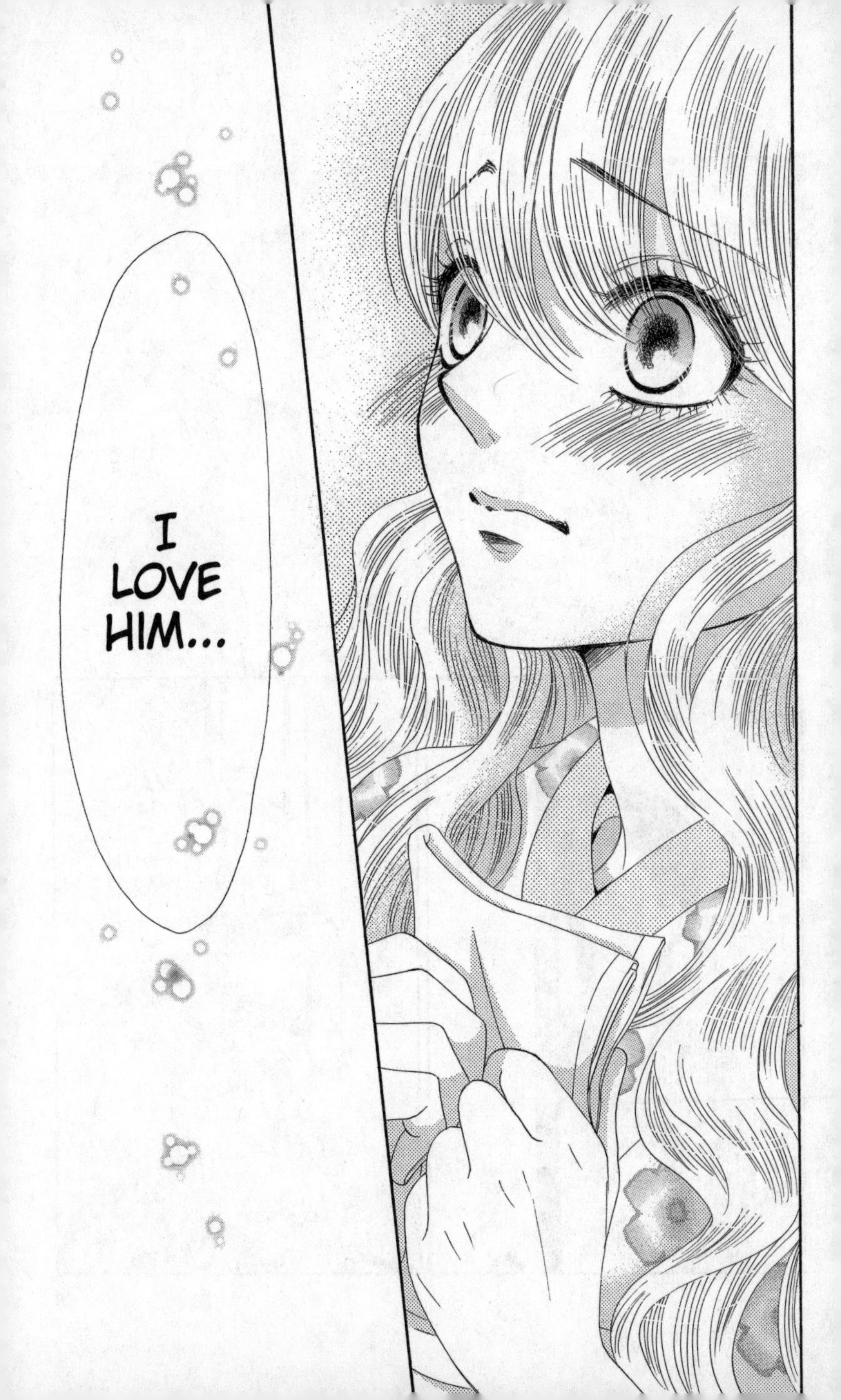
I LOVE HIM...

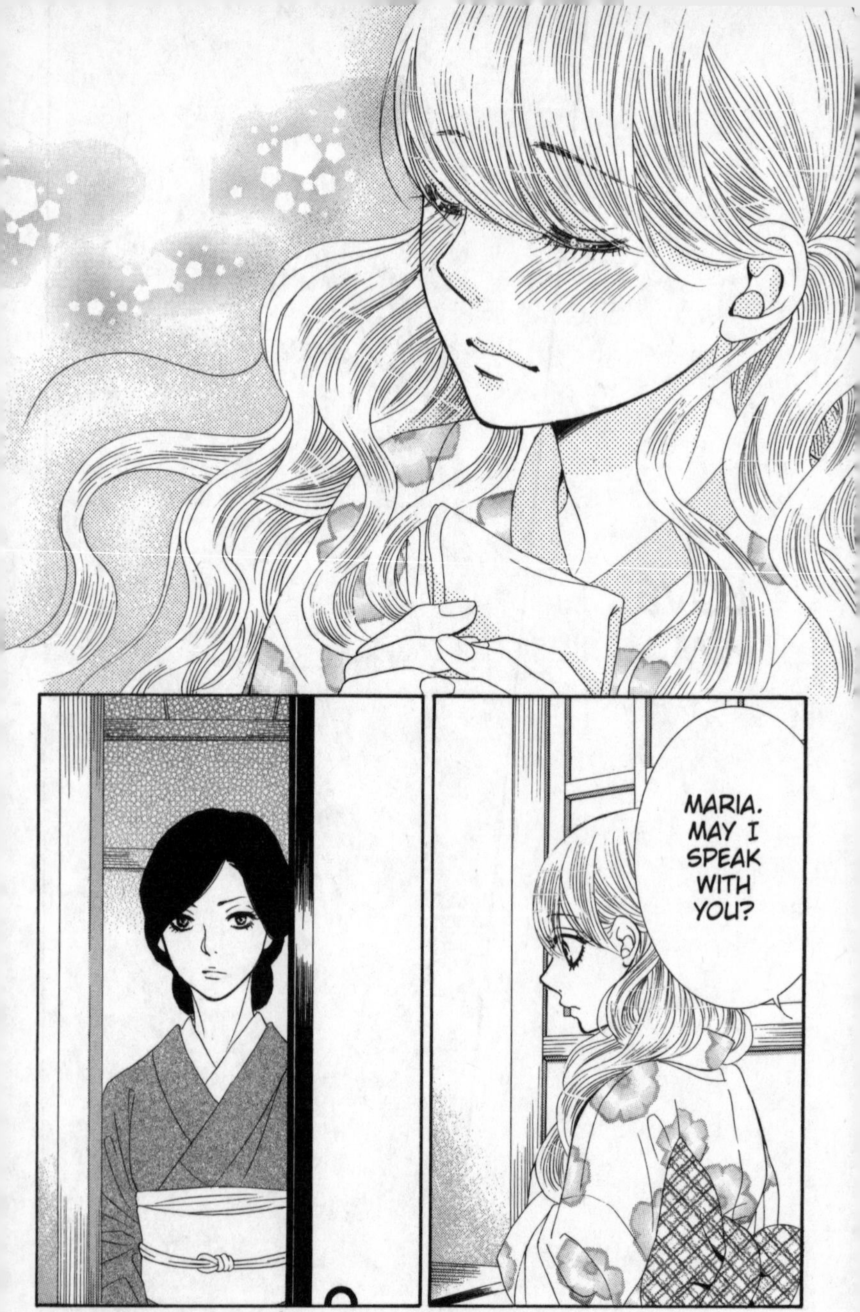
MARIA. MAY I SPEAK WITH YOU?

M-MOTHER!?

OH, THAT'S...

I DON'T RECOGNIZE THIS HANDKERCHIEF.

R. M

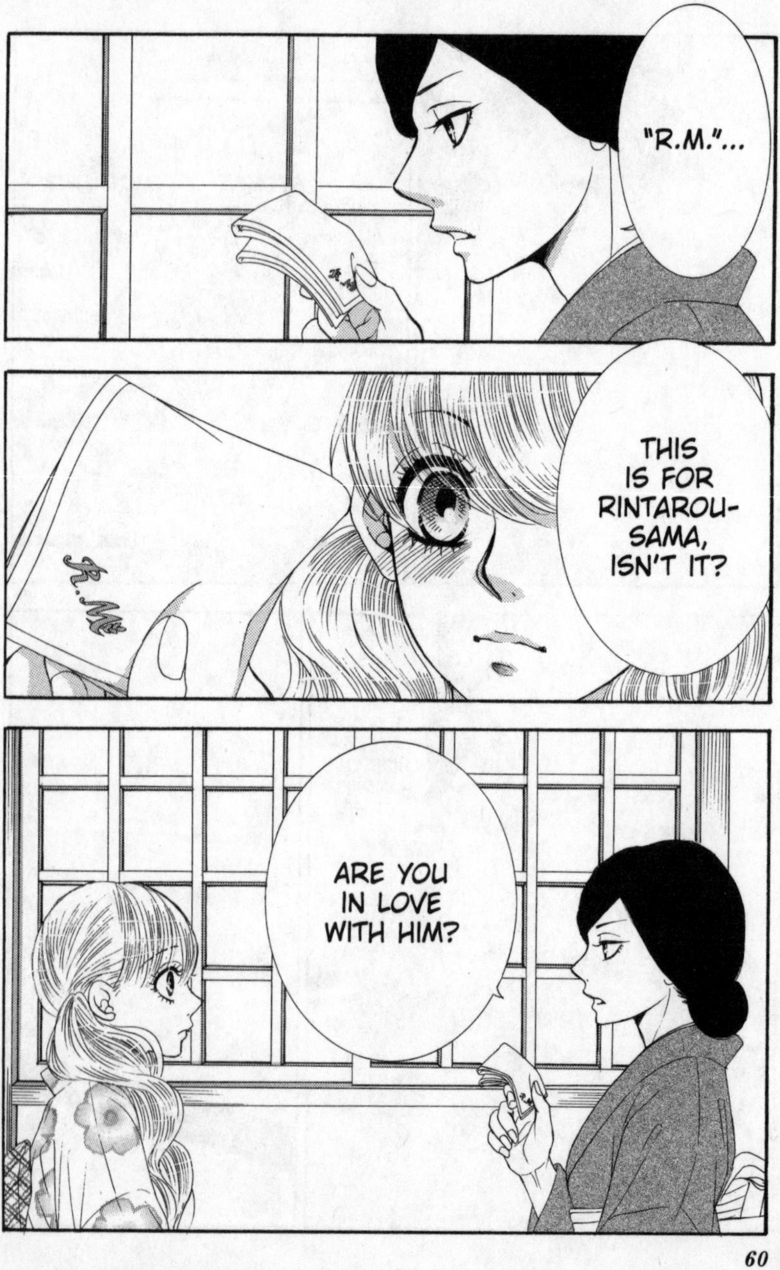
"R.M."...
THIS IS FOR RINTAROU-SAMA, ISN'T IT?
ARE YOU IN LOVE WITH HIM?

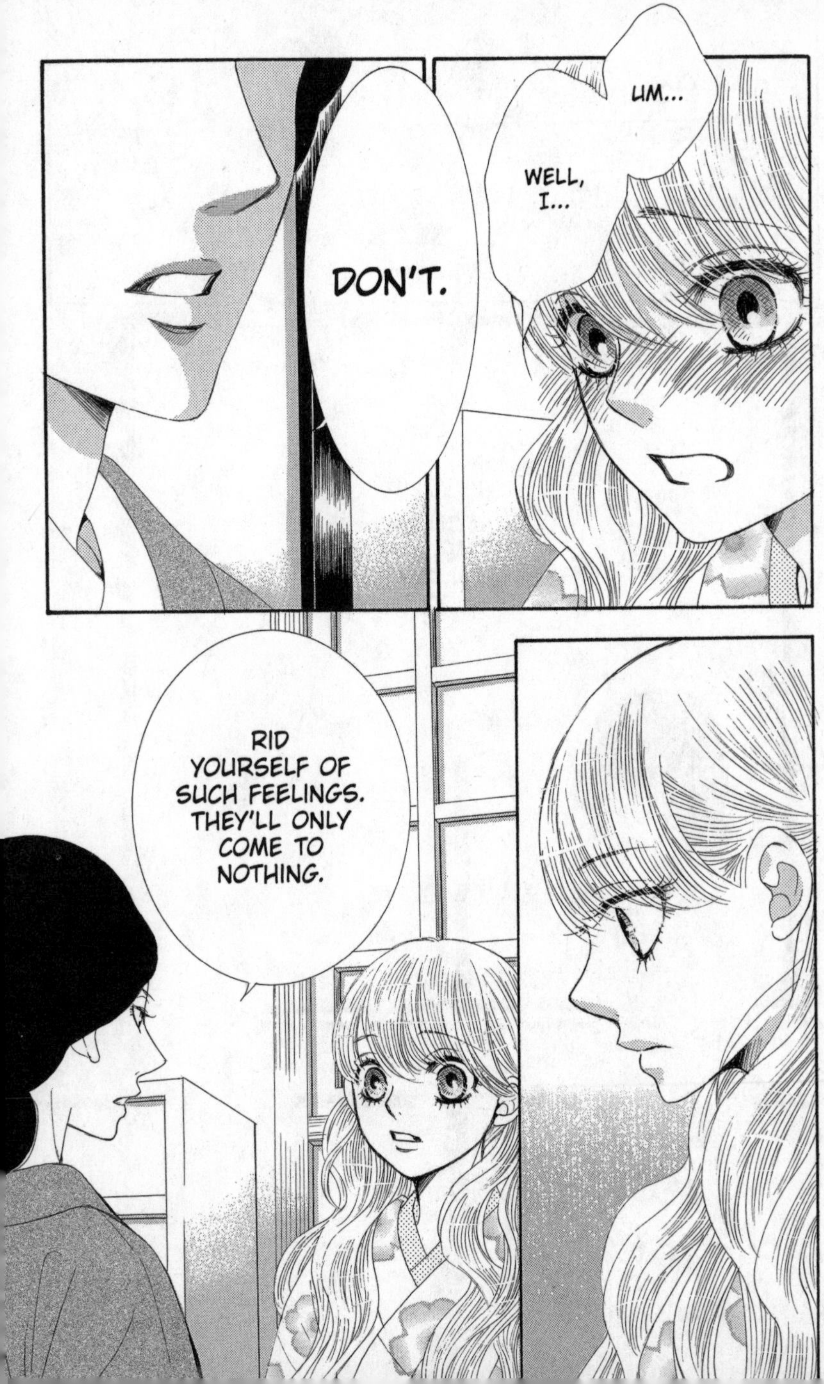
UM...
WELL, I...
DON'T.
RID YOURSELF OF SUCH FEELINGS. THEY'LL ONLY COME TO NOTHING.

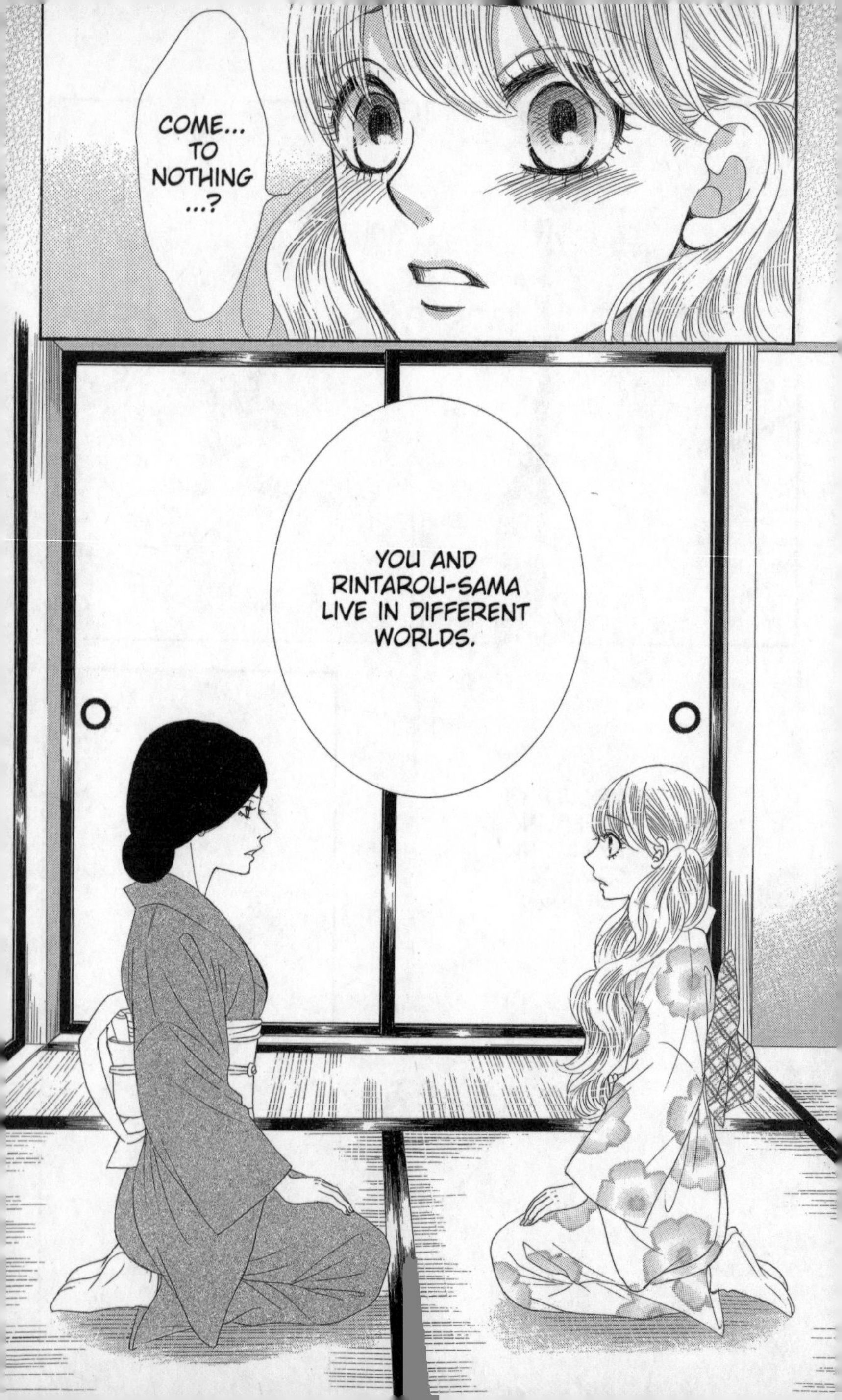
COME... TO NOTHING ...?
YOU AND RINTAROU-SAMA LIVE IN DIFFERENT WORLDS.

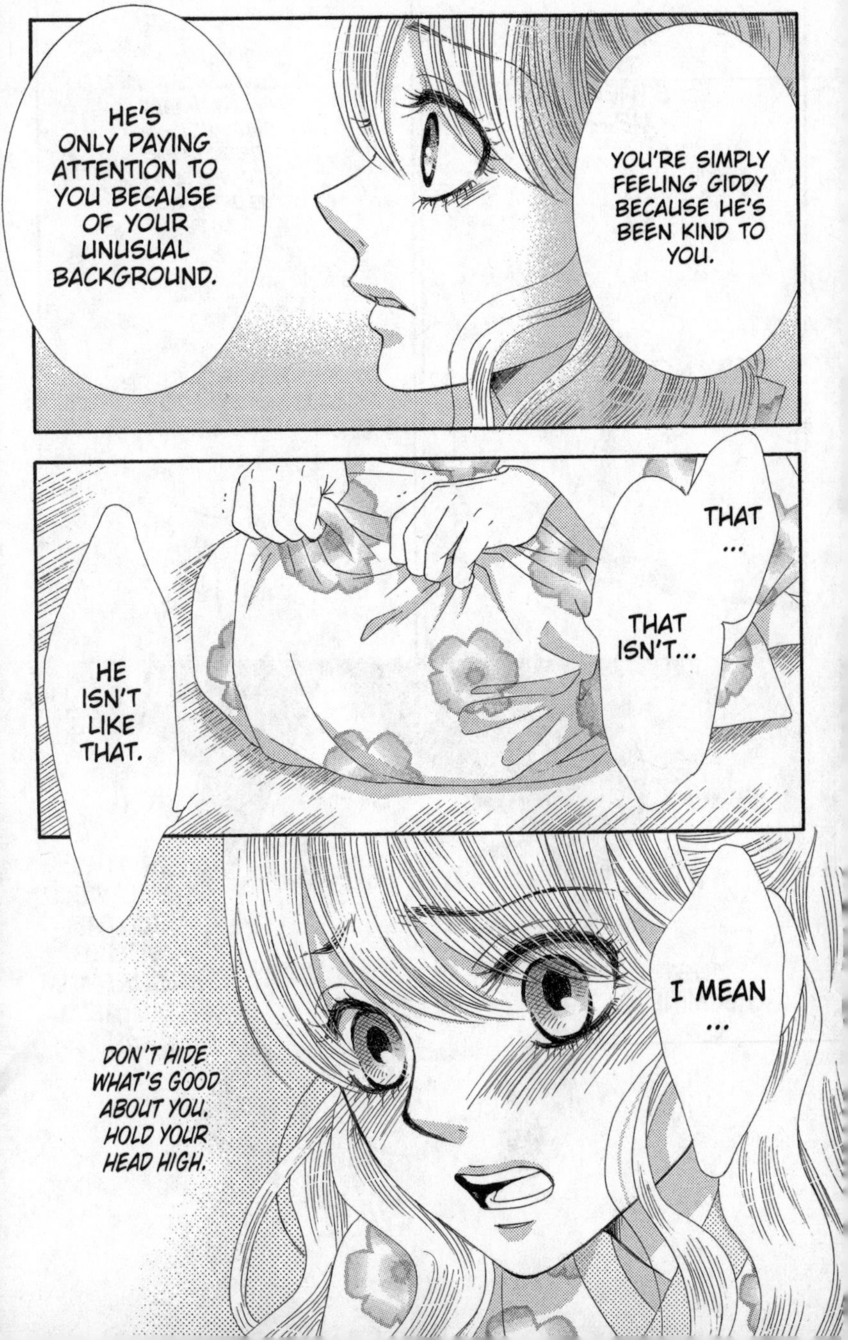
YOU'RE SIMPLY FEELING GIDDY BECAUSE HE'S BEEN KIND TO YOU.
HE'S ONLY PAYING ATTENTION TO YOU BECAUSE OF YOUR UNUSUAL BACKGROUND.
THAT ...
THAT ISN'T...
HE ISN'T LIKE THAT.
I MEAN ...
DON'T HIDE WHAT'S GOOD ABOUT YOU. HOLD YOUR HEAD HIGH.

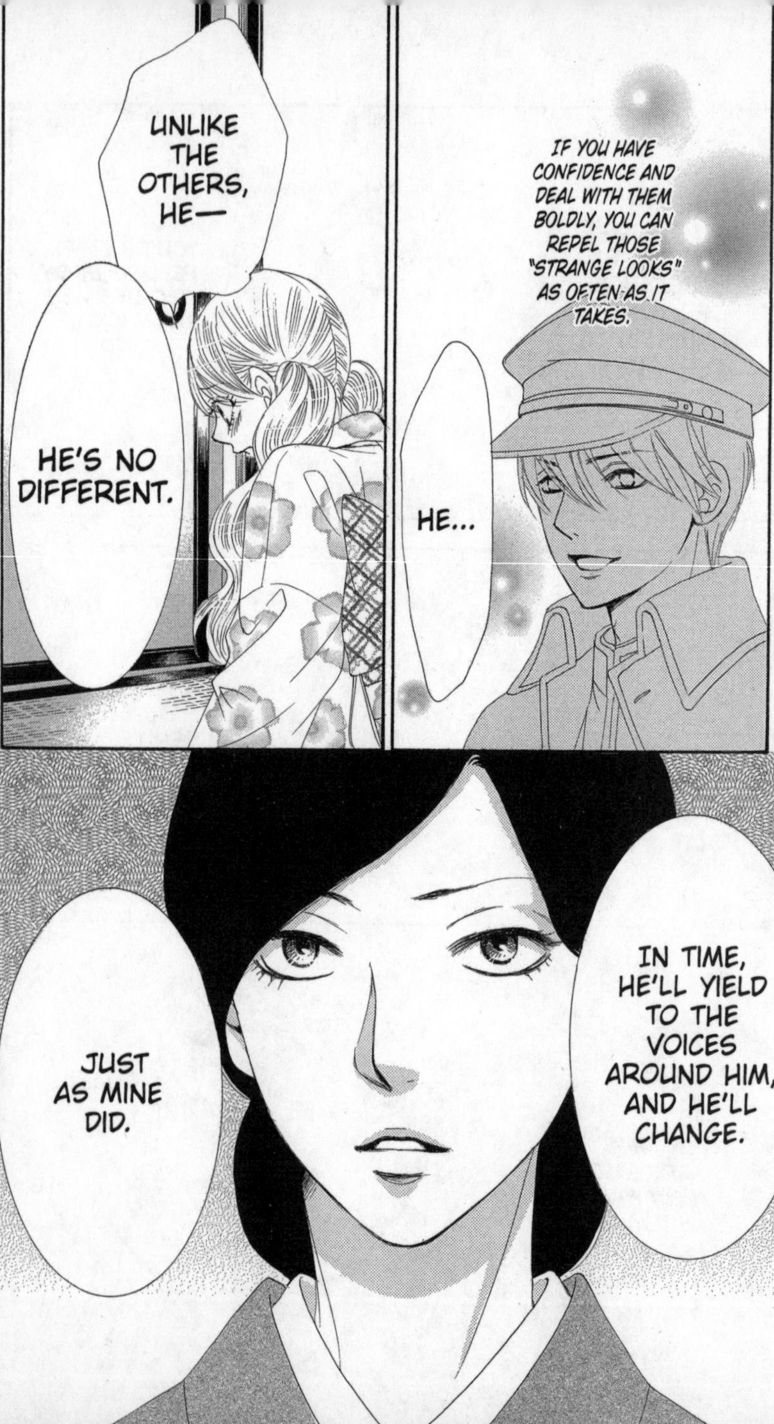
IF YOU HAVE CONFIDENCE AND DEAL WITH THEM BOLDLY, YOU CAN REPEL THOSE "STRANGE LOOKS" AS OFTEN AS IT TAKES.
HE...
UNLIKE THE OTHERS, HE—
HE'S NO DIFFERENT.
IN TIME, HE'LL YIELD TO THE VOICES AROUND HIM, AND HE'LL CHANGE.
JUST AS MINE DID.

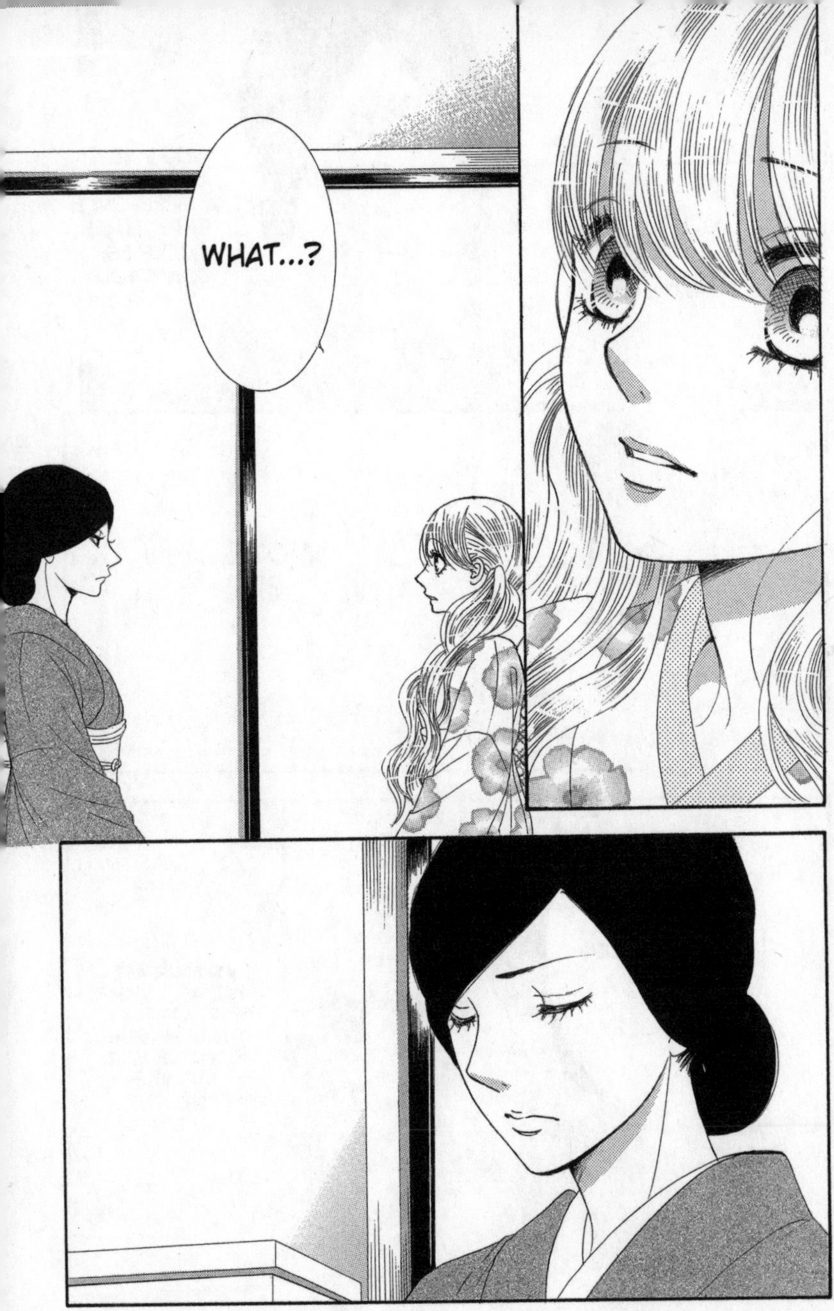
WHAT...?

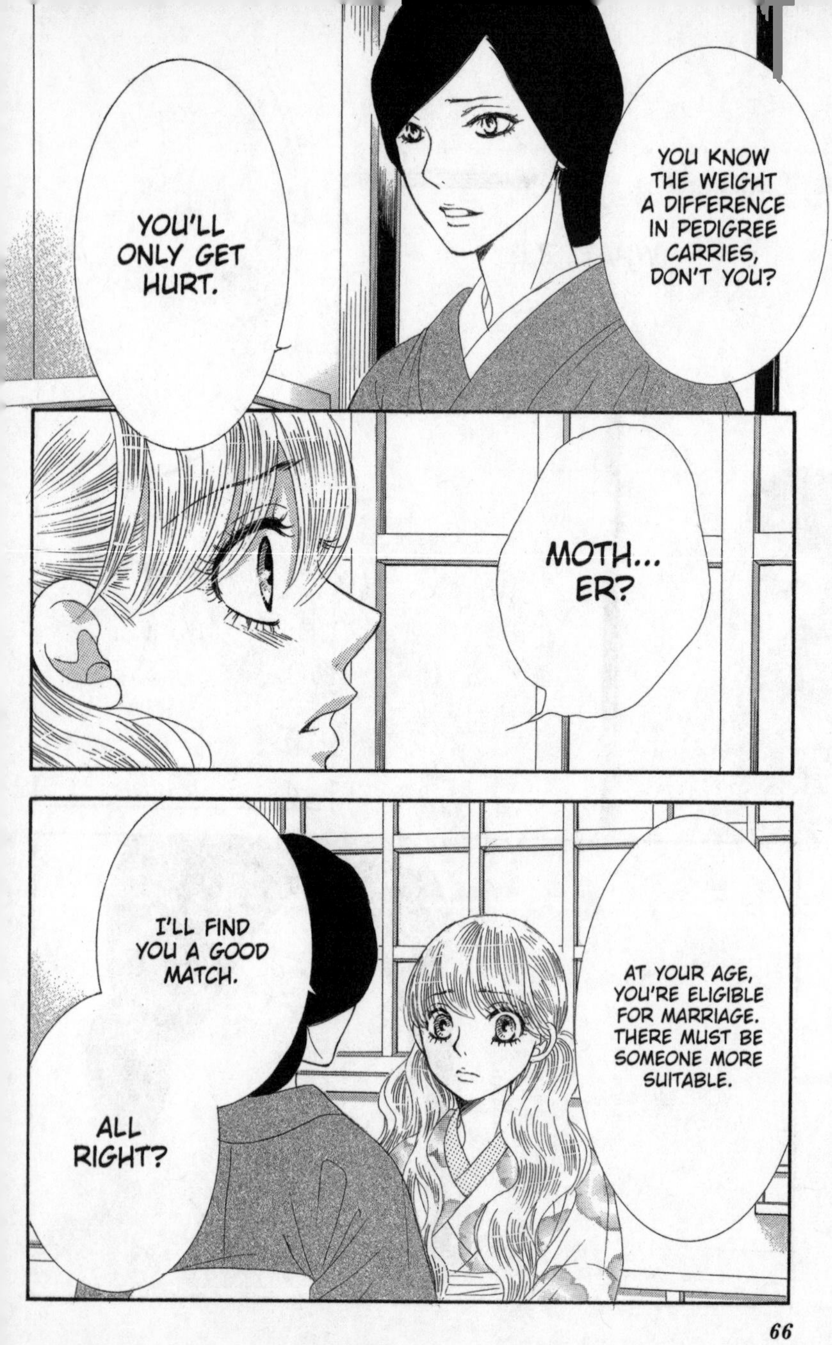
YOU KNOW THE WEIGHT A DIFFERENCE IN PEDIGREE CARRIES, DON'T YOU?
YOU'LL ONLY GET HURT.
MOTH... ER?
AT YOUR AGE, YOU'RE ELIGIBLE FOR MARRIAGE. THERE MUST BE SOMEONE MORE SUITABLE.
I'LL FIND YOU A GOOD MATCH.
ALL RIGHT?

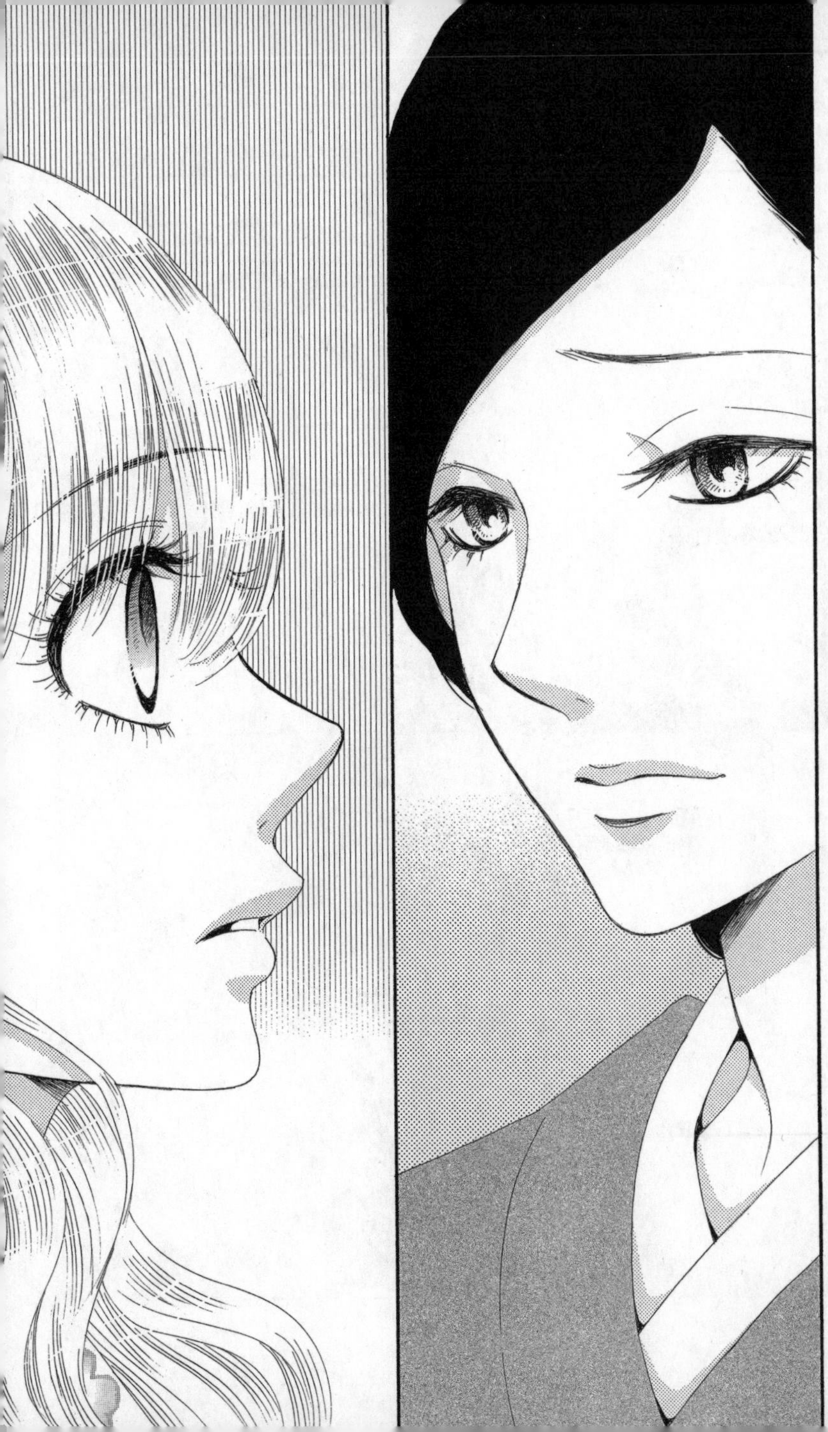

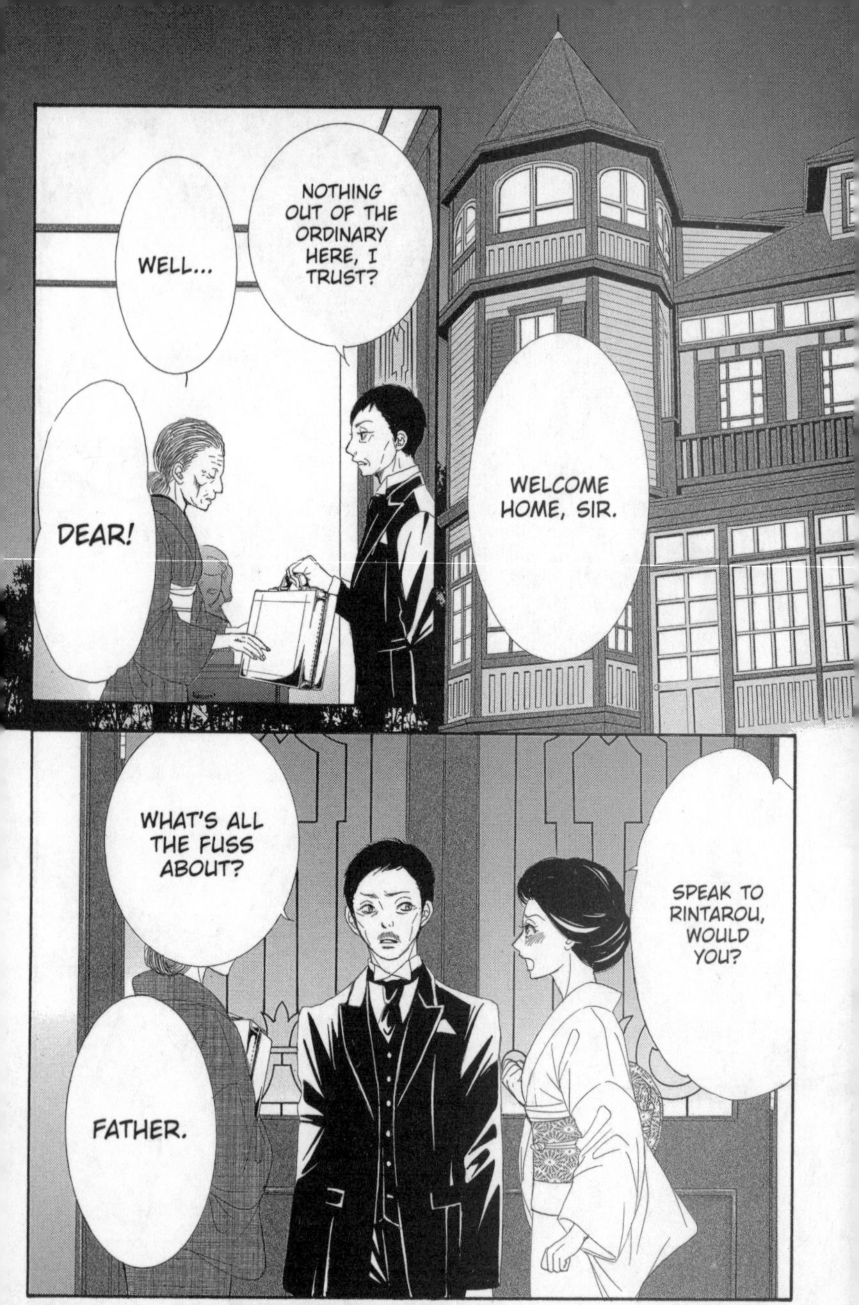
WELCOME HOME, SIR.
NOTHING OUT OF THE ORDINARY HERE, I TRUST?
WELL...
DEAR!
SPEAK TO RINTAROU, WOULD YOU?
WHAT'S ALL THE FUSS ABOUT?
FATHER.

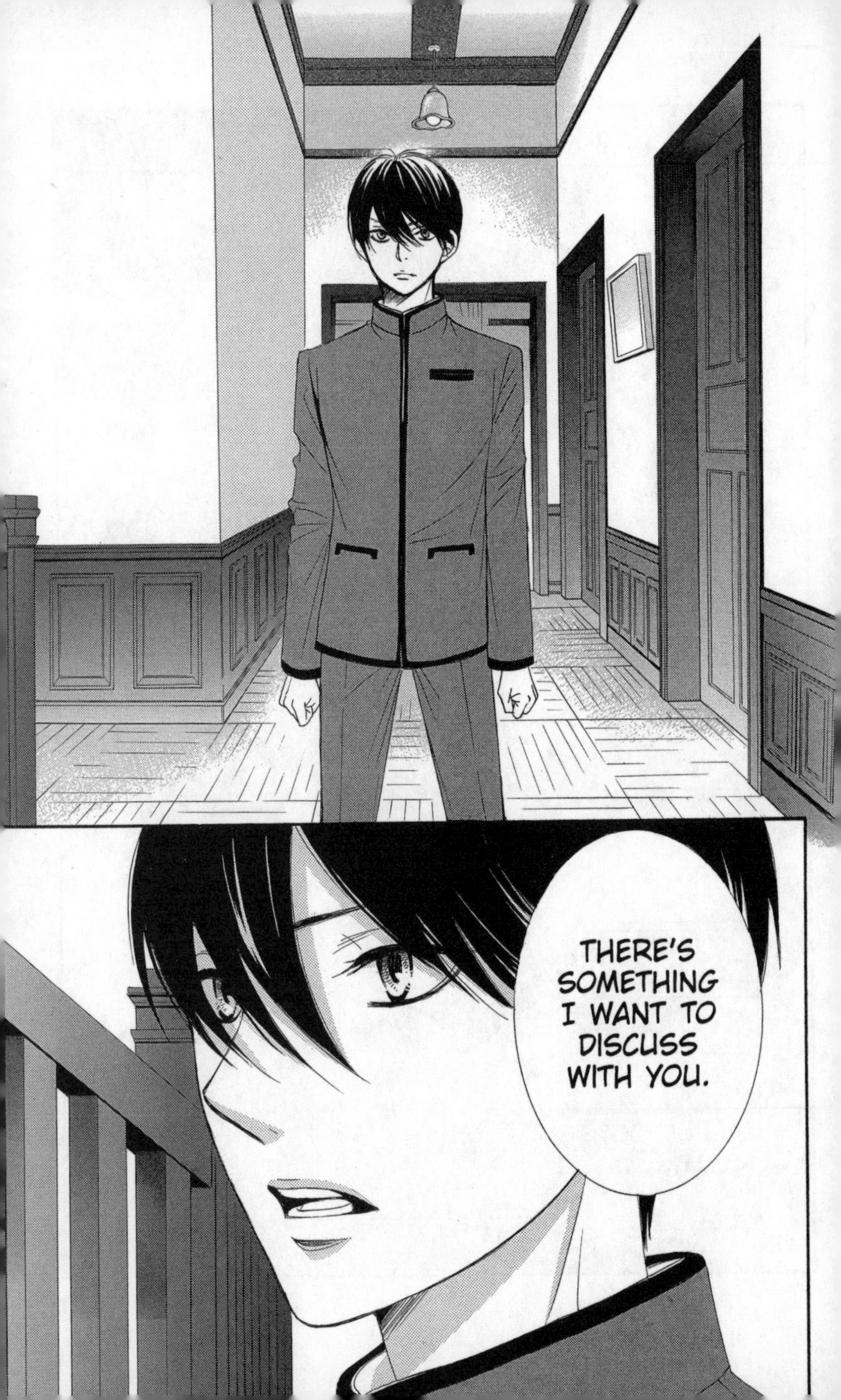
THERE'S SOMETHING I WANT TO DISCUSS WITH YOU.

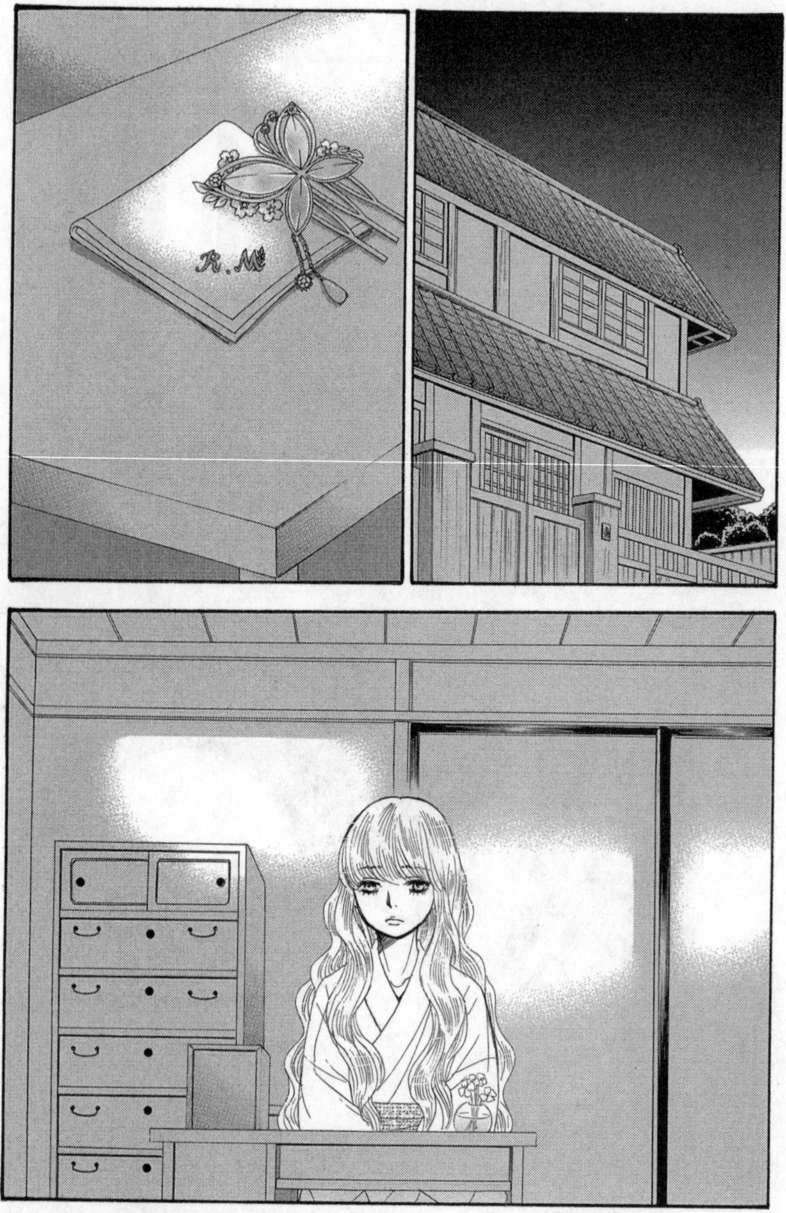
R.M

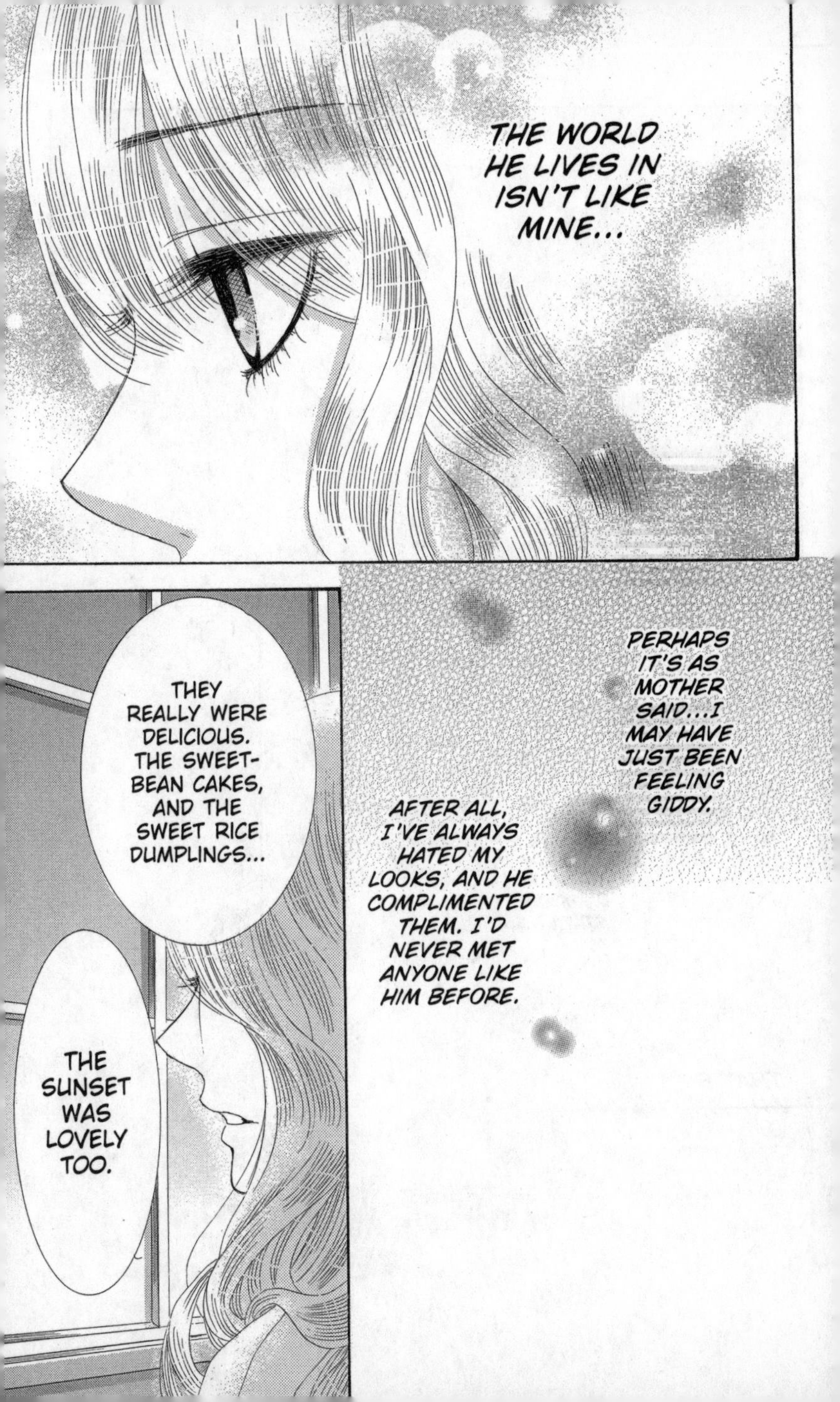
THE WORLD HE LIVES IN ISN'T LIKE MINE...
PERHAPS IT'S AS MOTHER SAID...I MAY HAVE JUST BEEN FEELING GIDDY.
AFTER ALL, I'VE ALWAYS HATED MY LOOKS, AND HE COMPLIMENTED THEM. I'D NEVER MET ANYONE LIKE HIM BEFORE.
THEY REALLY WERE DELICIOUS. THE SWEET-BEAN CAKES, AND THE SWEET RICE DUMPLINGS...
THE SUNSET WAS LOVELY TOO.

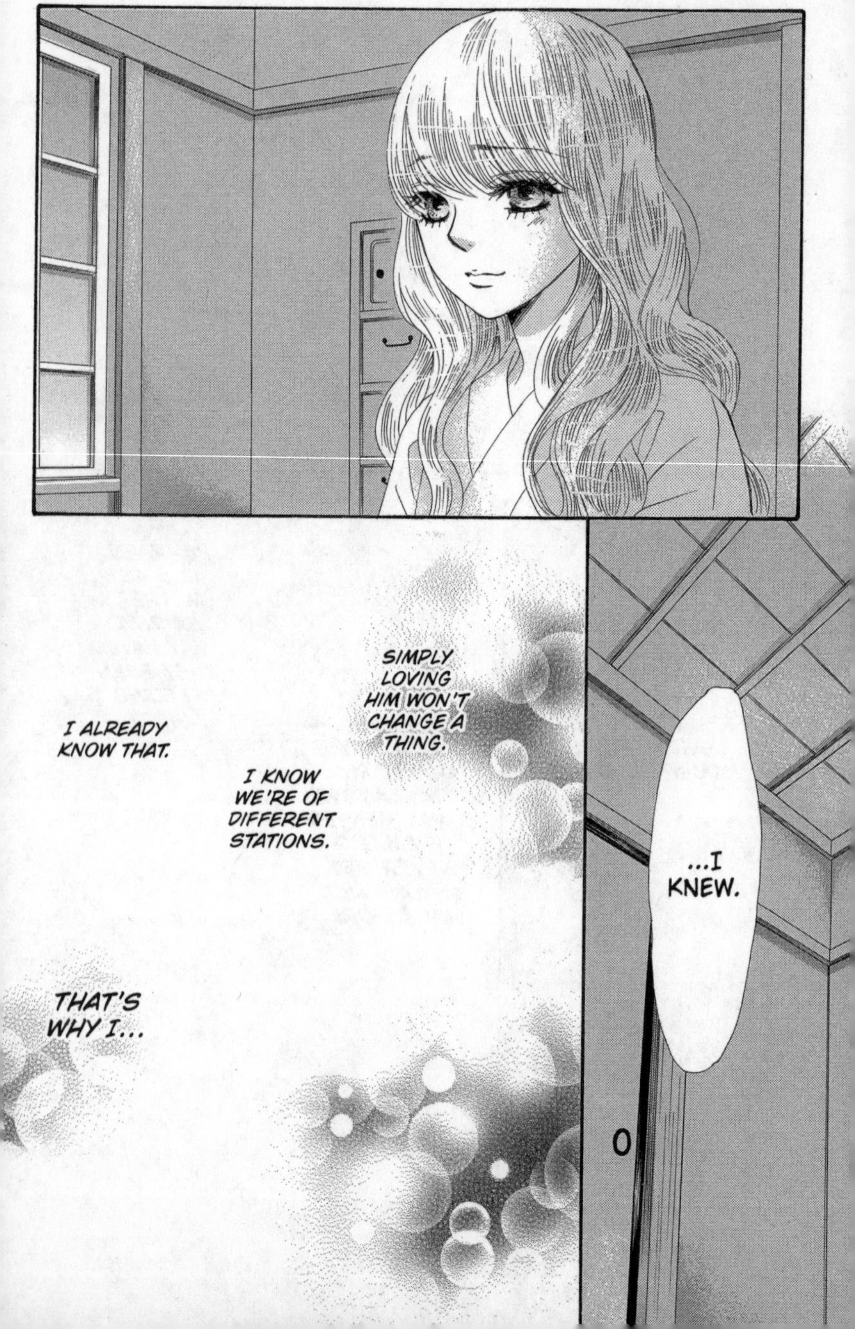
...I KNEW.
SIMPLY LOVING HIM WON'T CHANGE A THING.
I KNOW WE'RE OF DIFFERENT STATIONS.
I ALREADY KNOW THAT.
THAT'S WHY I...

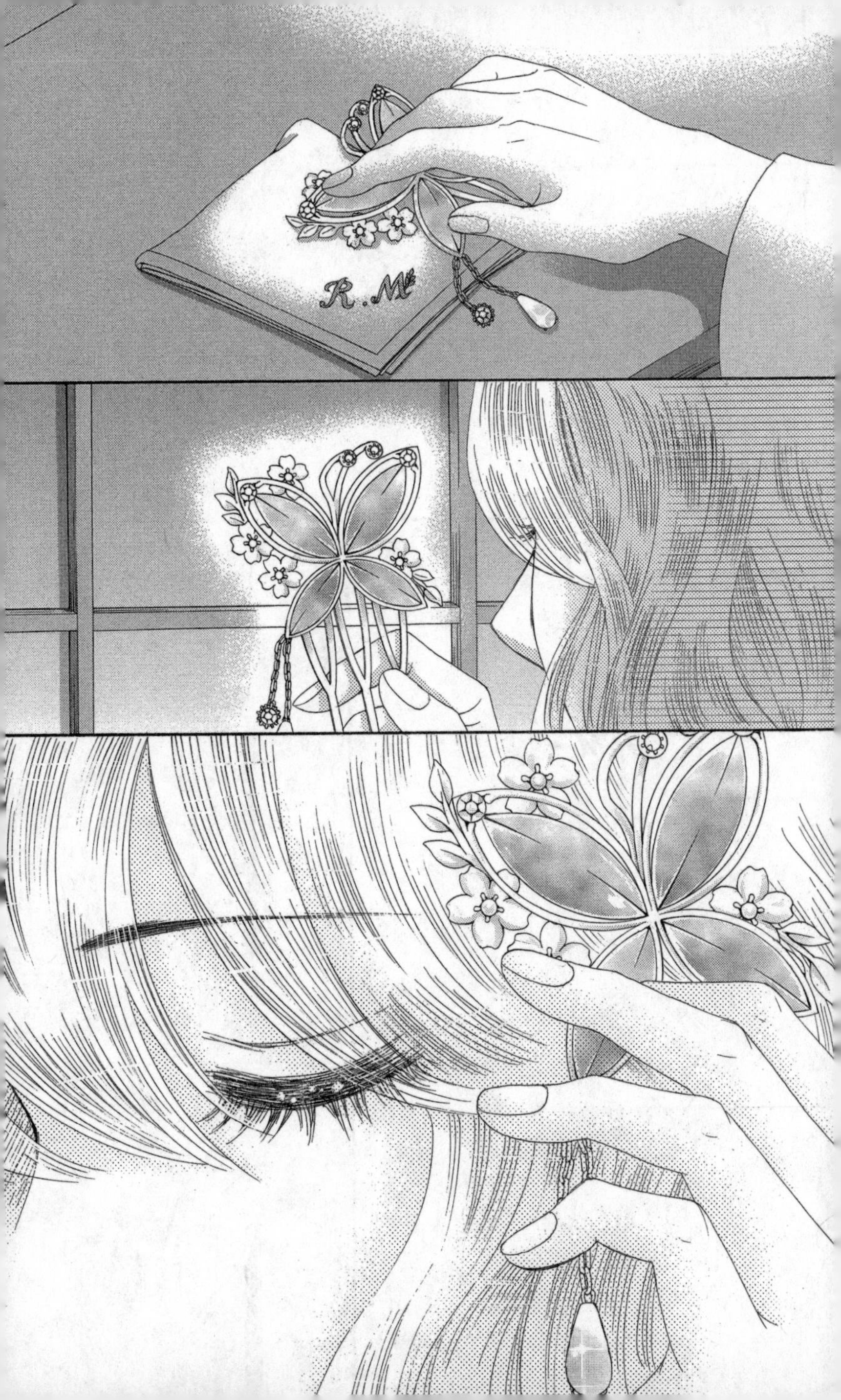
R.M

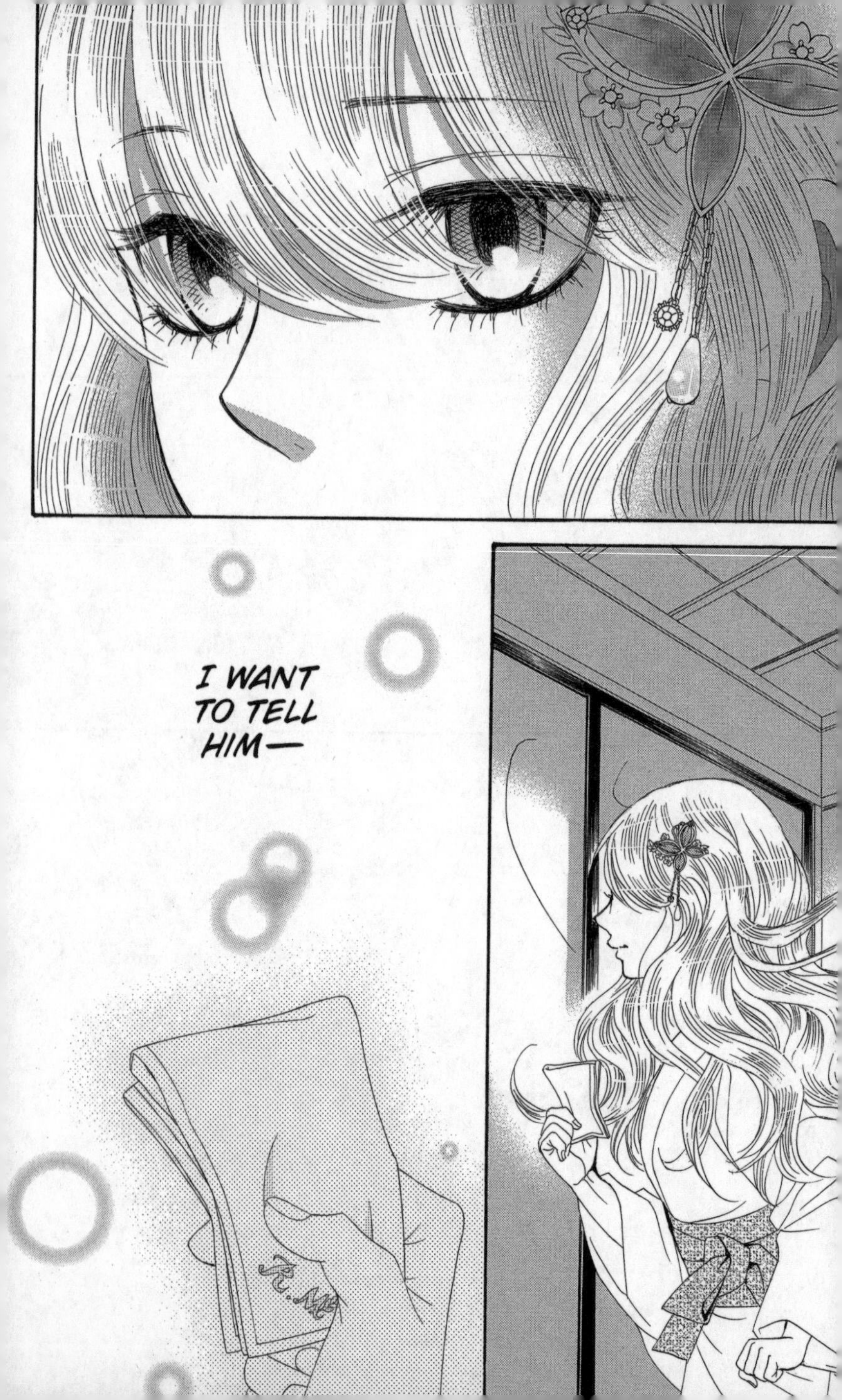
I WANT TO TELL HIM—

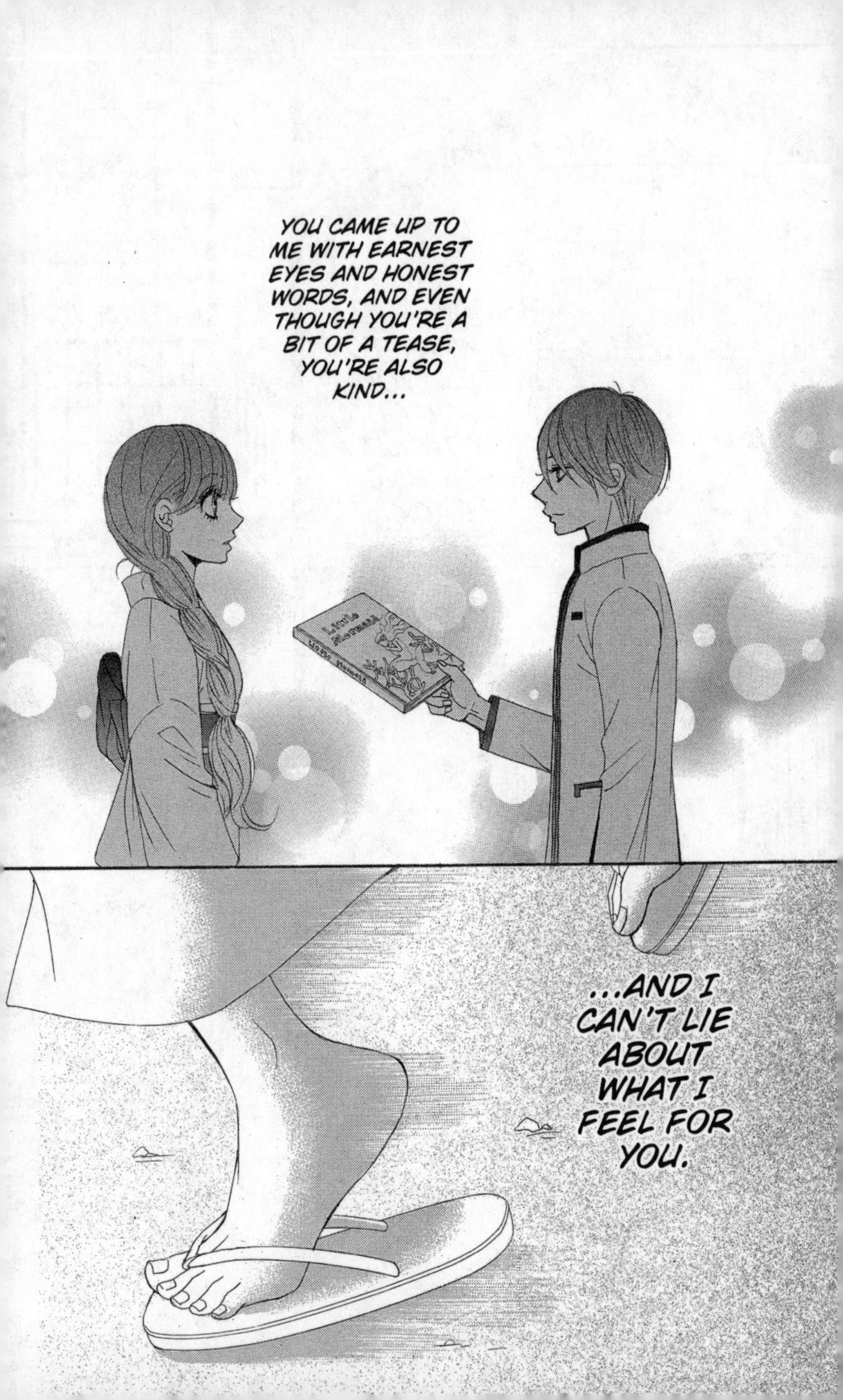
YOU CAME UP TO ME WITH EARNEST EYES AND HONEST WORDS, AND EVEN THOUGH YOU'RE A BIT OF A TEASE, YOU'RE ALSO KIND...
...AND I CAN'T LIE ABOUT WHAT I FEEL FOR YOU.

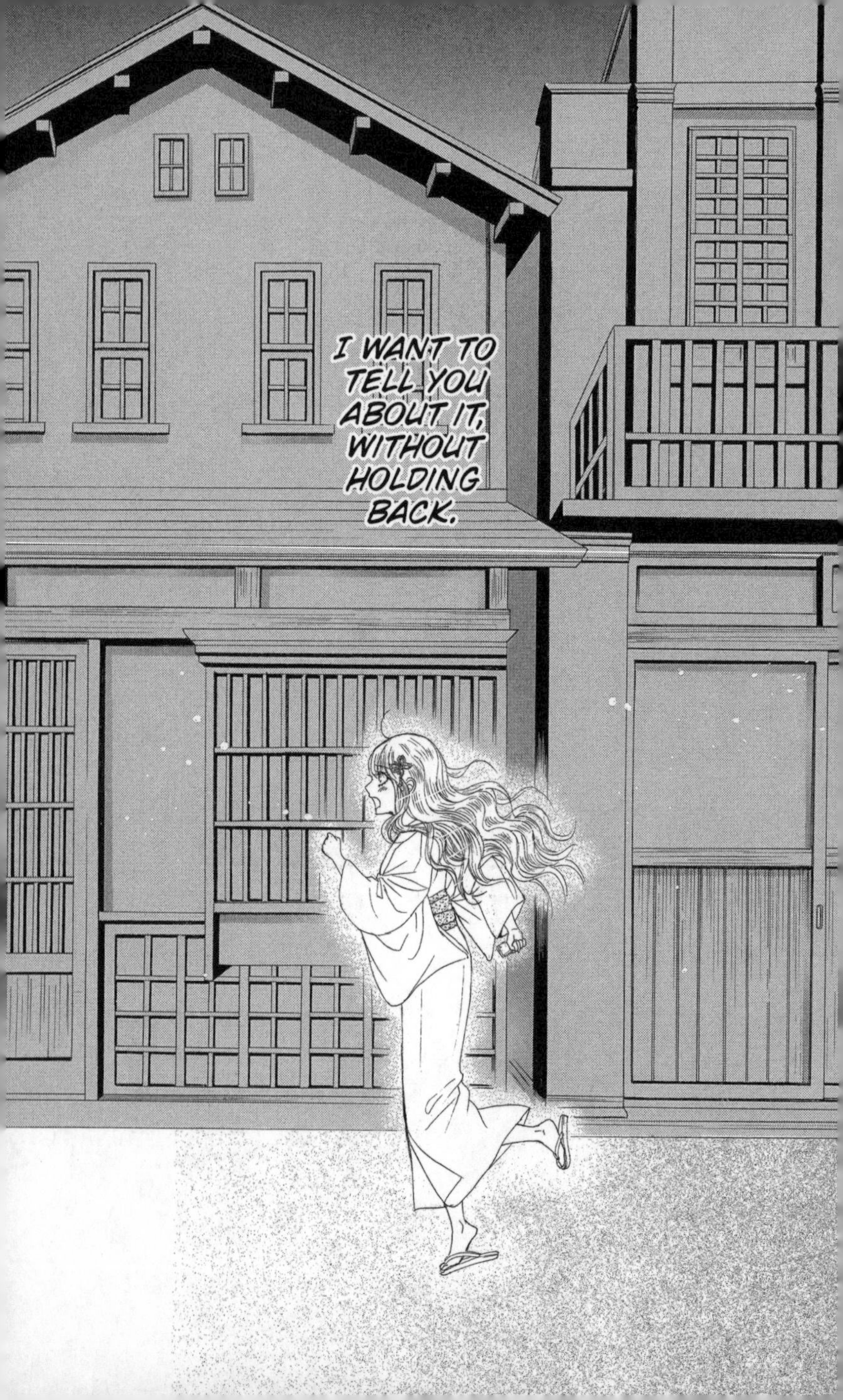
I WANT TO TELL YOU ABOUT IT, WITHOUT HOLDING BACK.

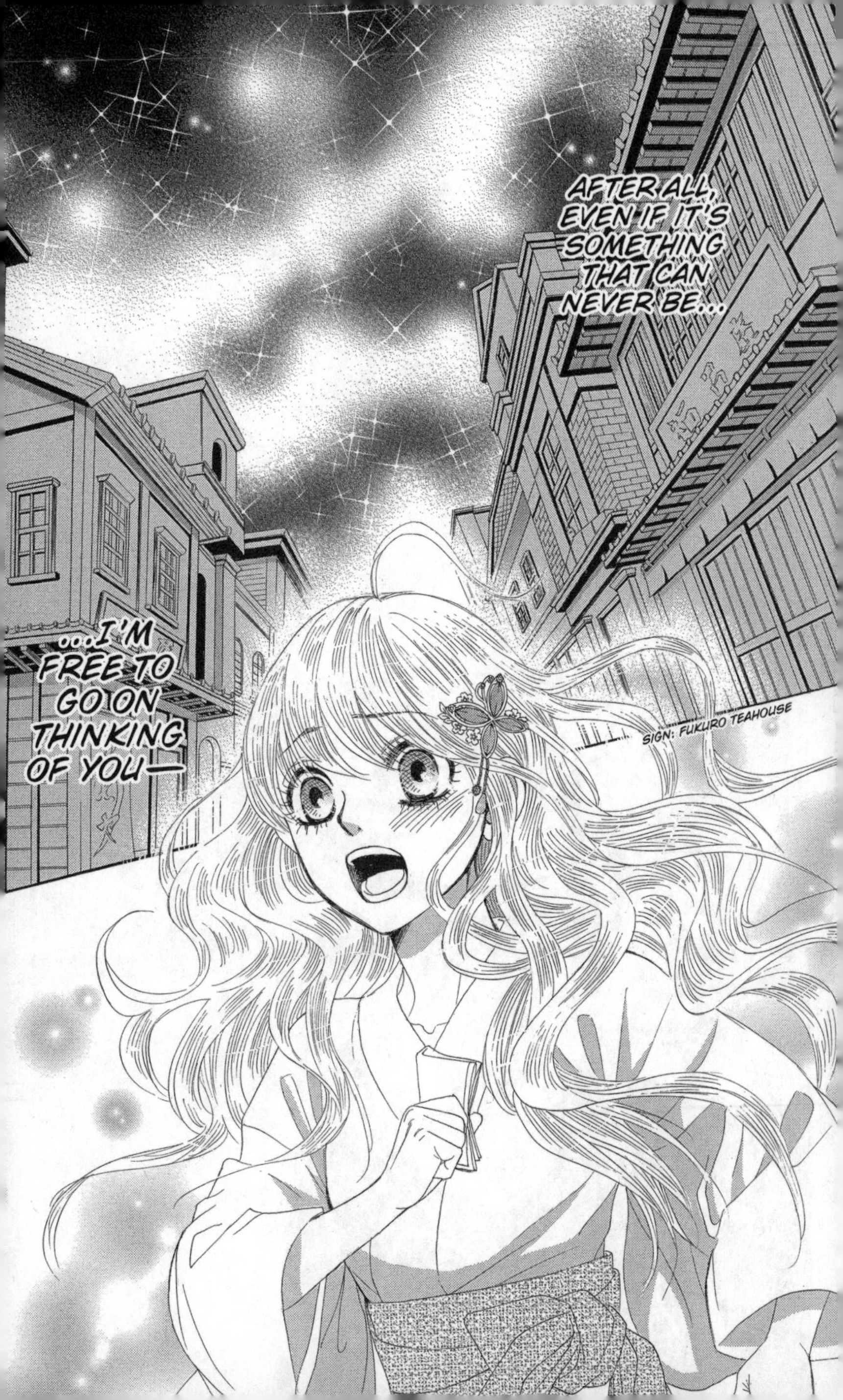
AFTER ALL, EVEN IF IT'S SOMETHING THAT CAN NEVER BE...
...I'M FREE TO GO ON THINKING OF YOU—
SIGN: FUKURO TEAHOUSE

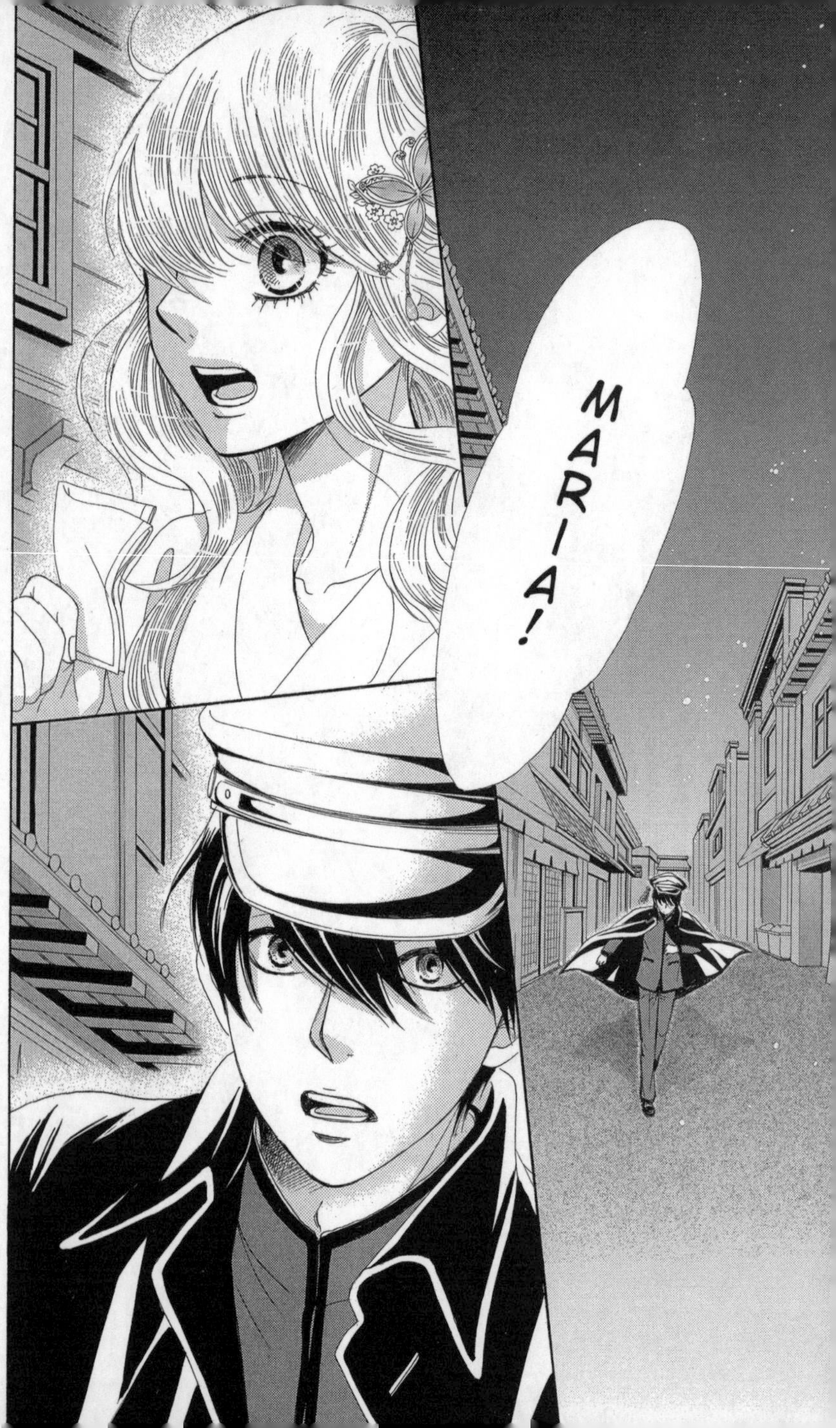
MARIA!

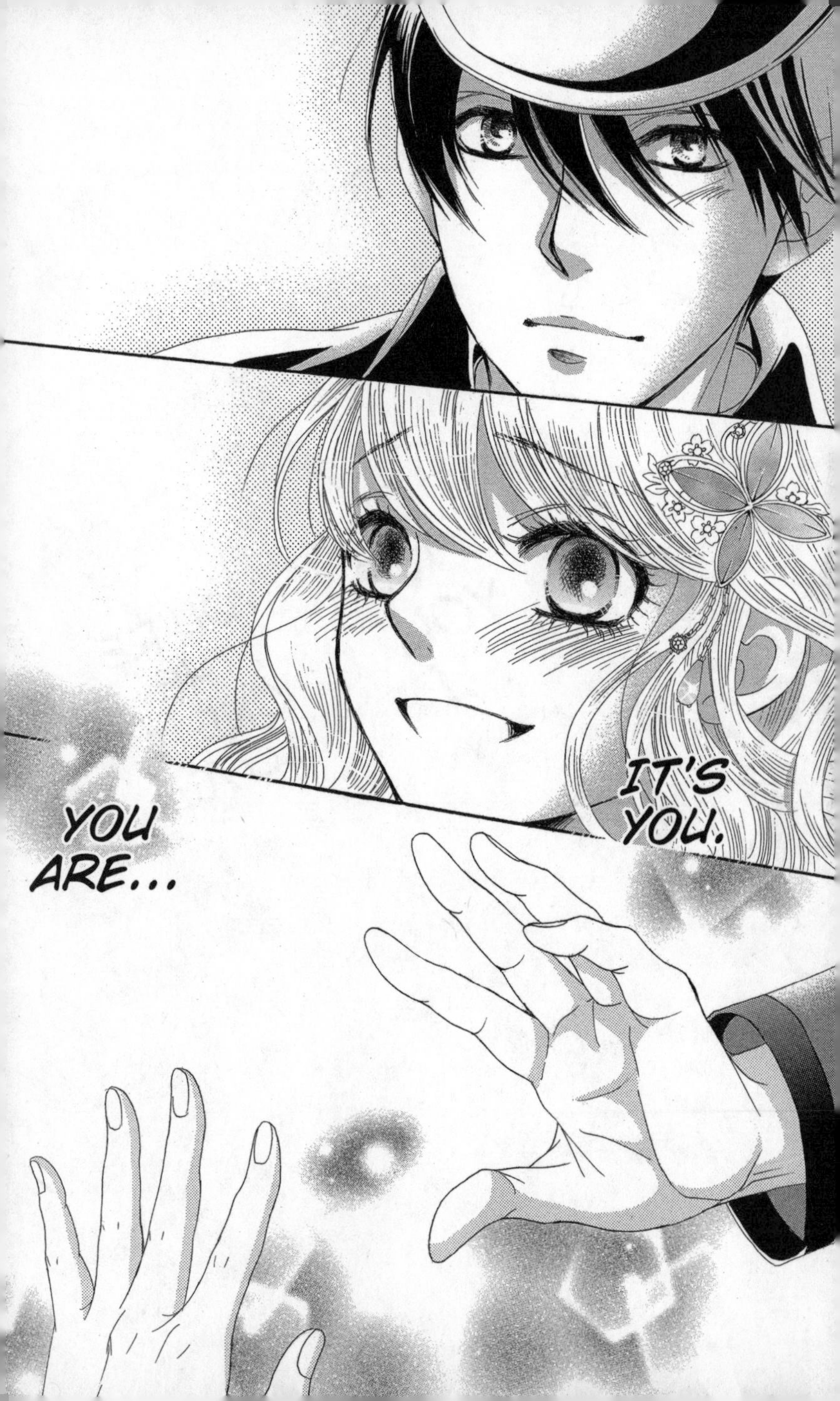
IT'S YOU.
YOU ARE...

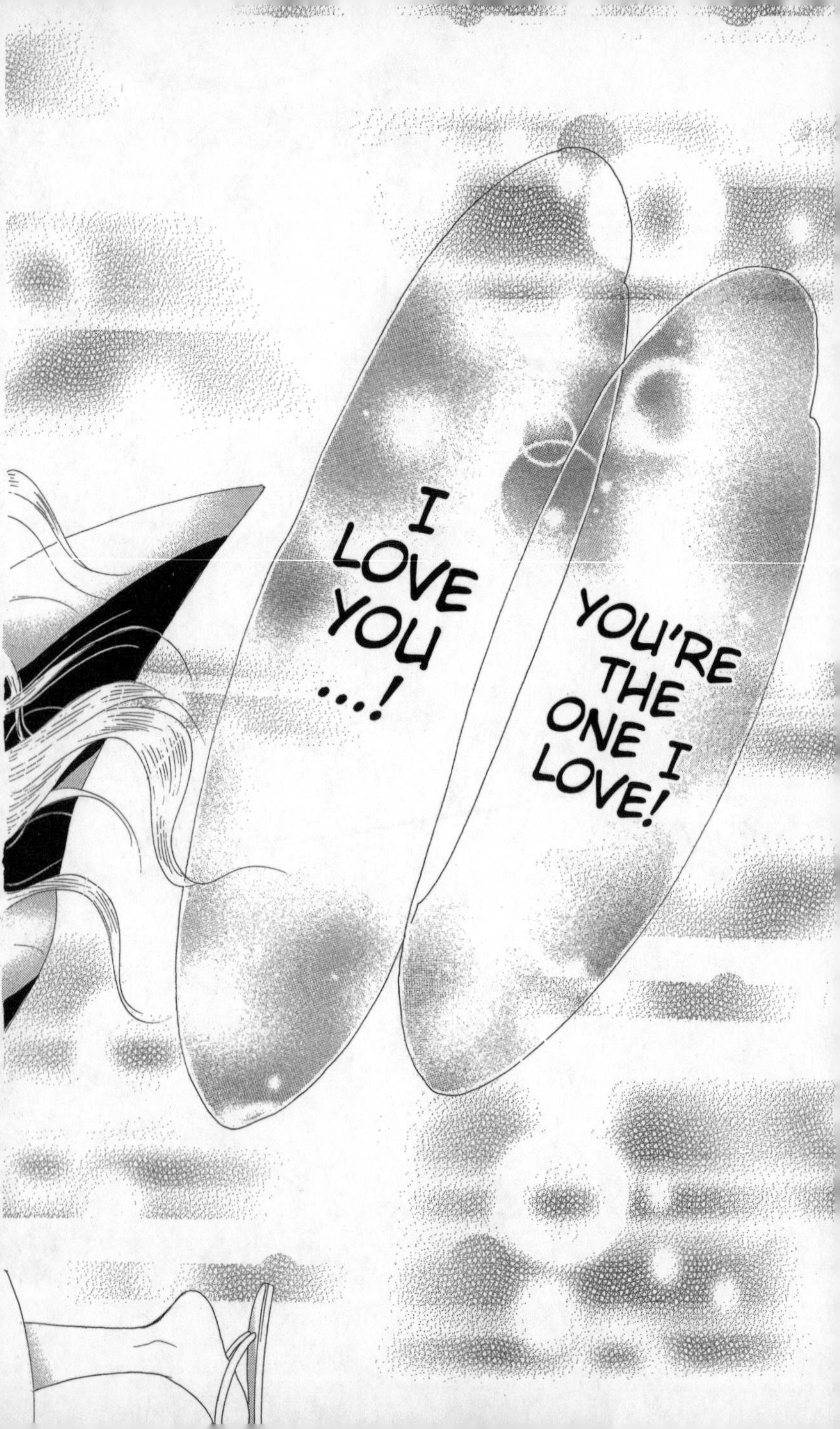
YOU'RE THE ONE I LOVE!
I LOVE YOU ...!

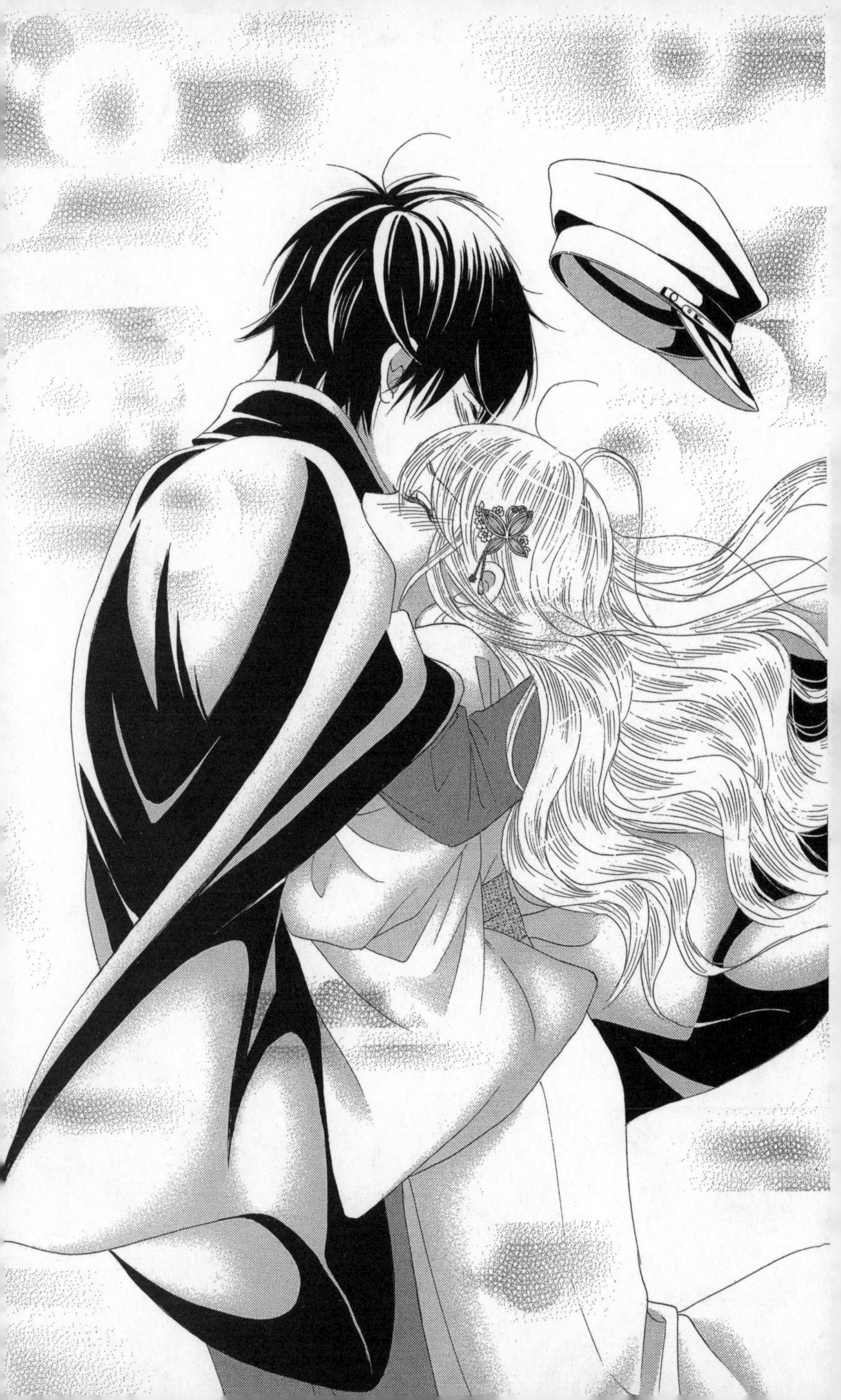

Episode 10

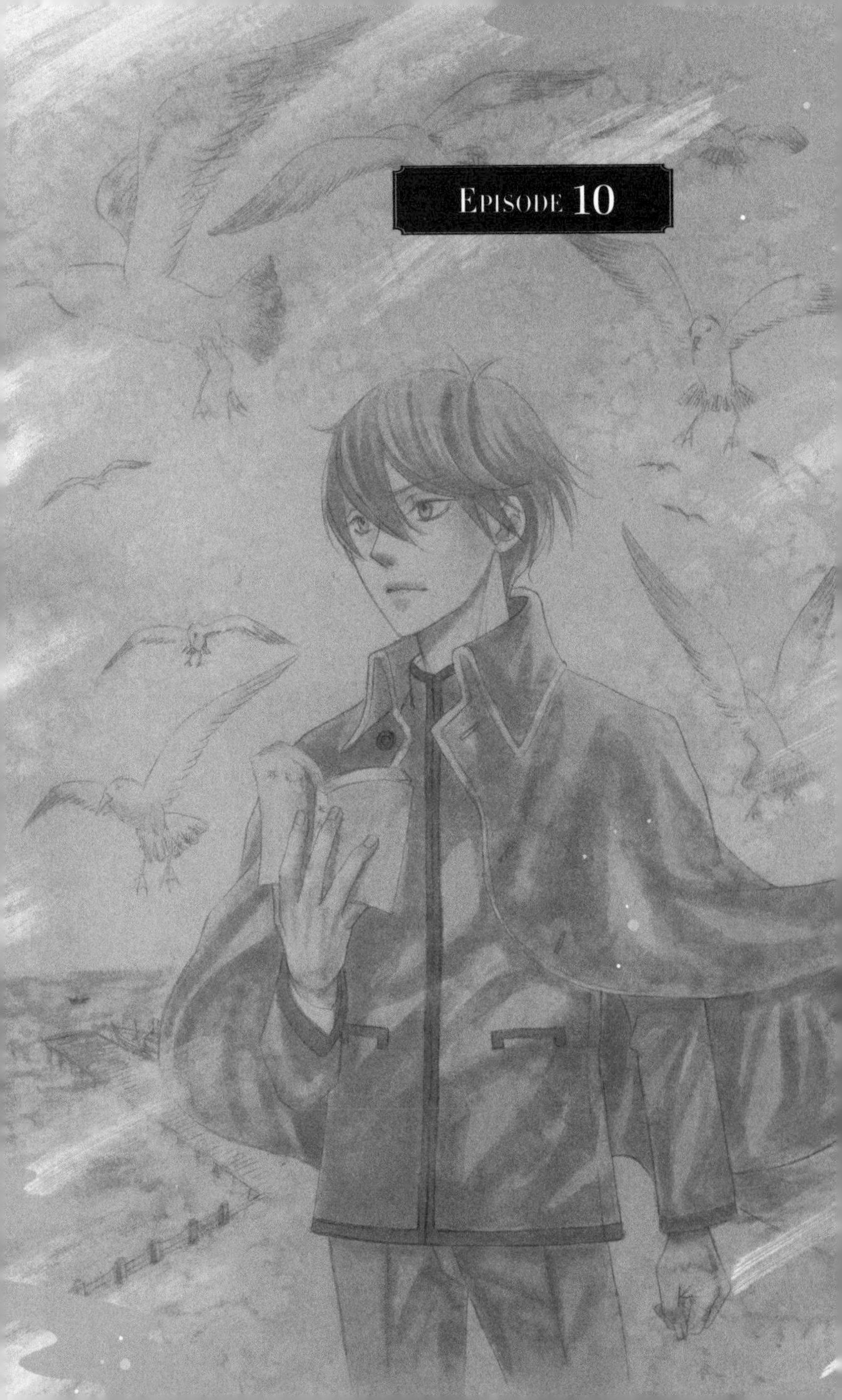

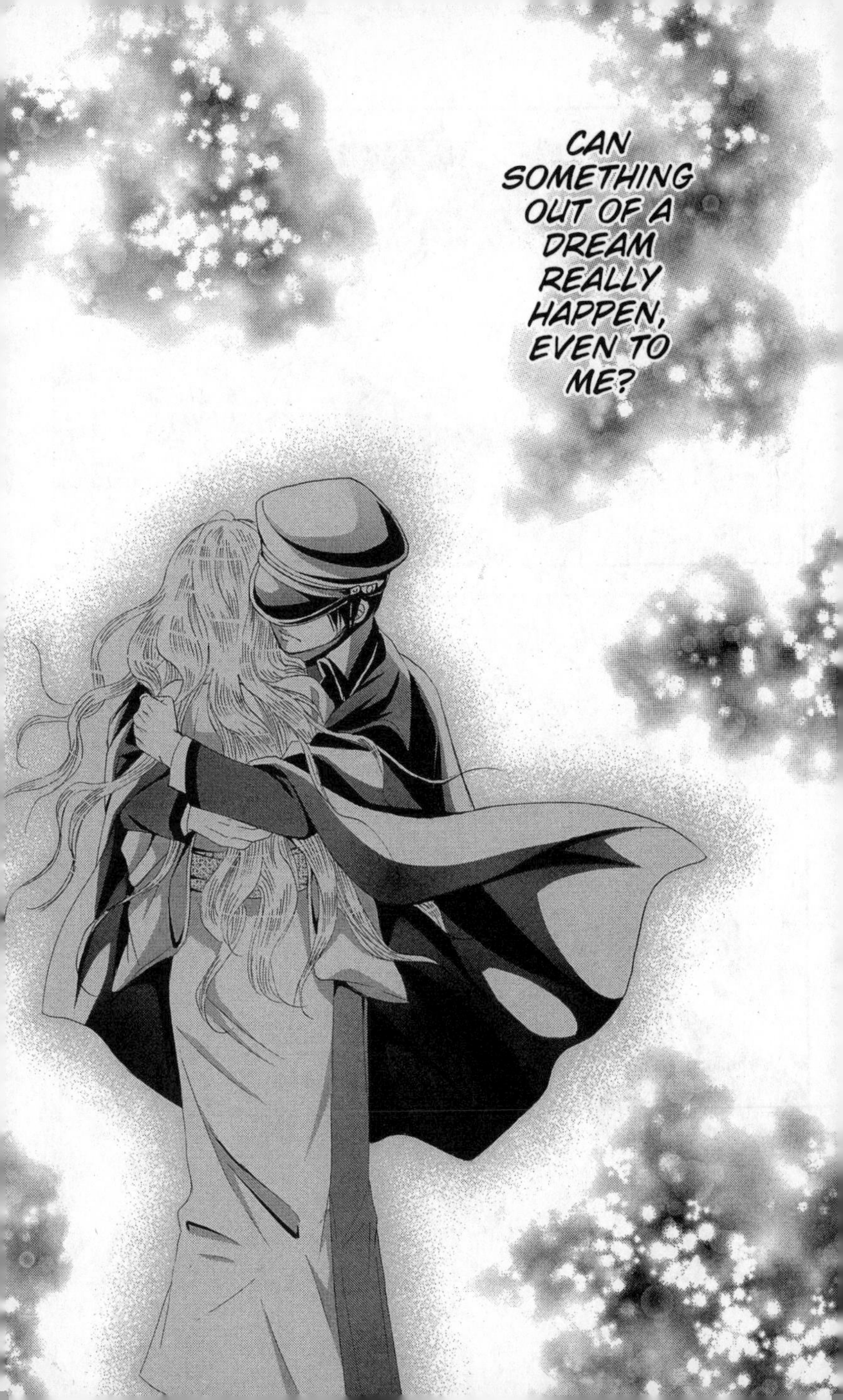
CAN SOMETHING OUT OF A DREAM REALLY HAPPEN, EVEN TO ME?

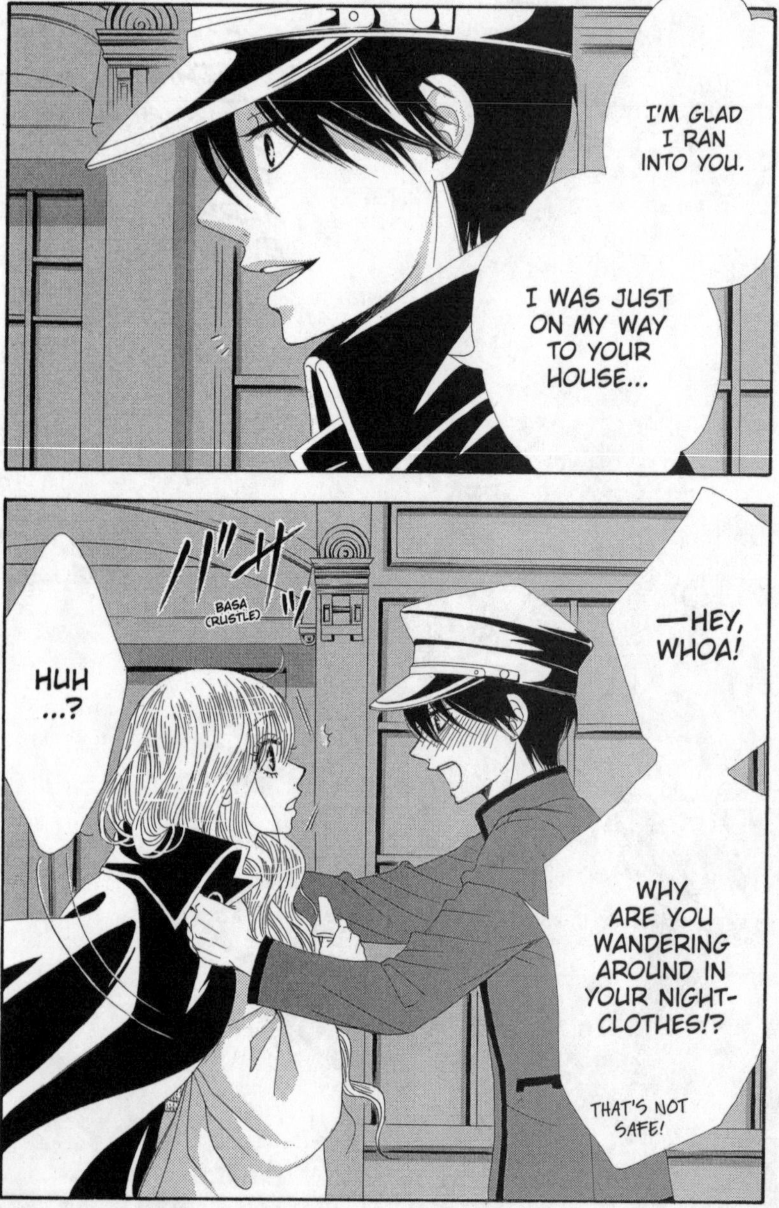
I'M GLAD I RAN INTO YOU.
I WAS JUST ON MY WAY TO YOUR HOUSE...
—HEY, WHOA!
BASA (RUSTLE)
HUH ...?
WHY ARE YOU WANDERING AROUND IN YOUR NIGHT-CLOTHES!?
THAT'S NOT SAFE!

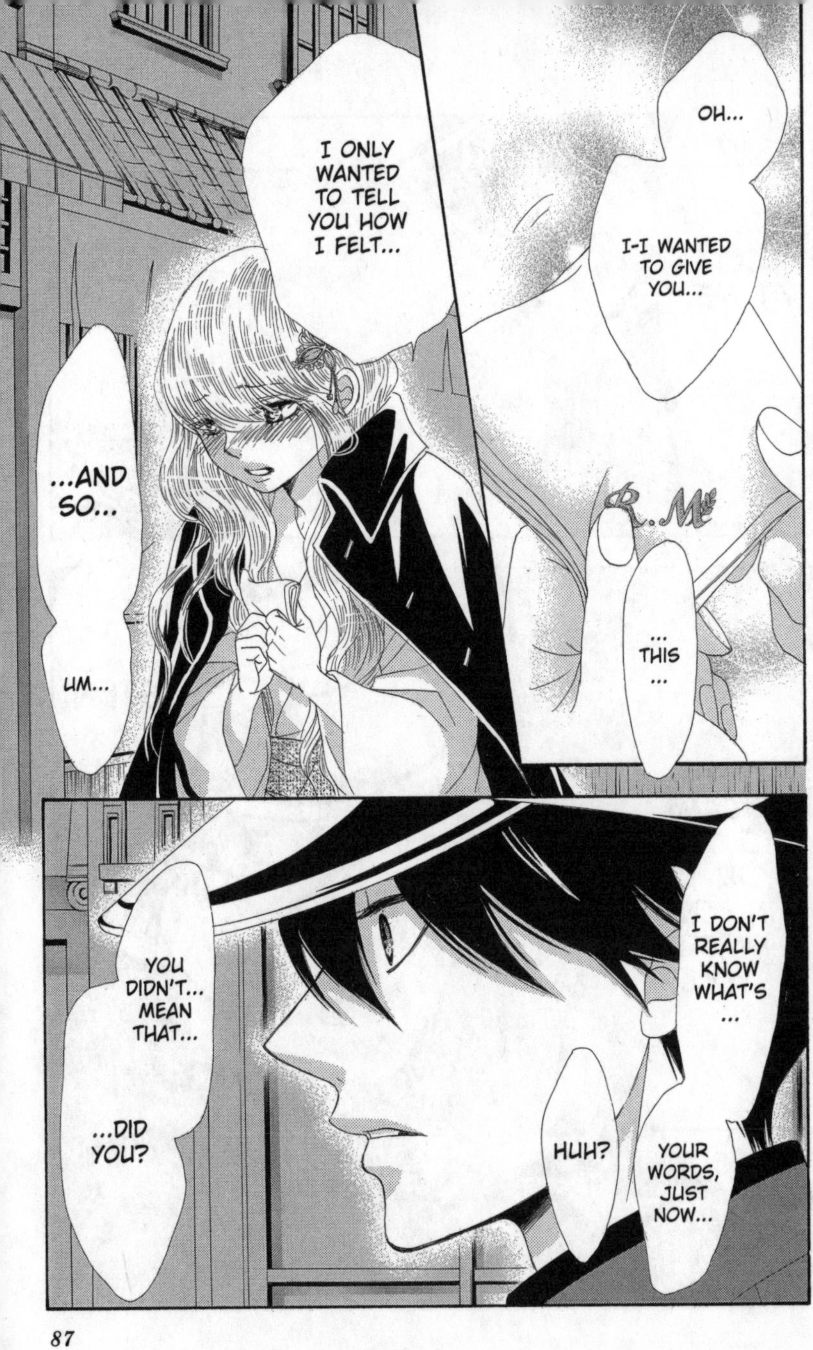
OH...
I-I WANTED TO GIVE YOU...
R..M
...THIS...
I ONLY WANTED TO TELL YOU HOW I FELT...
...AND SO...
UM...
I DON'T REALLY KNOW WHAT'S...
YOUR WORDS, JUST NOW...
HUH?
YOU DIDN'T... MEAN THAT...
...DID YOU?

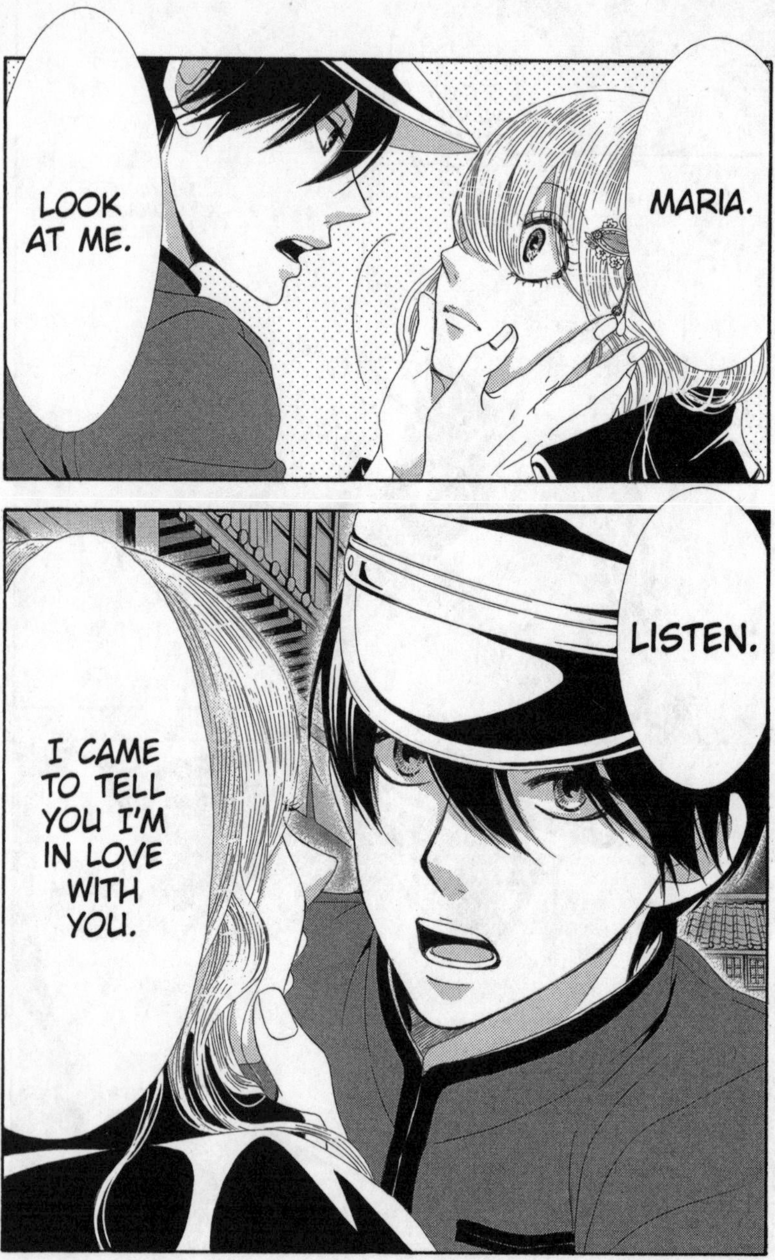
MARIA.
LOOK AT ME.
LISTEN.
I CAME TO TELL YOU I'M IN LOVE WITH YOU.

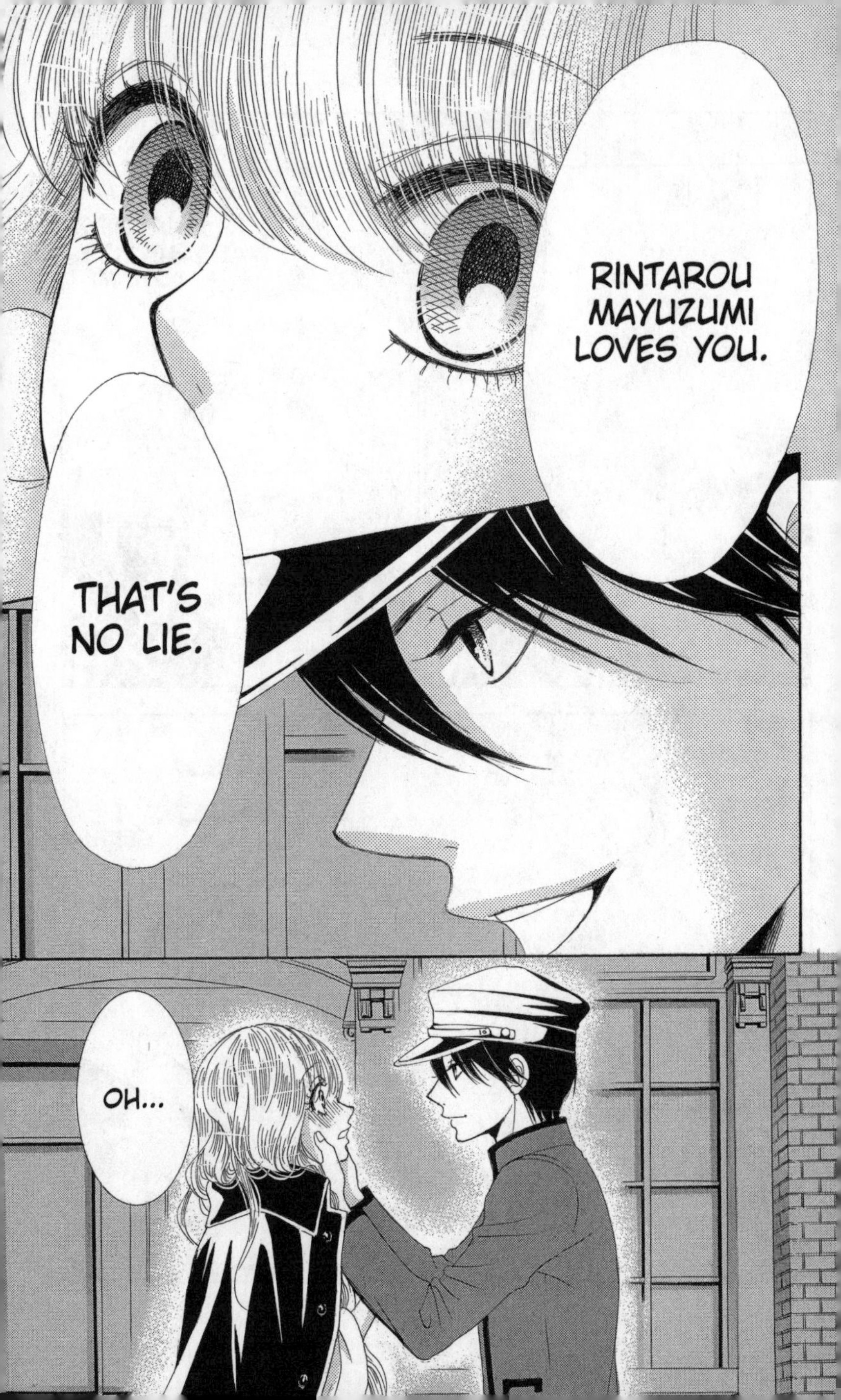
RINTAROU MAYUZUMI LOVES YOU.
THAT'S NO LIE.
OH...

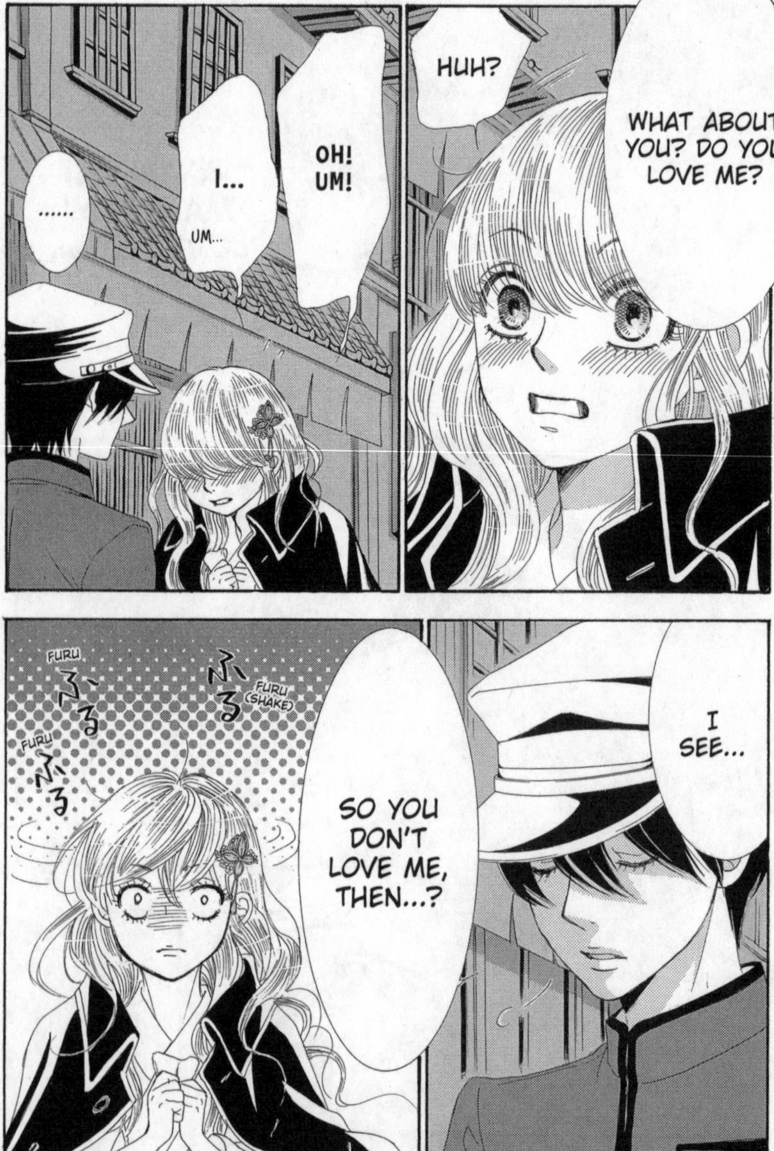
WHAT ABOUT YOU? DO YOU LOVE ME?
HUH?
OH! UM!
I...
UM...
......
I SEE...
SO YOU DON'T LOVE ME, THEN...?
ふる FURU (SHAKE)
ふる FURU
ふる FURU

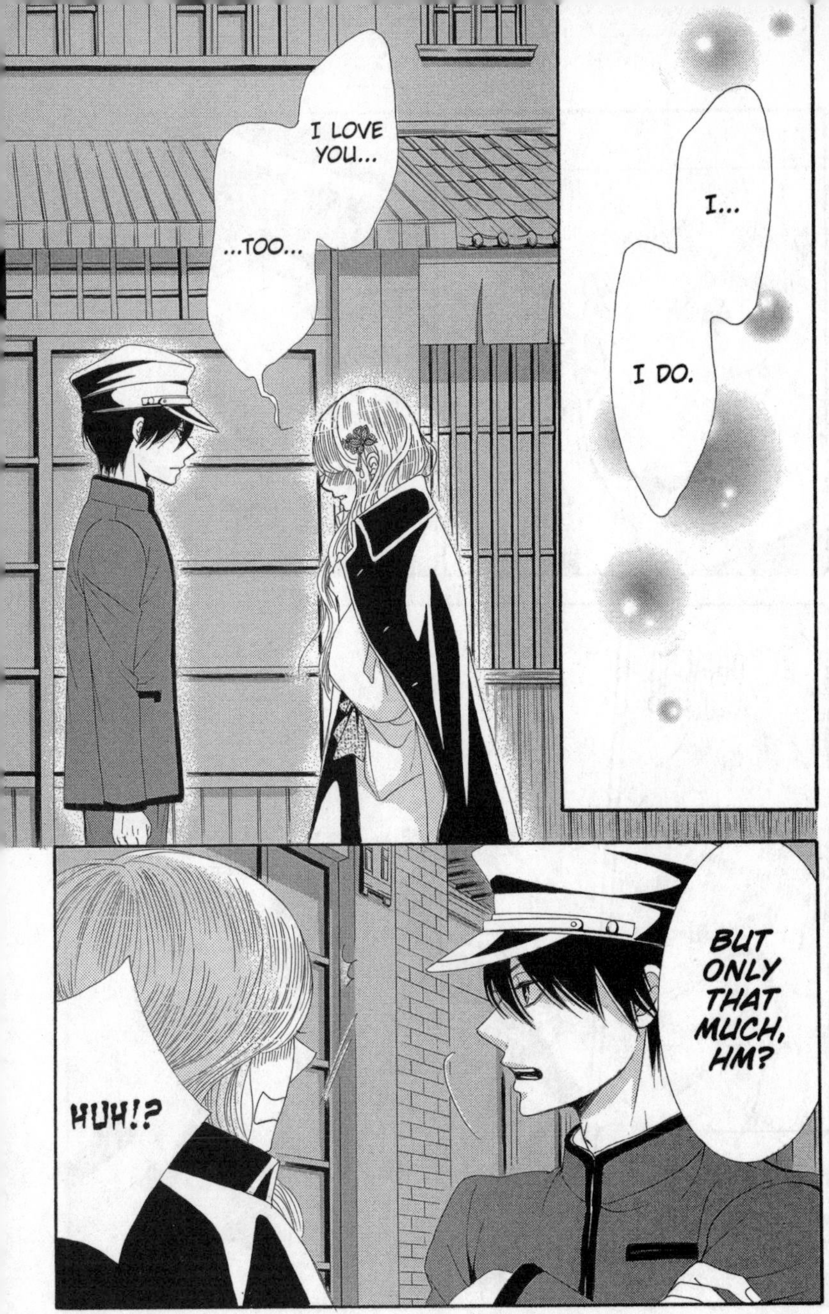
I...
I DO.
I LOVE YOU...
...TOO...
BUT ONLY THAT MUCH, HM?
HUH!?

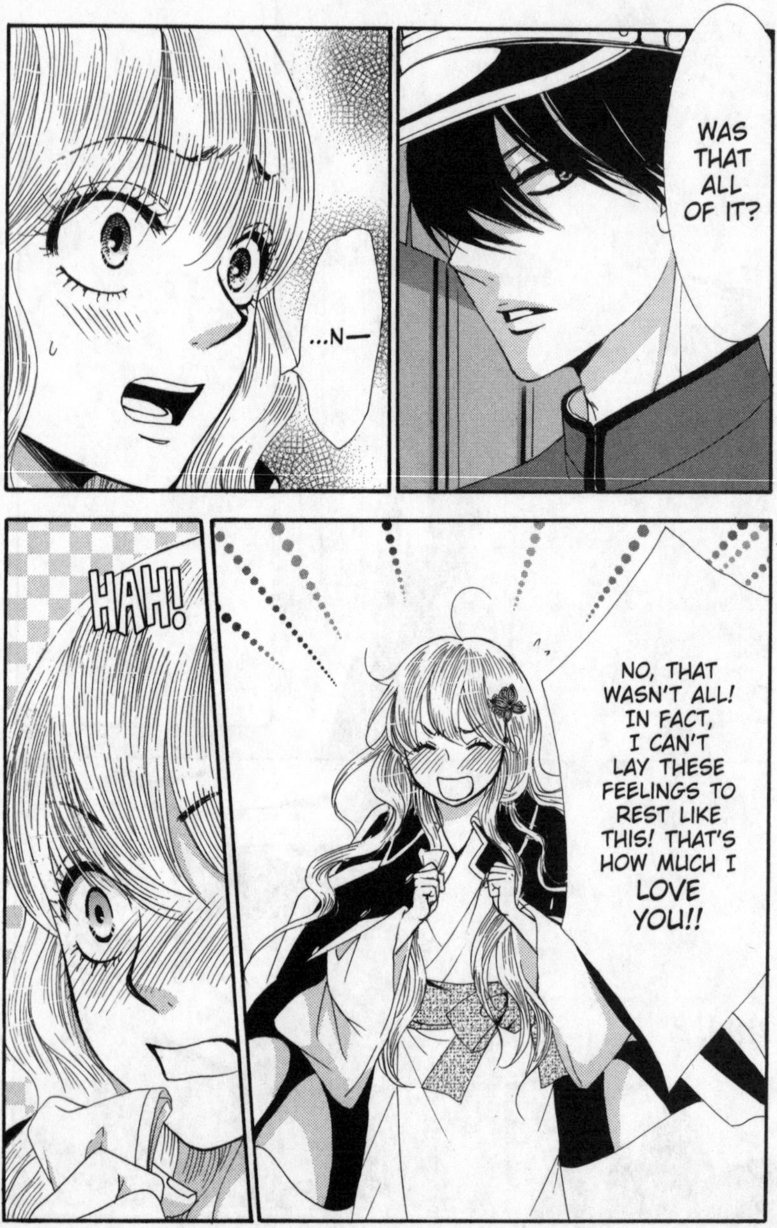
WAS THAT ALL OF IT?
...N—
NO, THAT WASN'T ALL! IN FACT, I CAN'T LAY THESE FEELINGS TO REST LIKE THIS! THAT'S HOW MUCH I LOVE YOU!!
HAH!

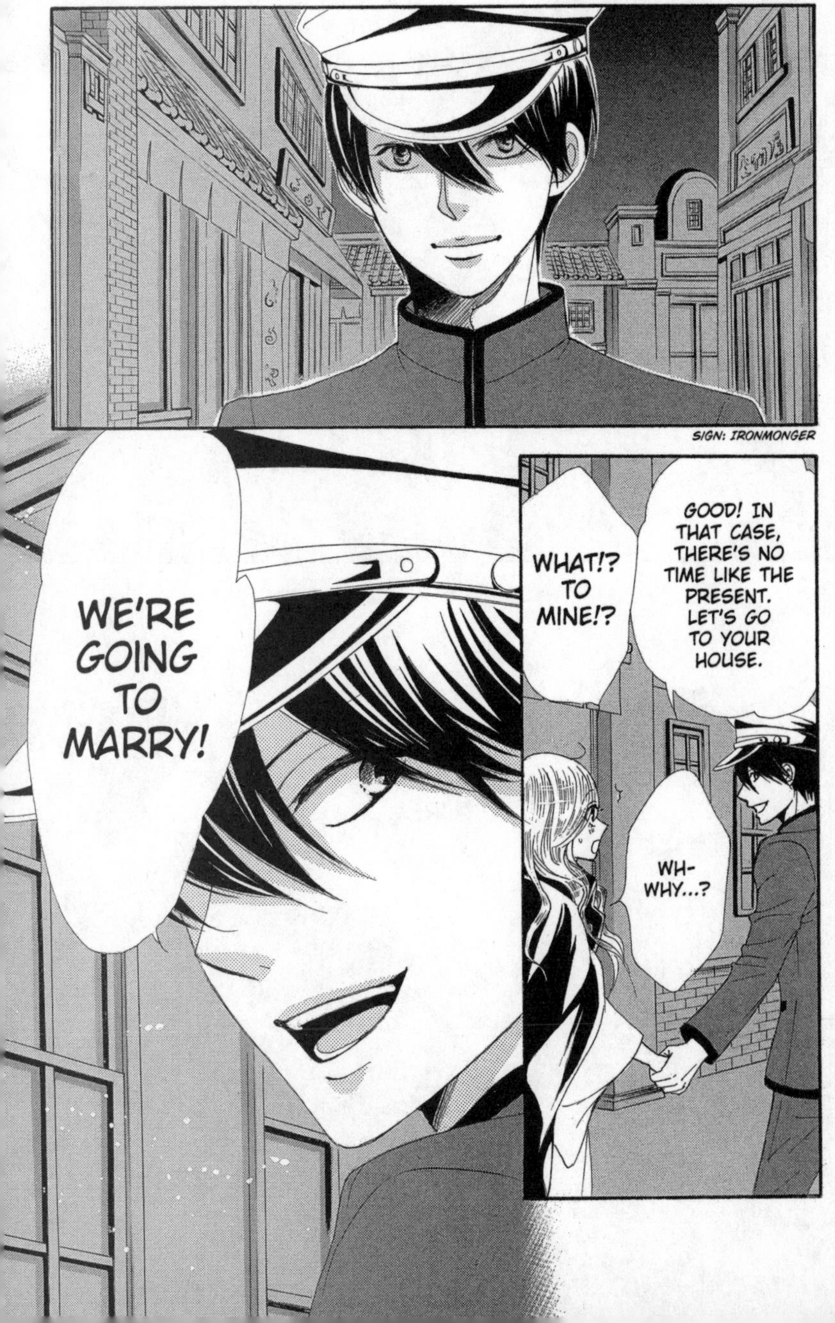
SIGN: IRONMONGER
GOOD! IN THAT CASE, THERE'S NO TIME LIKE THE PRESENT. LET'S GO TO YOUR HOUSE.
WHAT!? TO MINE!?
WH- WHY...?
WE'RE GOING TO MARRY!

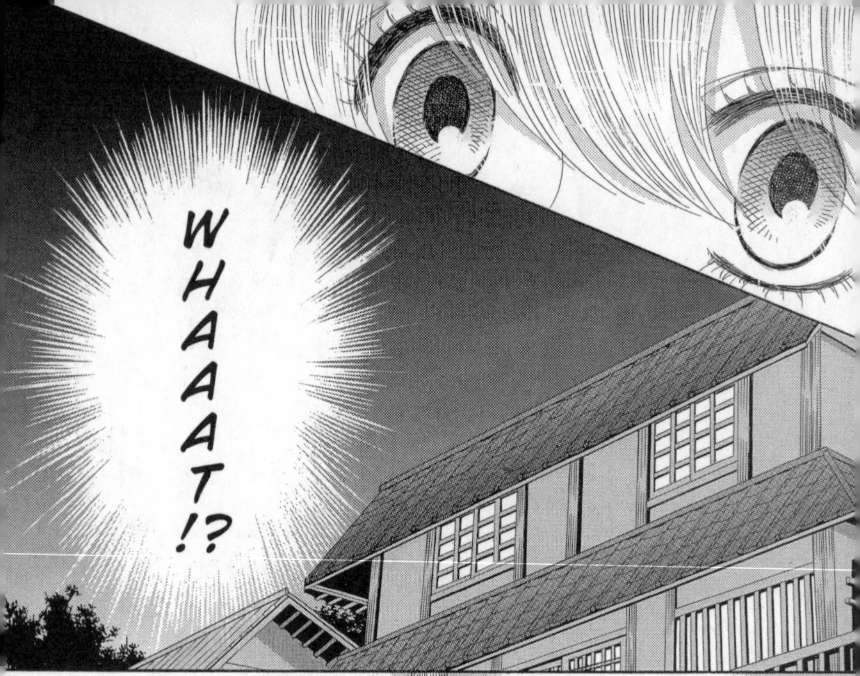
WHAAAT!?
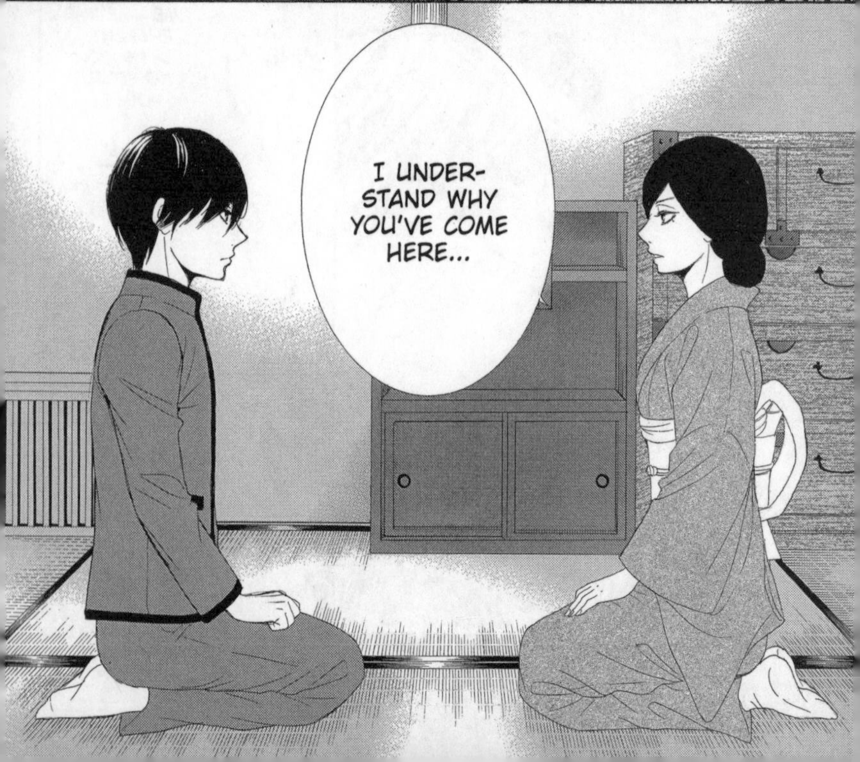
I UNDER-STAND WHY YOU'VE COME HERE...

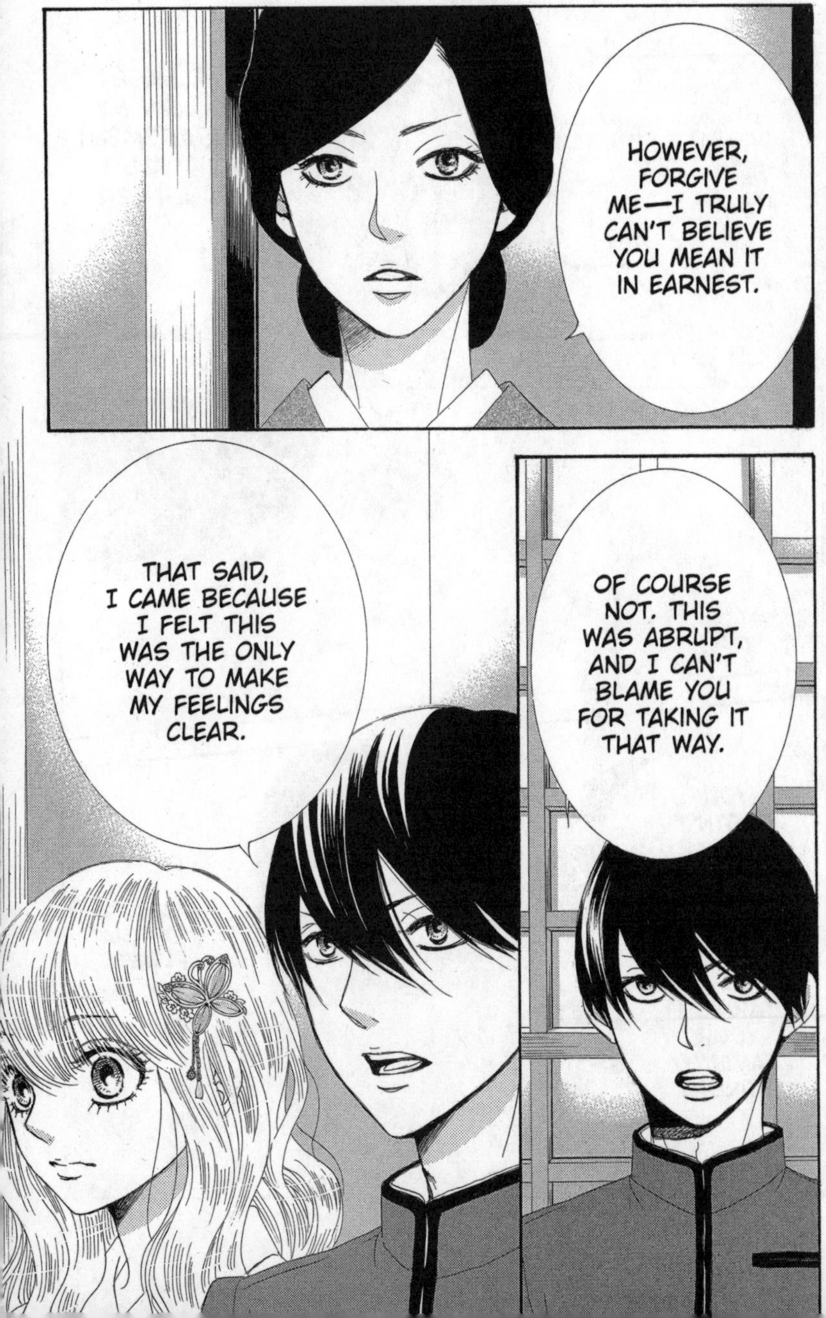
HOWEVER, FORGIVE ME—I TRULY CAN'T BELIEVE YOU MEAN IT IN EARNEST.
OF COURSE NOT. THIS WAS ABRUPT, AND I CAN'T BLAME YOU FOR TAKING IT THAT WAY.
THAT SAID, I CAME BECAUSE I FELT THIS WAS THE ONLY WAY TO MAKE MY FEELINGS CLEAR.

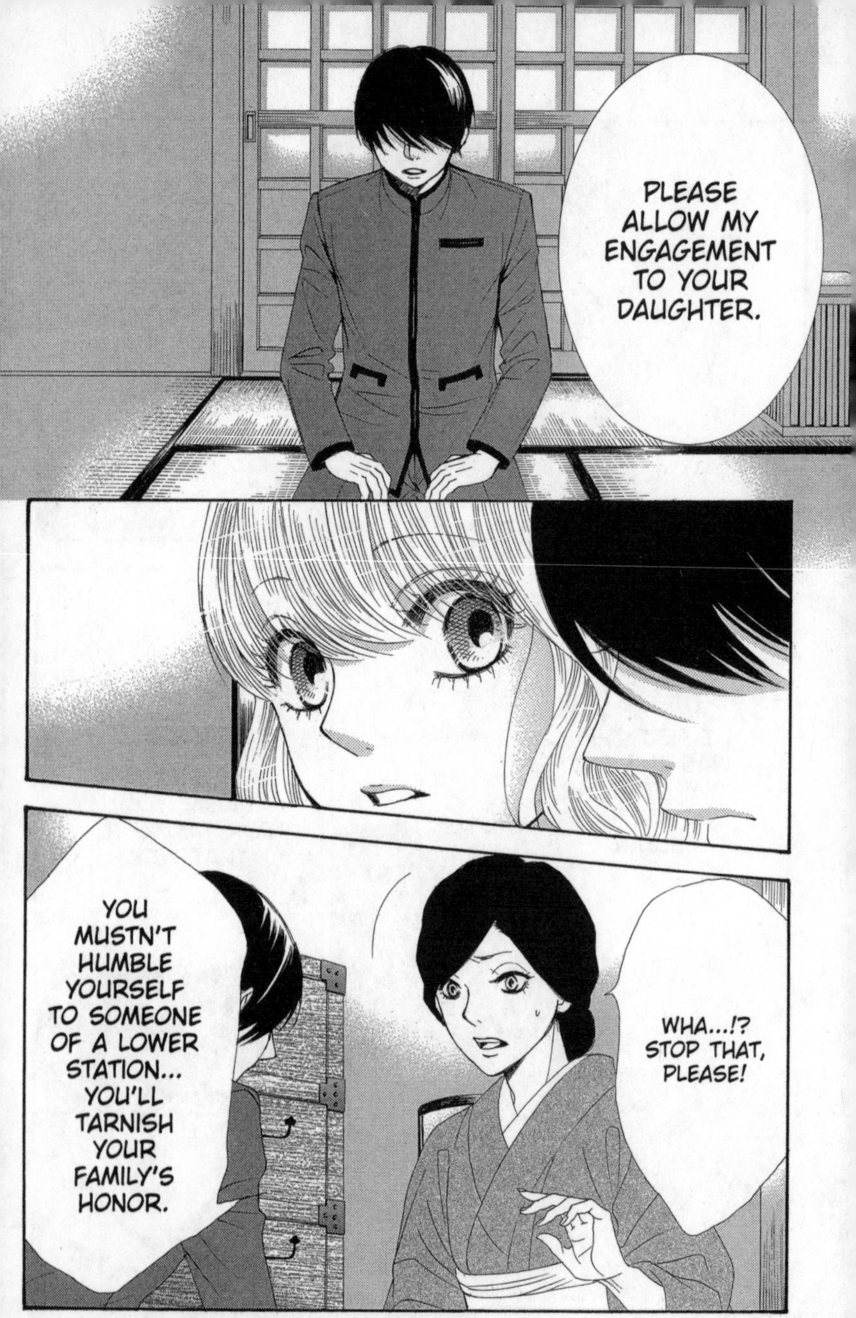
PLEASE ALLOW MY ENGAGEMENT TO YOUR DAUGHTER.
WHA...!? STOP THAT, PLEASE!
YOU MUSTN'T HUMBLE YOURSELF TO SOMEONE OF A LOWER STATION... YOU'LL TARNISH YOUR FAMILY'S HONOR.

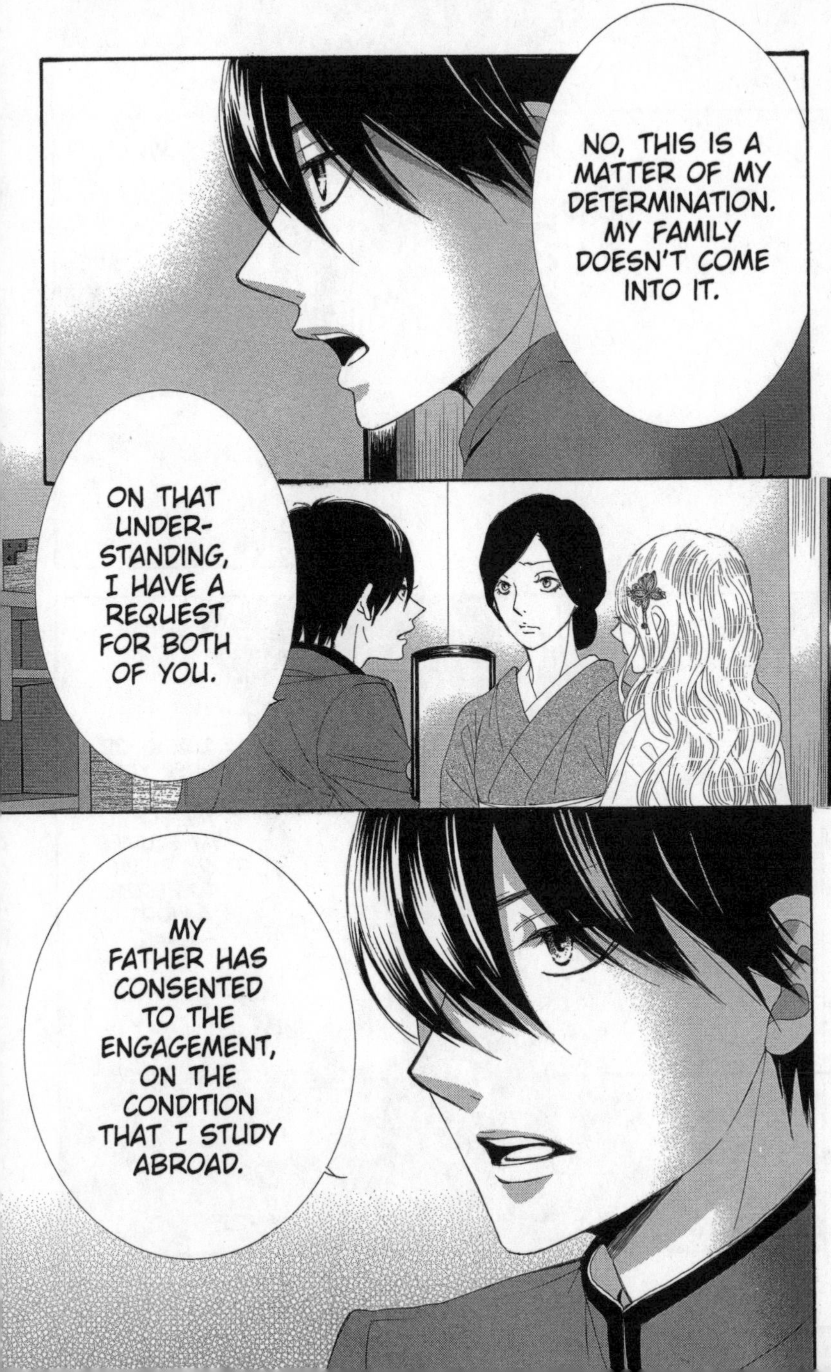
NO, THIS IS A MATTER OF MY DETERMINATION. MY FAMILY DOESN'T COME INTO IT.
ON THAT UNDER-STANDING, I HAVE A REQUEST FOR BOTH OF YOU.
MY FATHER HAS CONSENTED TO THE ENGAGEMENT, ON THE CONDITION THAT I STUDY ABROAD.

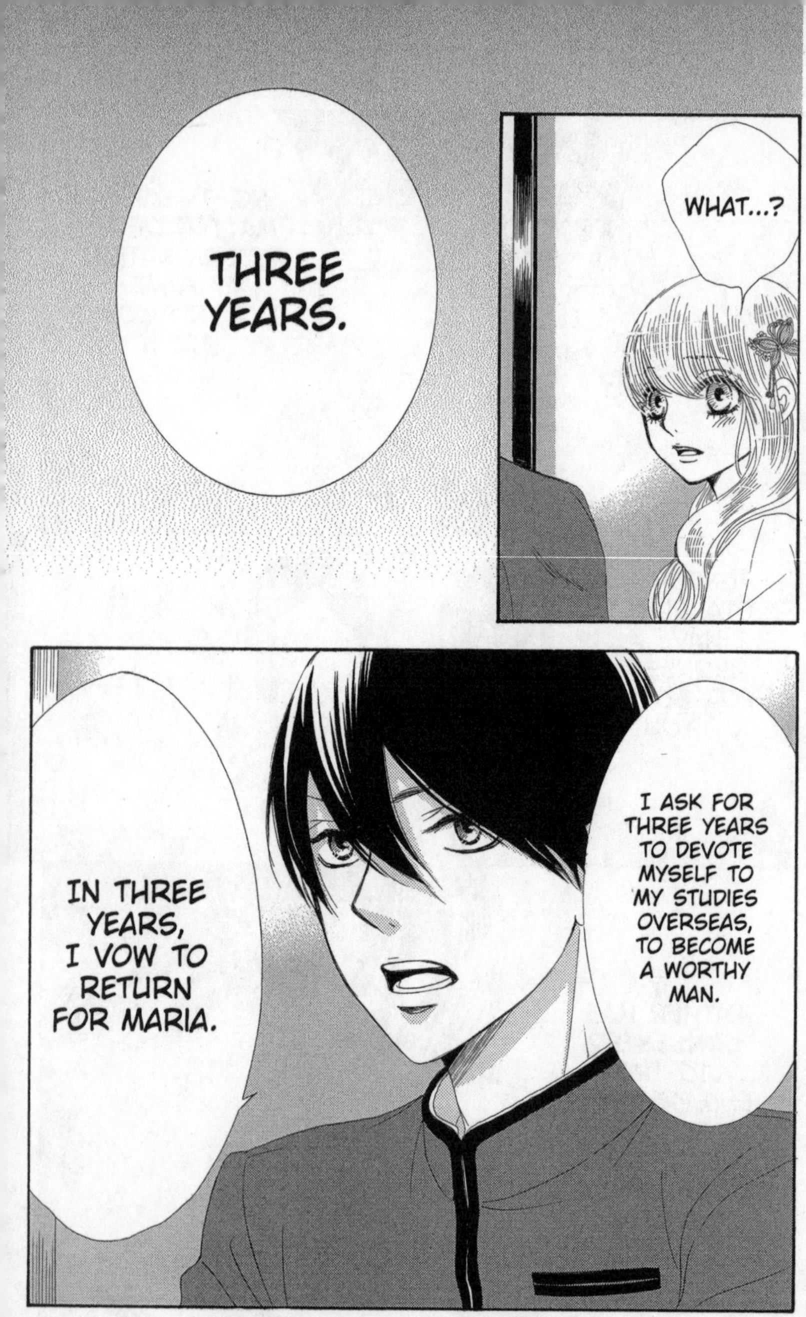
WHAT...?
THREE YEARS.
I ASK FOR THREE YEARS TO DEVOTE MYSELF TO MY STUDIES OVERSEAS, TO BECOME A WORTHY MAN.
IN THREE YEARS, I VOW TO RETURN FOR MARIA.

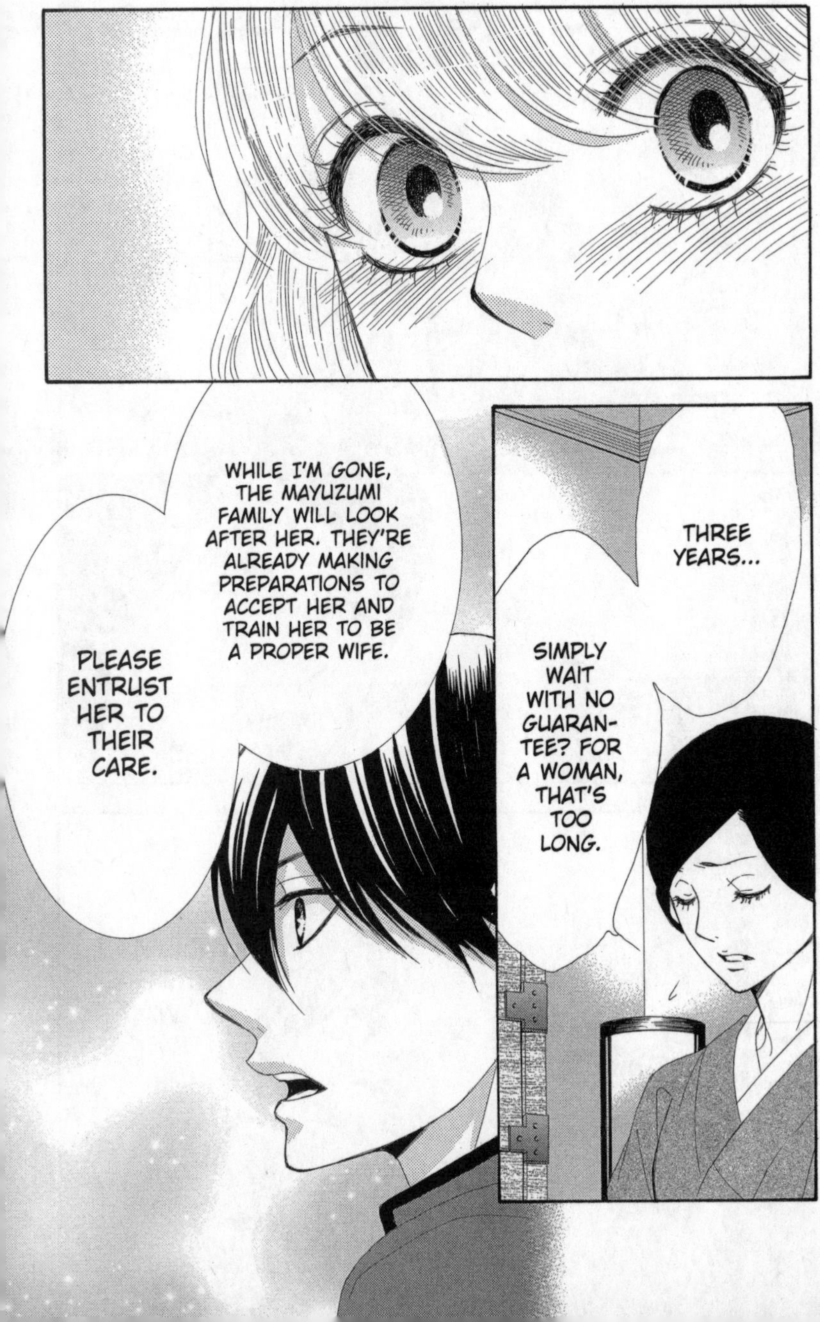
THREE YEARS...
SIMPLY WAIT WITH NO GUARAN-TEE? FOR A WOMAN, THAT'S TOO LONG.
WHILE I'M GONE, THE MAYUZUMI FAMILY WILL LOOK AFTER HER. THEY'RE ALREADY MAKING PREPARATIONS TO ACCEPT HER AND TRAIN HER TO BE A PROPER WIFE.
PLEASE ENTRUST HER TO THEIR CARE.

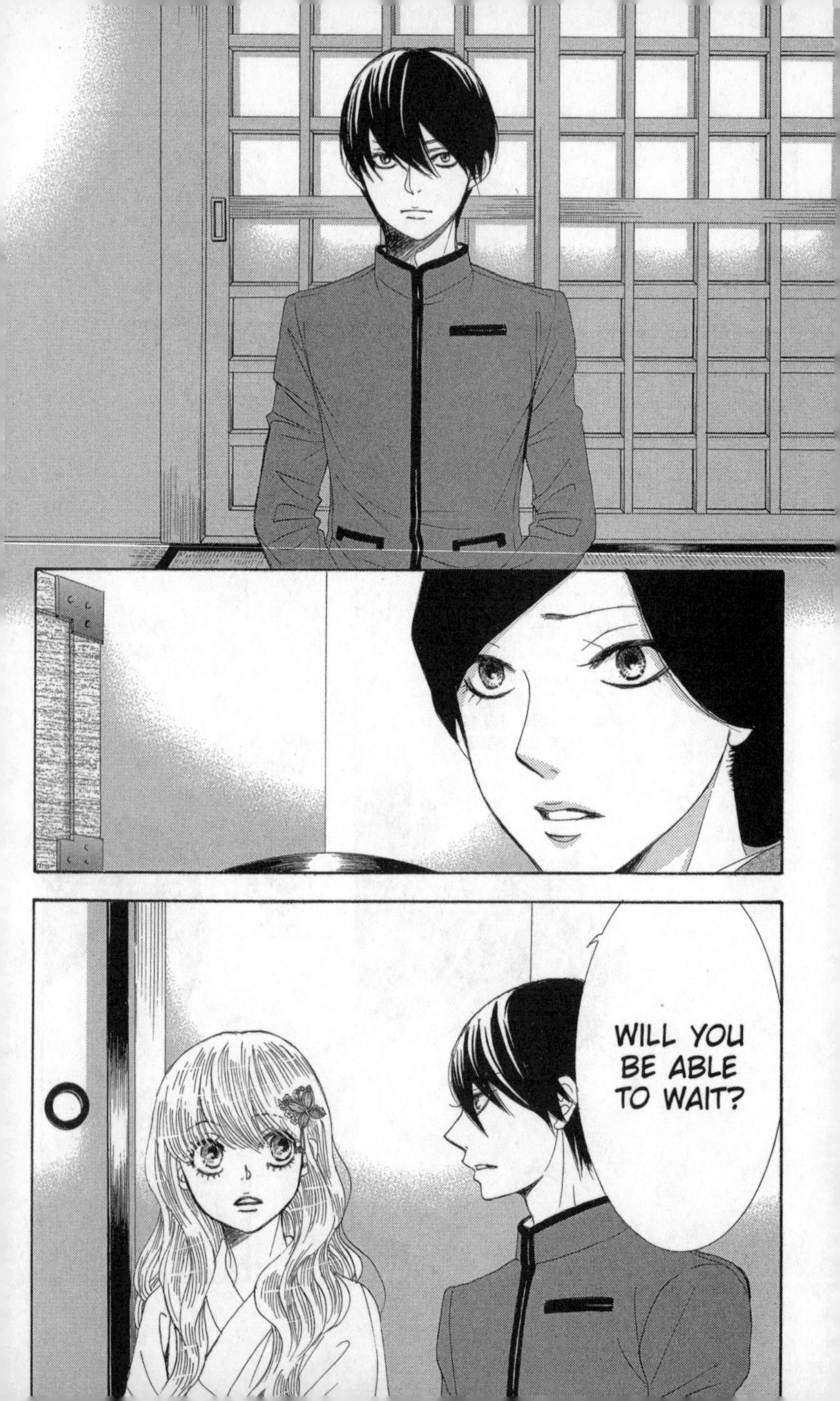
WILL YOU BE ABLE TO WAIT?

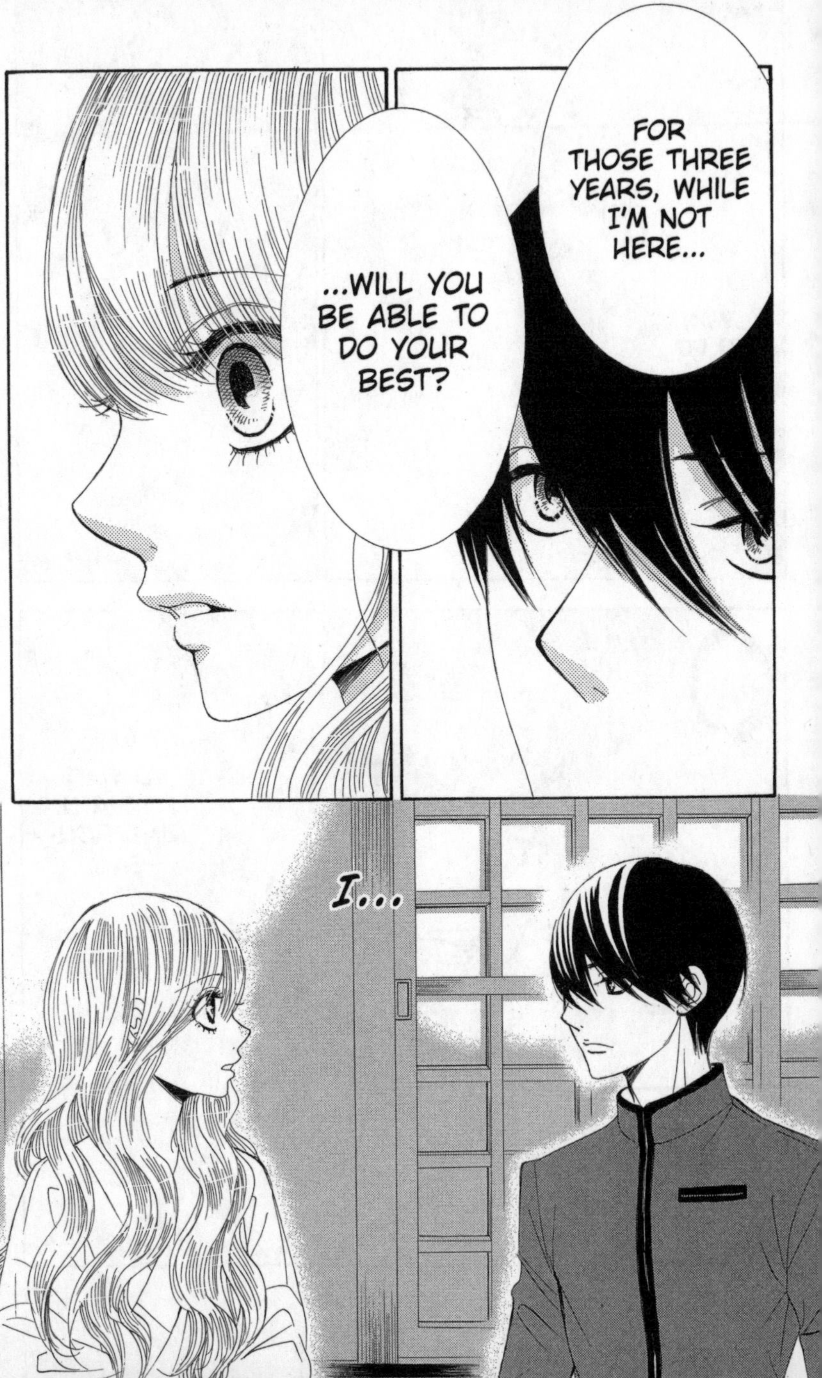
FOR THOSE THREE YEARS, WHILE I'M NOT HERE...
...WILL YOU BE ABLE TO DO YOUR BEST?
I...

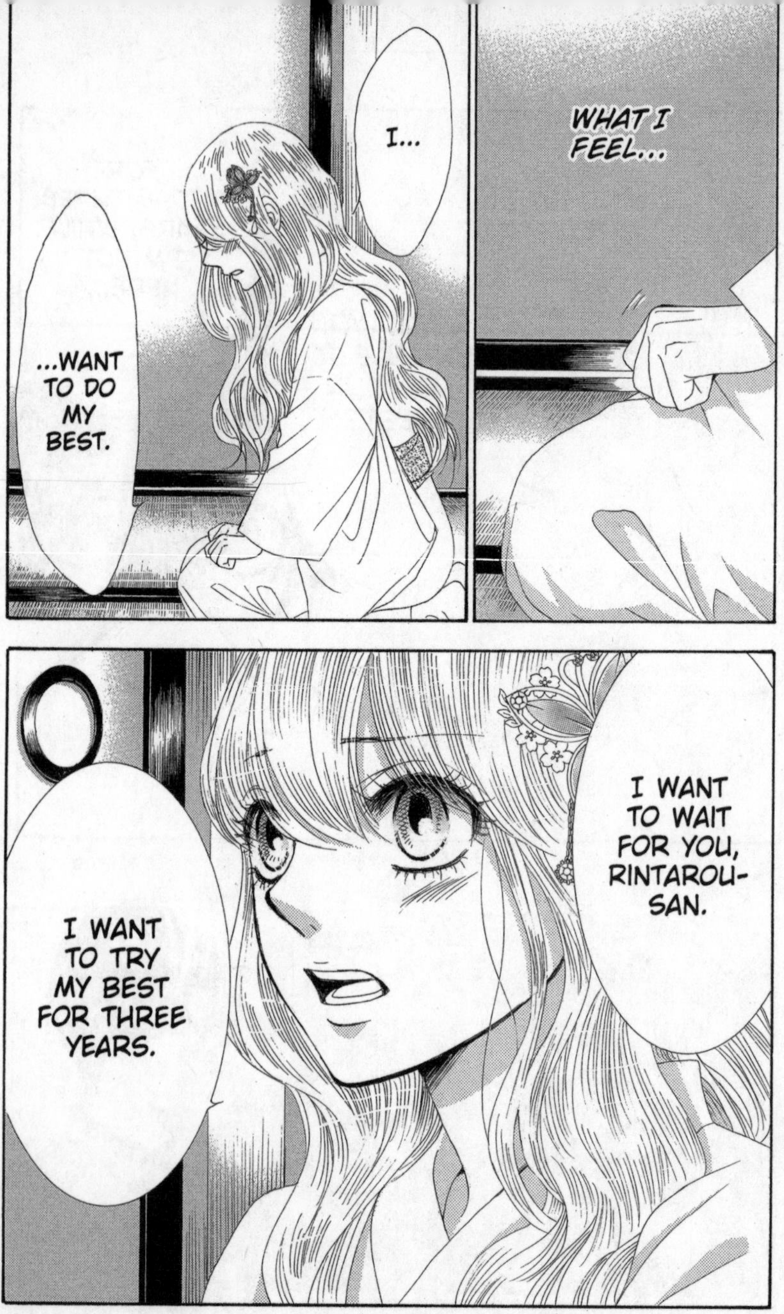
WHAT I FEEL...
I...
...WANT TO DO MY BEST.
I WANT TO WAIT FOR YOU, RINTAROU-SAN.
I WANT TO TRY MY BEST FOR THREE YEARS.

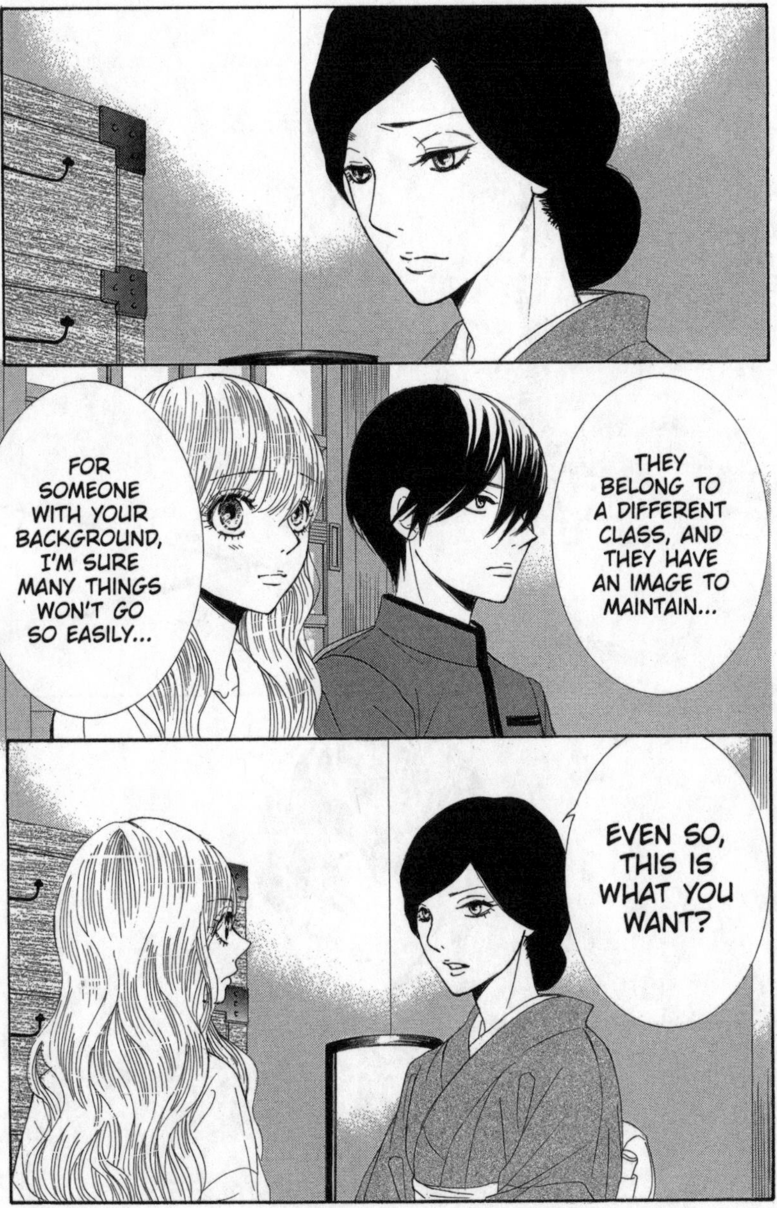
THEY BELONG TO A DIFFERENT CLASS, AND THEY HAVE AN IMAGE TO MAINTAIN...
FOR SOMEONE WITH YOUR BACKGROUND, I'M SURE MANY THINGS WON'T GO SO EASILY...
EVEN SO, THIS IS WHAT YOU WANT?

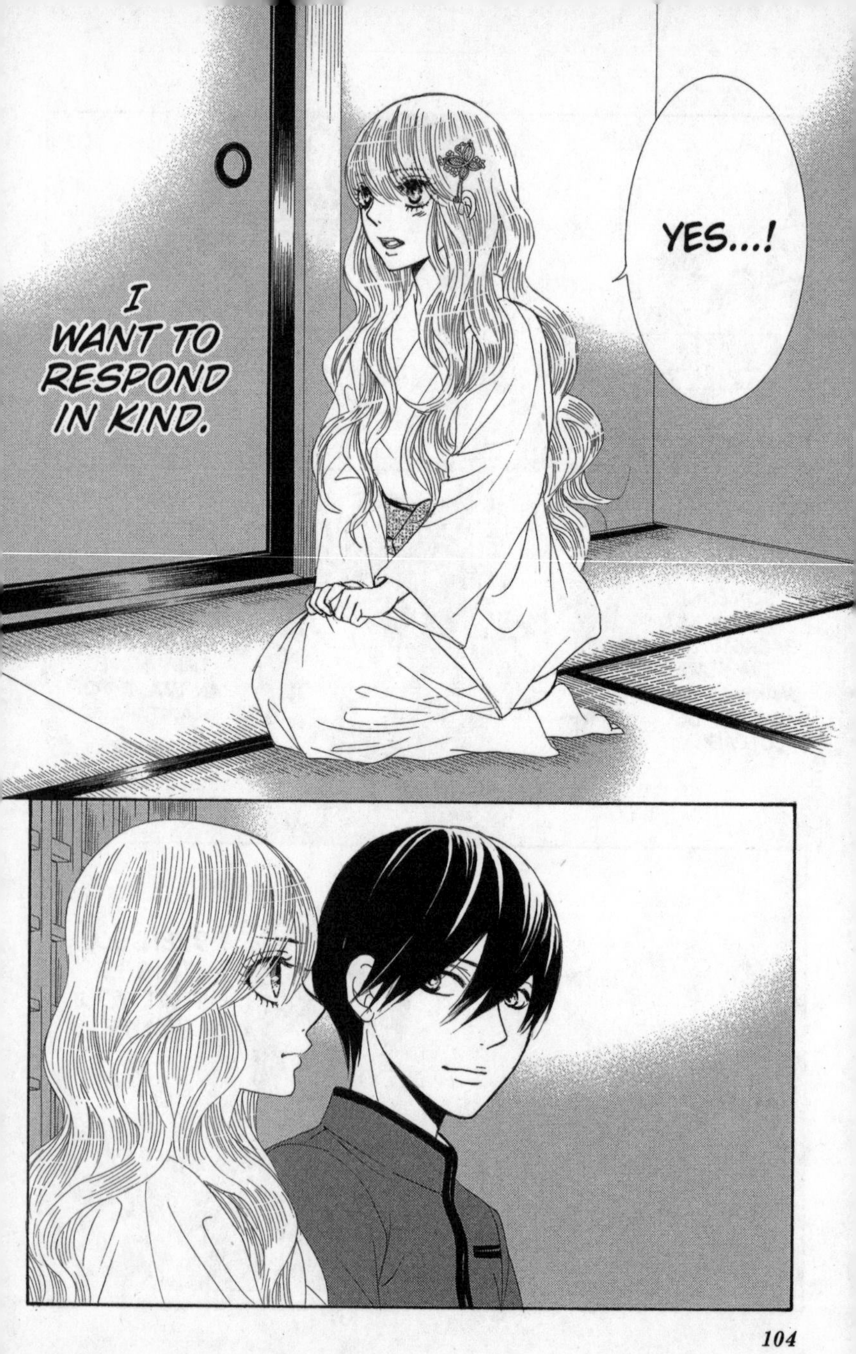
YES...!
I WANT TO RESPOND IN KIND.

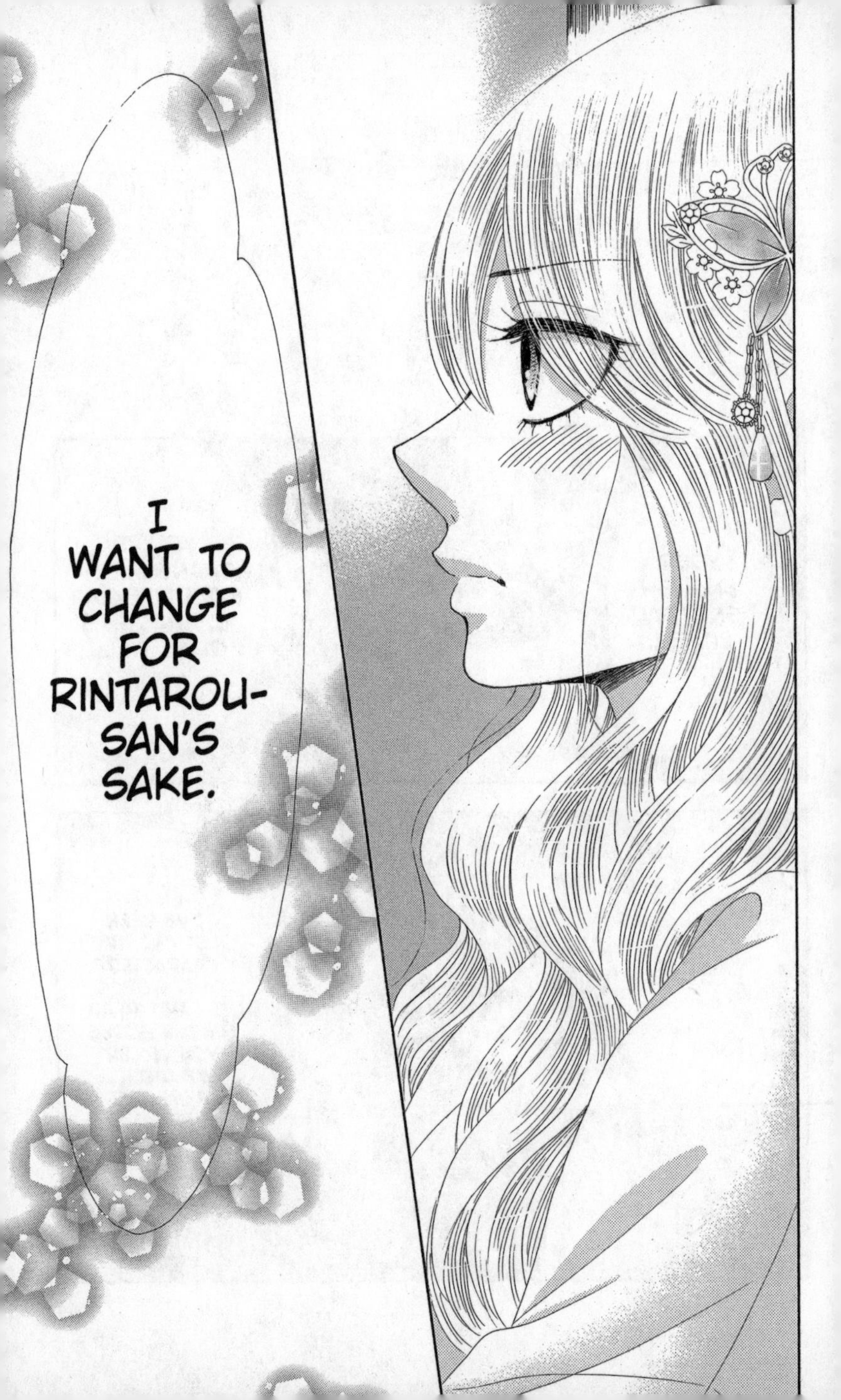
I WANT TO CHANGE FOR RINTAROU-SAN'S SAKE.

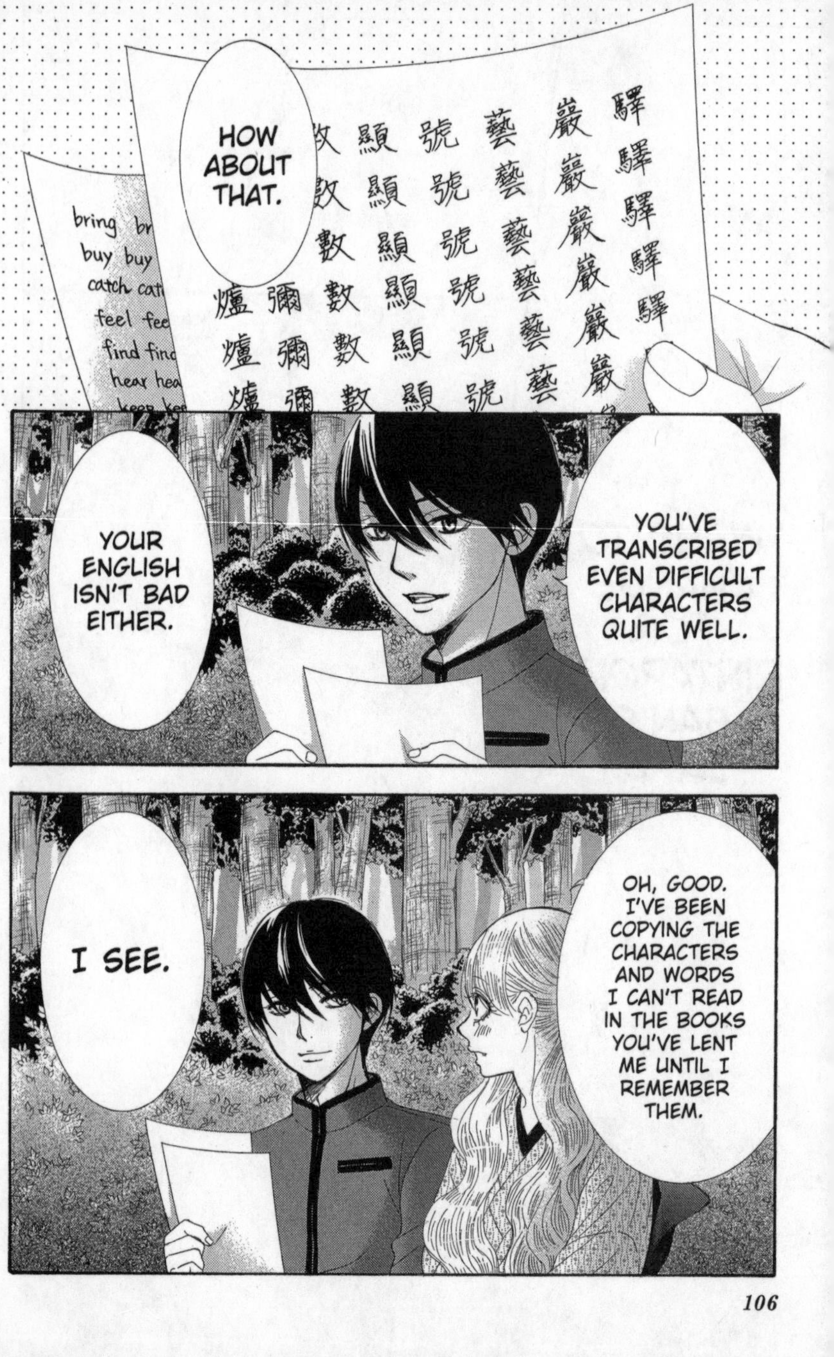
HOW ABOUT THAT.
YOU'VE TRANSCRIBED EVEN DIFFICULT CHARACTERS QUITE WELL.
YOUR ENGLISH ISN'T BAD EITHER.
OH, GOOD. I'VE BEEN COPYING THE CHARACTERS AND WORDS I CAN'T READ IN THE BOOKS YOU'VE LENT ME UNTIL I REMEMBER THEM.
I SEE.

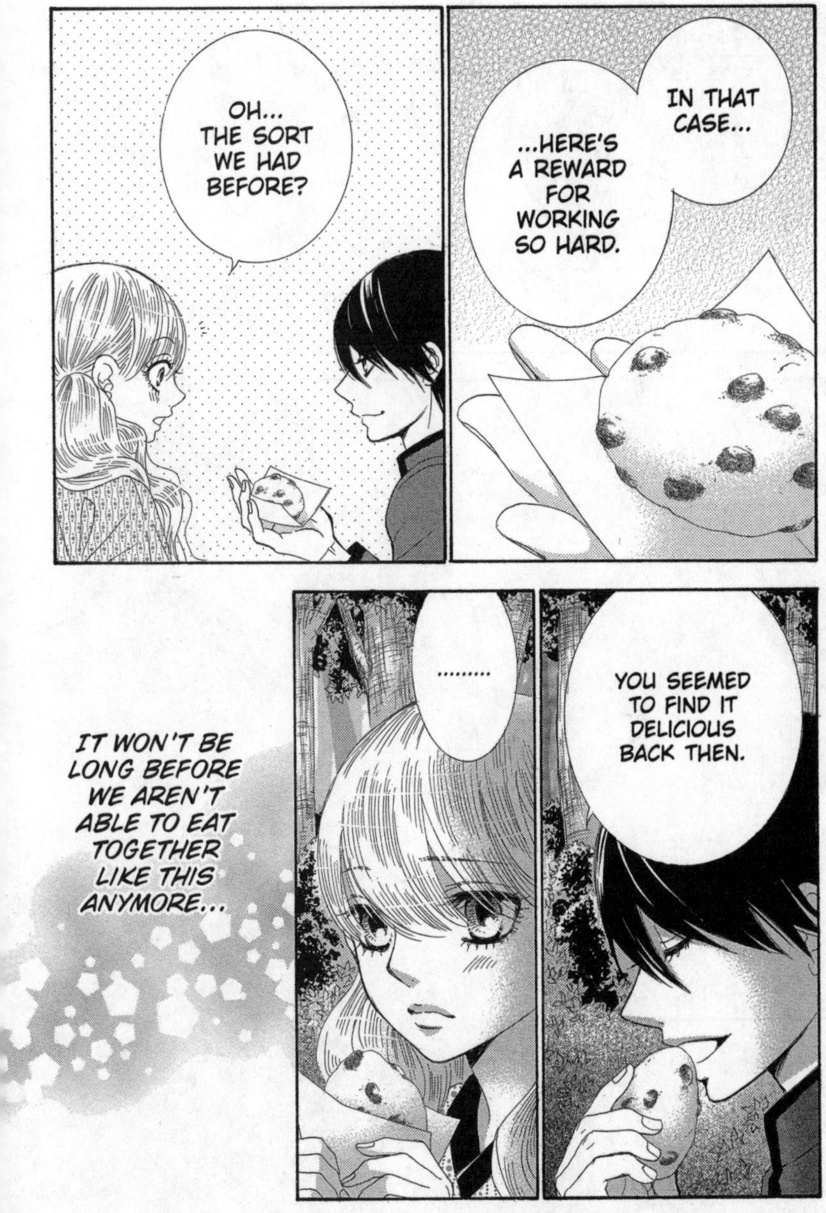
IN THAT CASE...
...HERE'S A REWARD FOR WORKING SO HARD.
OH... THE SORT WE HAD BEFORE?
YOU SEEMED TO FIND IT DELICIOUS BACK THEN.
....
IT WON'T BE LONG BEFORE WE AREN'T ABLE TO EAT TOGETHER LIKE THIS ANYMORE...

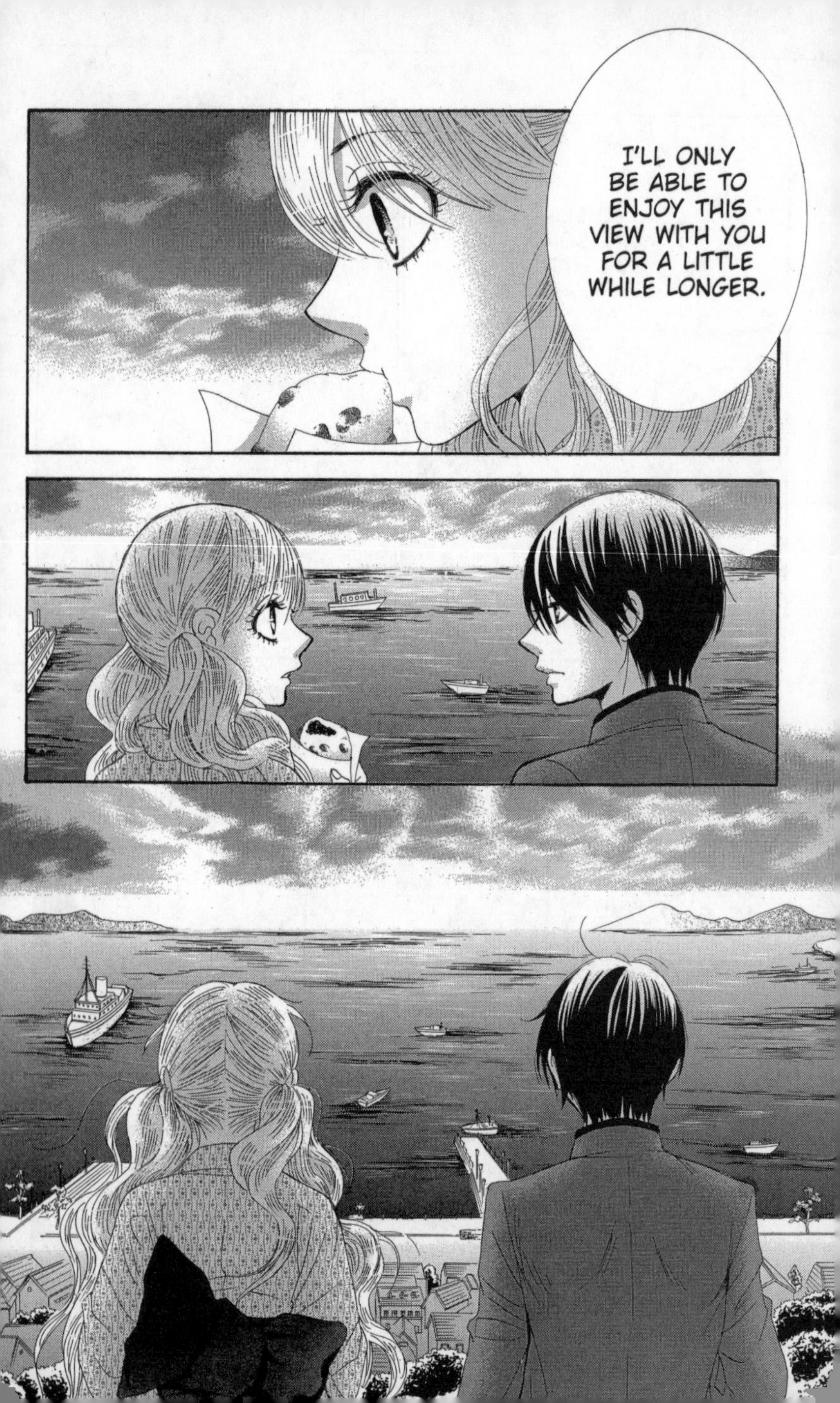
I'LL ONLY BE ABLE TO ENJOY THIS VIEW WITH YOU FOR A LITTLE WHILE LONGER.

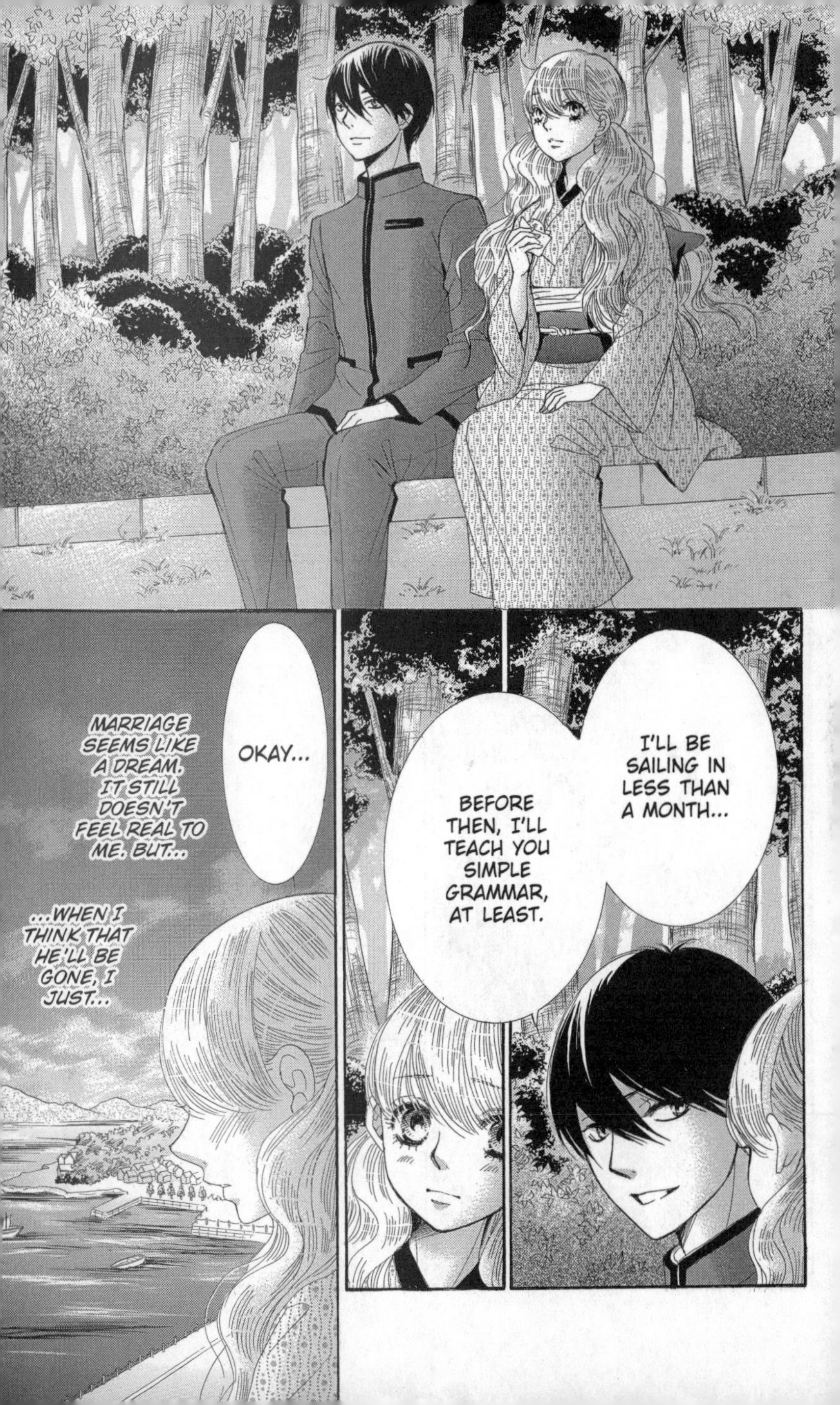
I'LL BE SAILING IN LESS THAN A MONTH...
BEFORE THEN, I'LL TEACH YOU SIMPLE GRAMMAR, AT LEAST.
OKAY...
MARRIAGE SEEMS LIKE A DREAM. IT STILL DOESN'T FEEL REAL TO ME. BUT...
...WHEN I THINK THAT HE'LL BE GONE, I JUST...

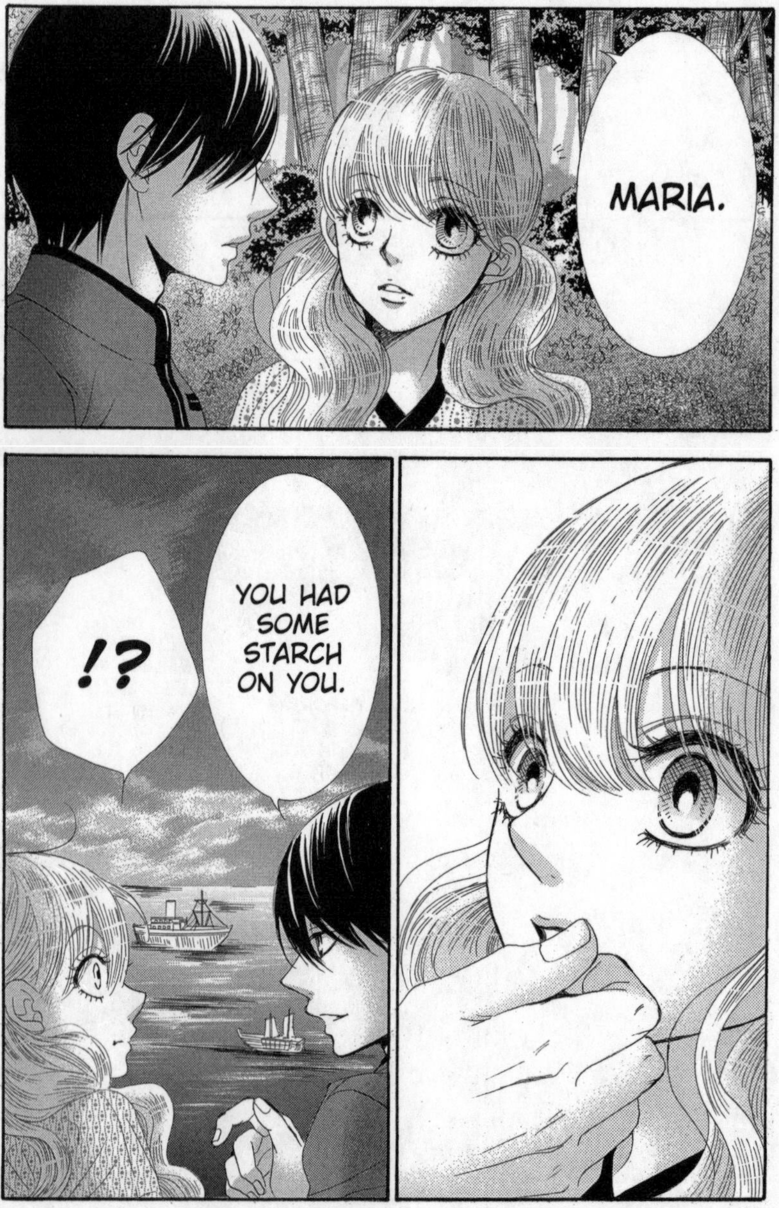
MARIA.
YOU HAD SOME STARCH ON YOU.
!?

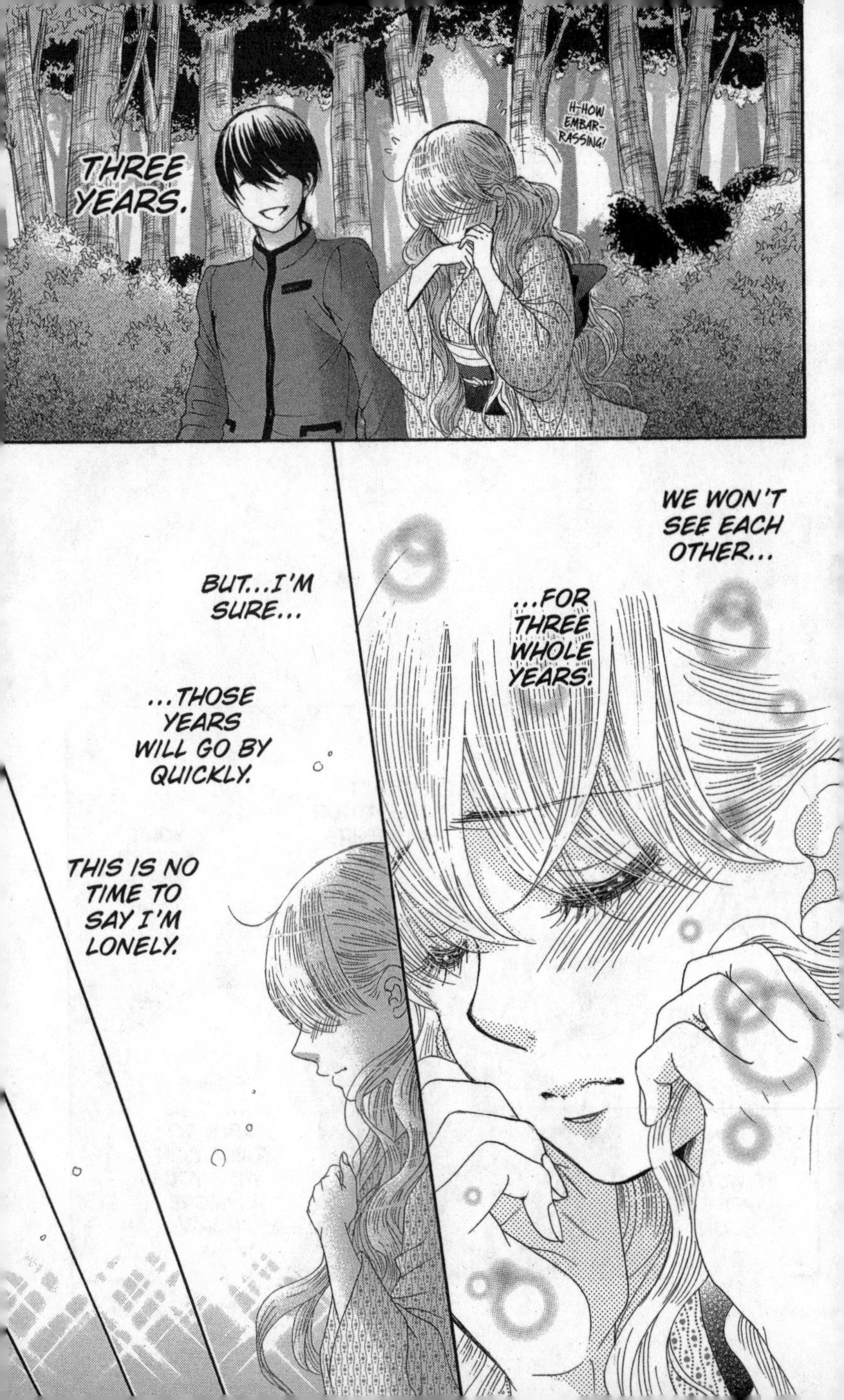
H-HOW EMBARRASSING!
THREE YEARS.
WE WON'T SEE EACH OTHER...
...FOR THREE WHOLE YEARS.
BUT...I'M SURE...
...THOSE YEARS WILL GO BY QUICKLY.
THIS IS NO TIME TO SAY I'M LONELY.

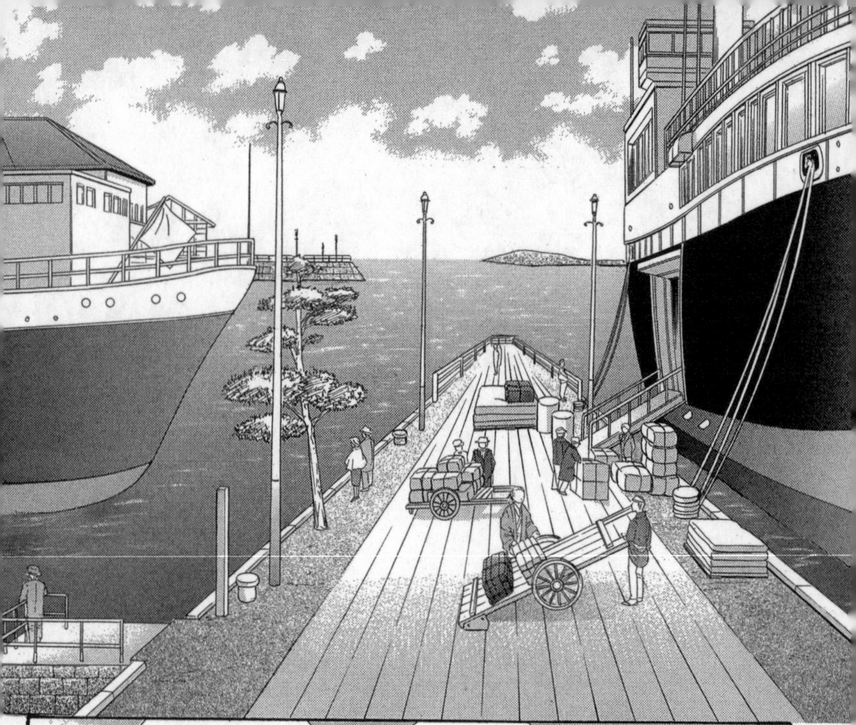

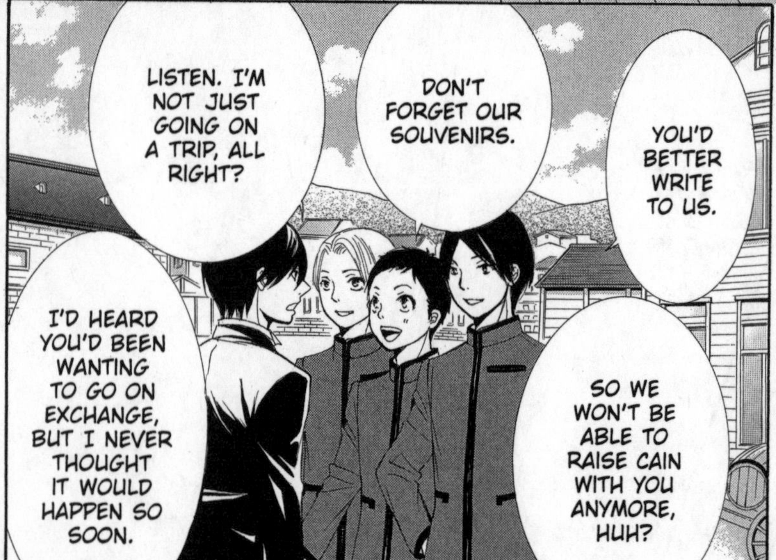
YOU'D BETTER WRITE TO US.
DON'T FORGET OUR SOUVENIRS.
LISTEN. I'M NOT JUST GOING ON A TRIP, ALL RIGHT?
SO WE WON'T BE ABLE TO RAISE CAIN WITH YOU ANYMORE, HUH?
I'D HEARD YOU'D BEEN WANTING TO GO ON EXCHANGE, BUT I NEVER THOUGHT IT WOULD HAPPEN SO SOON.

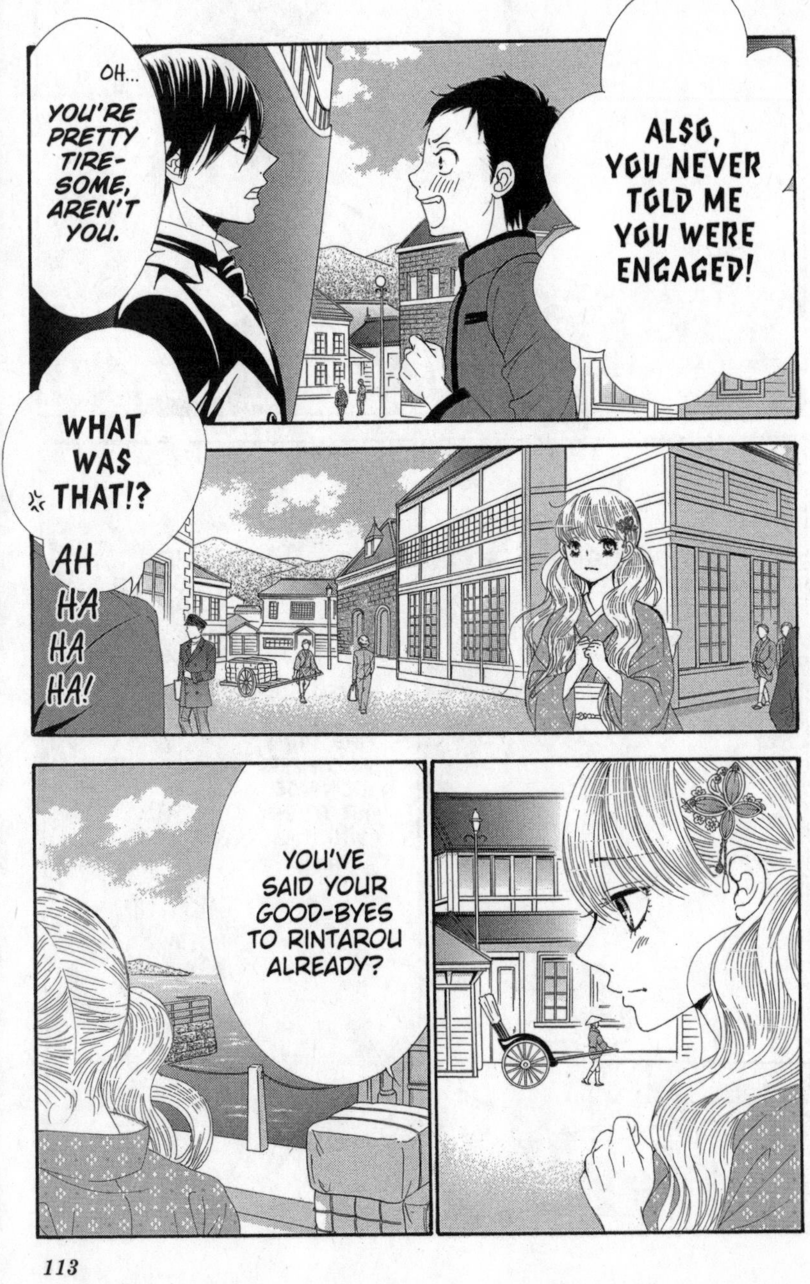
ALSO, YOU NEVER TOLD ME YOU WERE ENGAGED!
OH... YOU'RE PRETTY TIRESOME, AREN'T YOU.
WHAT WAS THAT!?
AH HA HA HA!
YOU'VE SAID YOUR GOOD-BYES TO RINTAROU ALREADY?

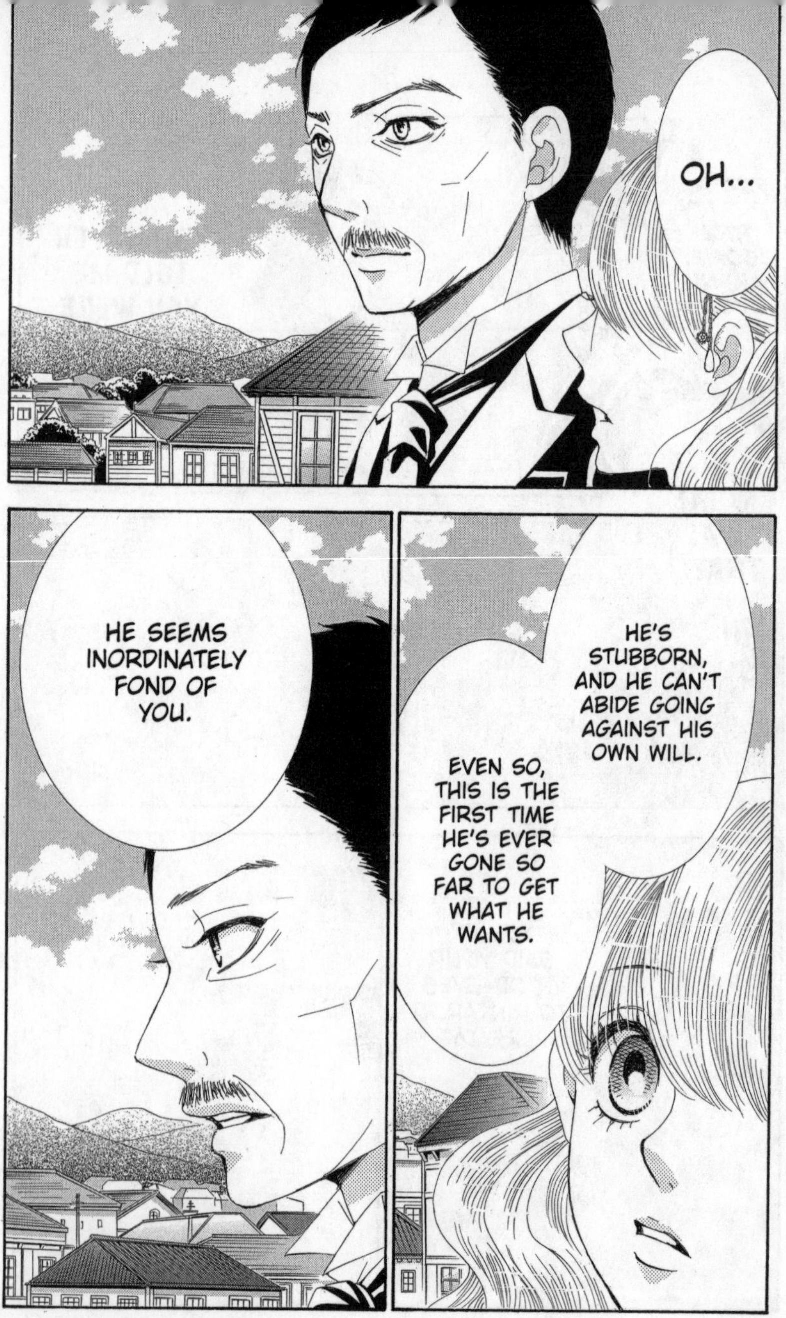
OH...
HE'S STUBBORN, AND HE CAN'T ABIDE GOING AGAINST HIS OWN WILL.
EVEN SO, THIS IS THE FIRST TIME HE'S EVER GONE SO FAR TO GET WHAT HE WANTS.
HE SEEMS INORDINATELY FOND OF YOU.

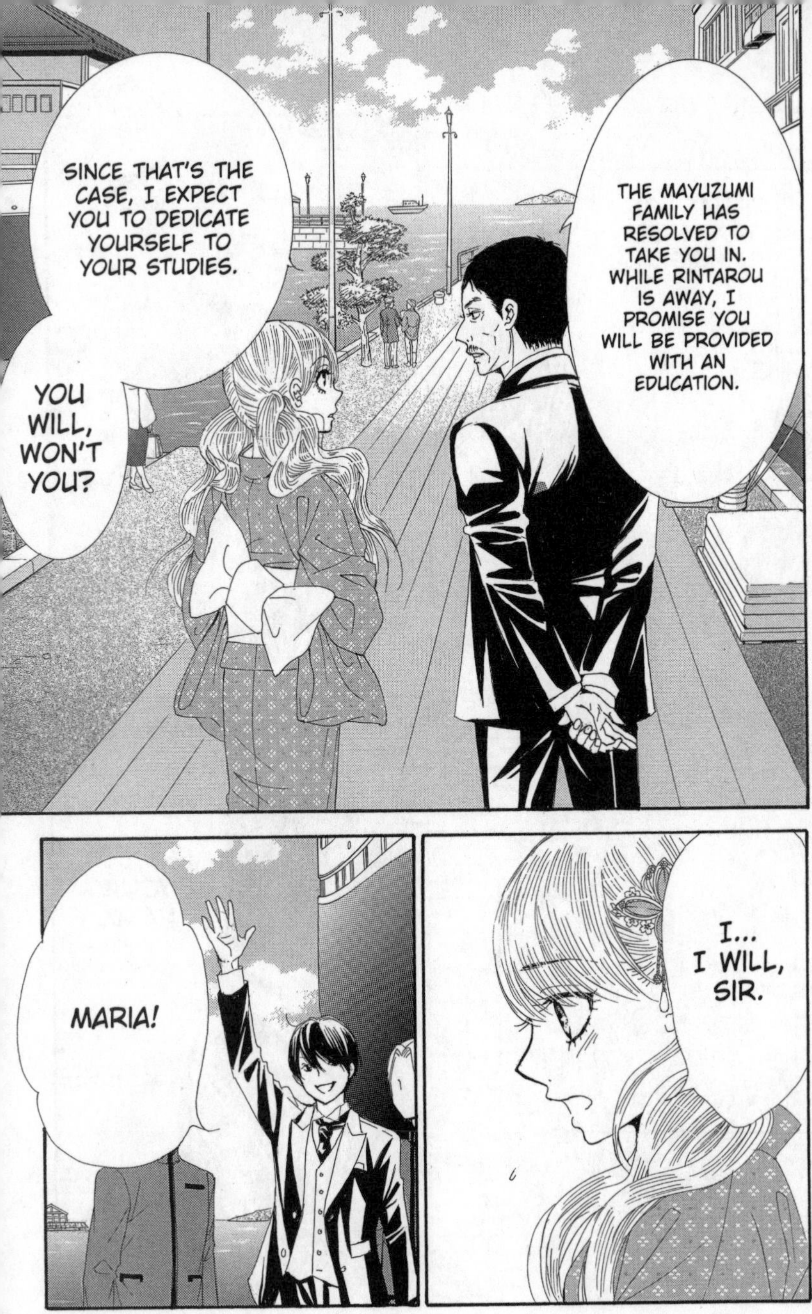
THE MAYUZUMI FAMILY HAS RESOLVED TO TAKE YOU IN. WHILE RINTAROU IS AWAY, I PROMISE YOU WILL BE PROVIDED WITH AN EDUCATION.
SINCE THAT'S THE CASE, I EXPECT YOU TO DEDICATE YOURSELF TO YOUR STUDIES.
YOU WILL, WON'T YOU?
I... I WILL, SIR.
MARIA!

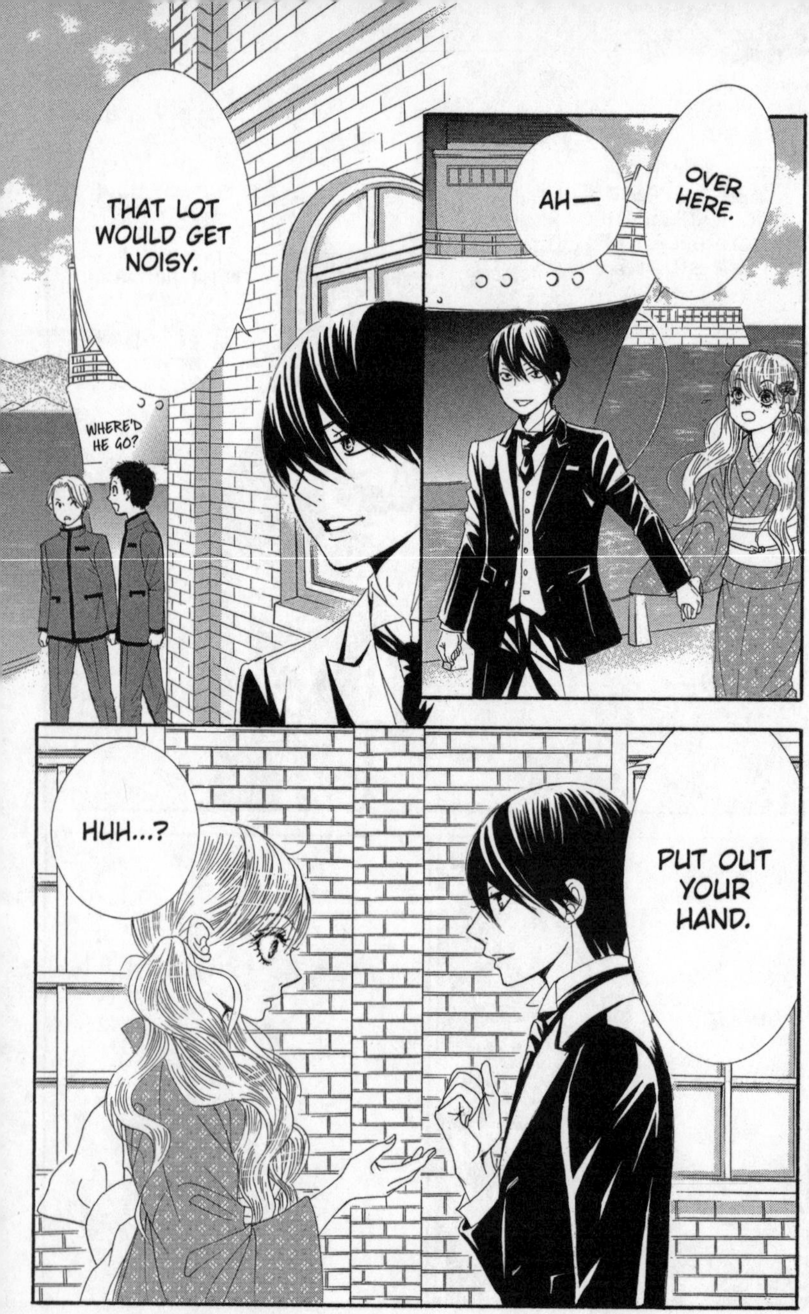
OVER HERE.
AH—
THAT LOT WOULD GET NOISY.
WHERE'D HE GO?
PUT OUT YOUR HAND.
HUH...?

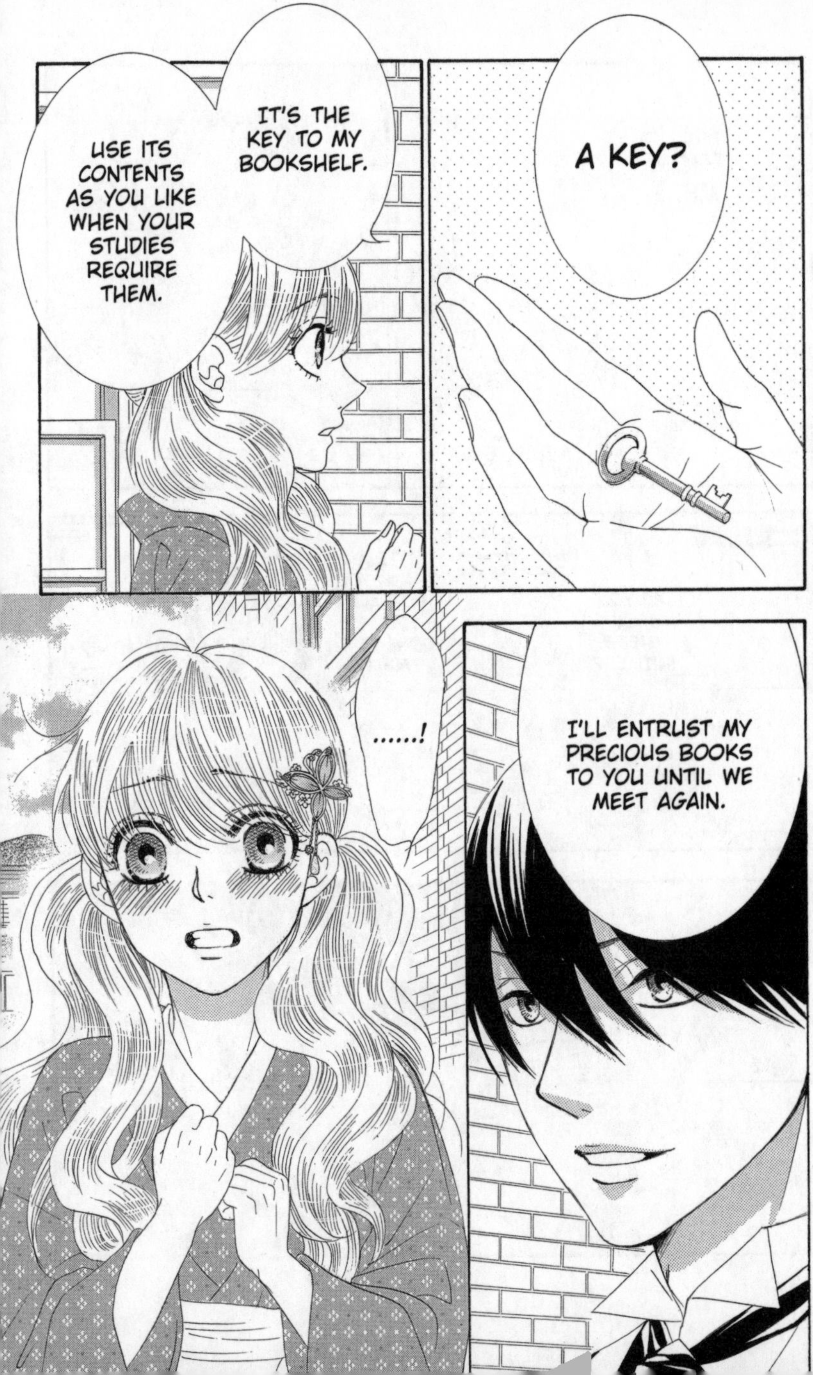
A KEY?
IT'S THE KEY TO MY BOOKSHELF.
USE ITS CONTENTS AS YOU LIKE WHEN YOUR STUDIES REQUIRE THEM.
I'LL ENTRUST MY PRECIOUS BOOKS TO YOU UNTIL WE MEET AGAIN.
......!

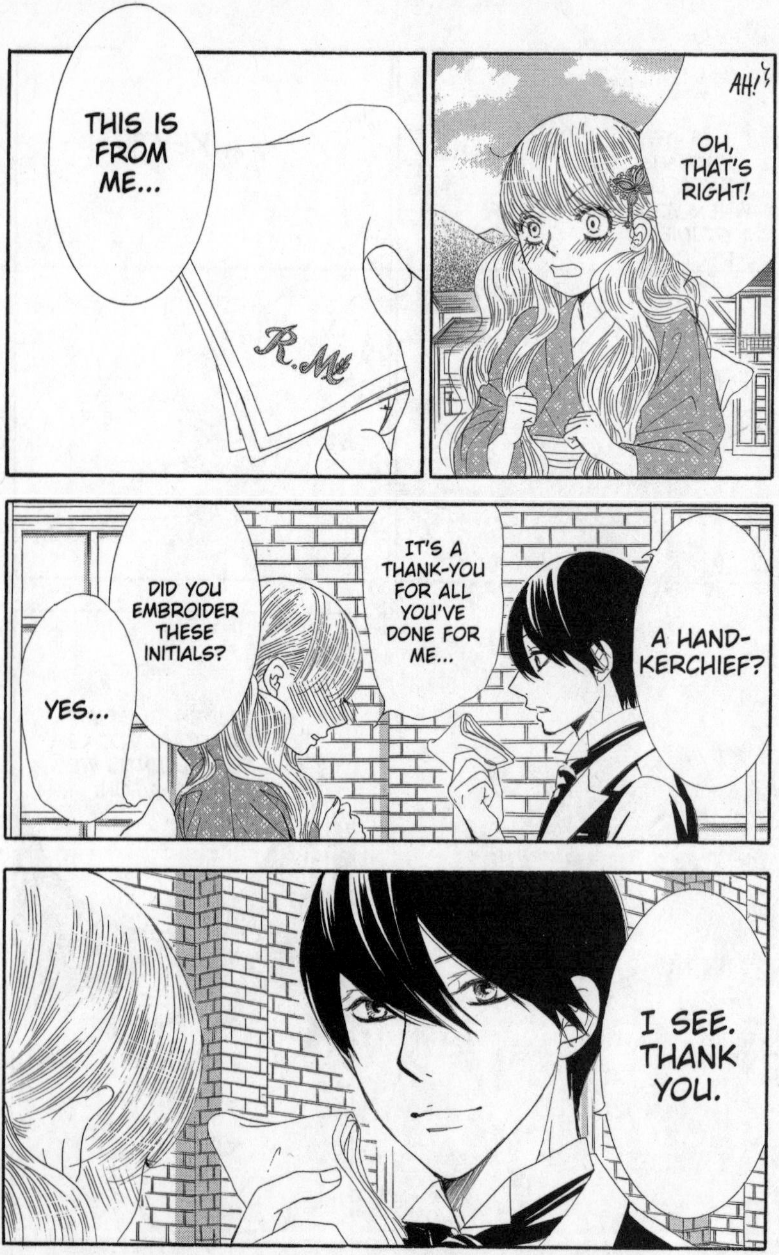
AH!
OH, THAT'S RIGHT!
THIS IS FROM ME...
R.M
A HAND-KERCHIEF?
IT'S A THANK-YOU FOR ALL YOU'VE DONE FOR ME...
DID YOU EMBROIDER THESE INITIALS?
YES...
I SEE. THANK YOU.

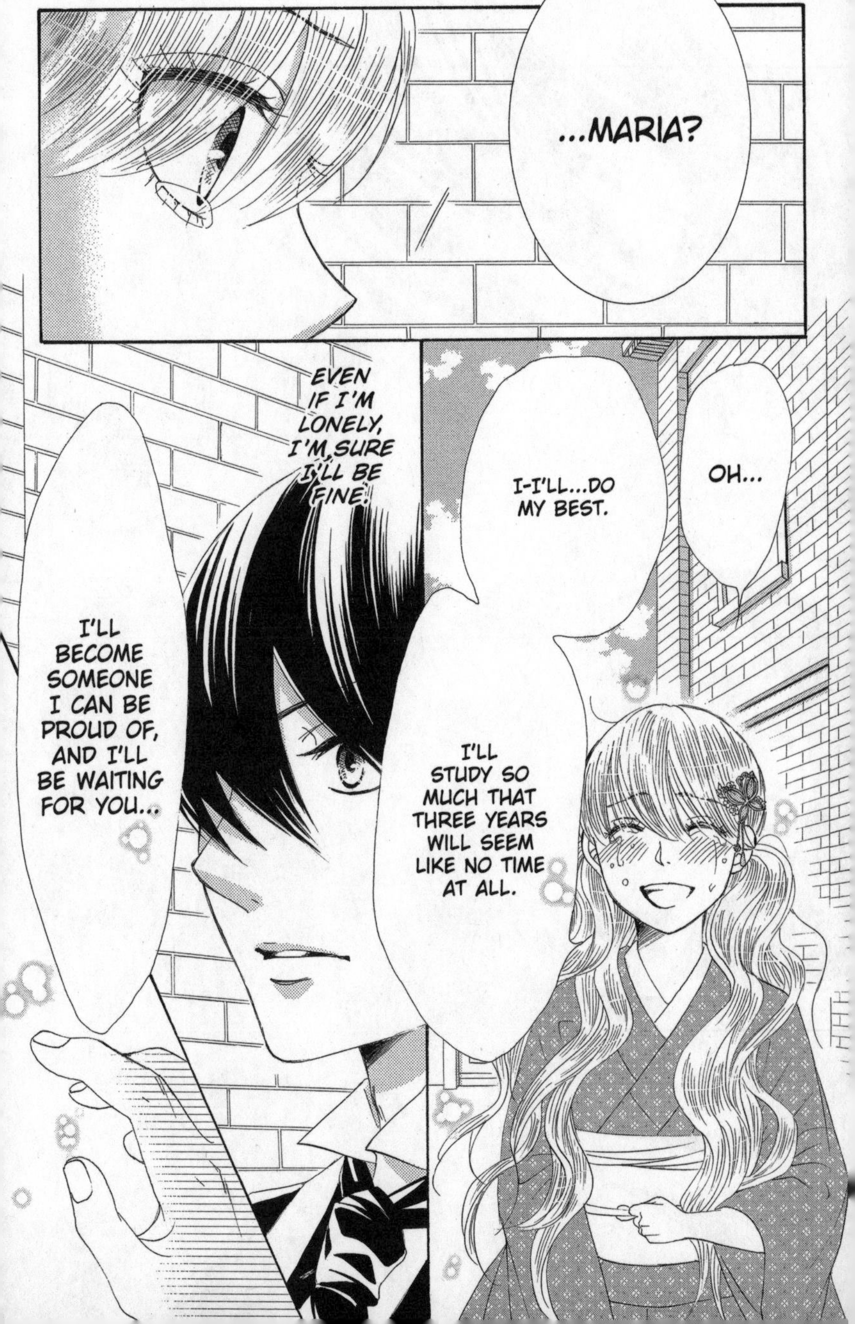
...MARIA?
OH...
I-I'LL...DO MY BEST.
I'LL STUDY SO MUCH THAT THREE YEARS WILL SEEM LIKE NO TIME AT ALL.
EVEN IF I'M LONELY, I'M SURE I'LL BE FINE.
I'LL BECOME SOMEONE I CAN BE PROUD OF, AND I'LL BE WAITING FOR YOU...

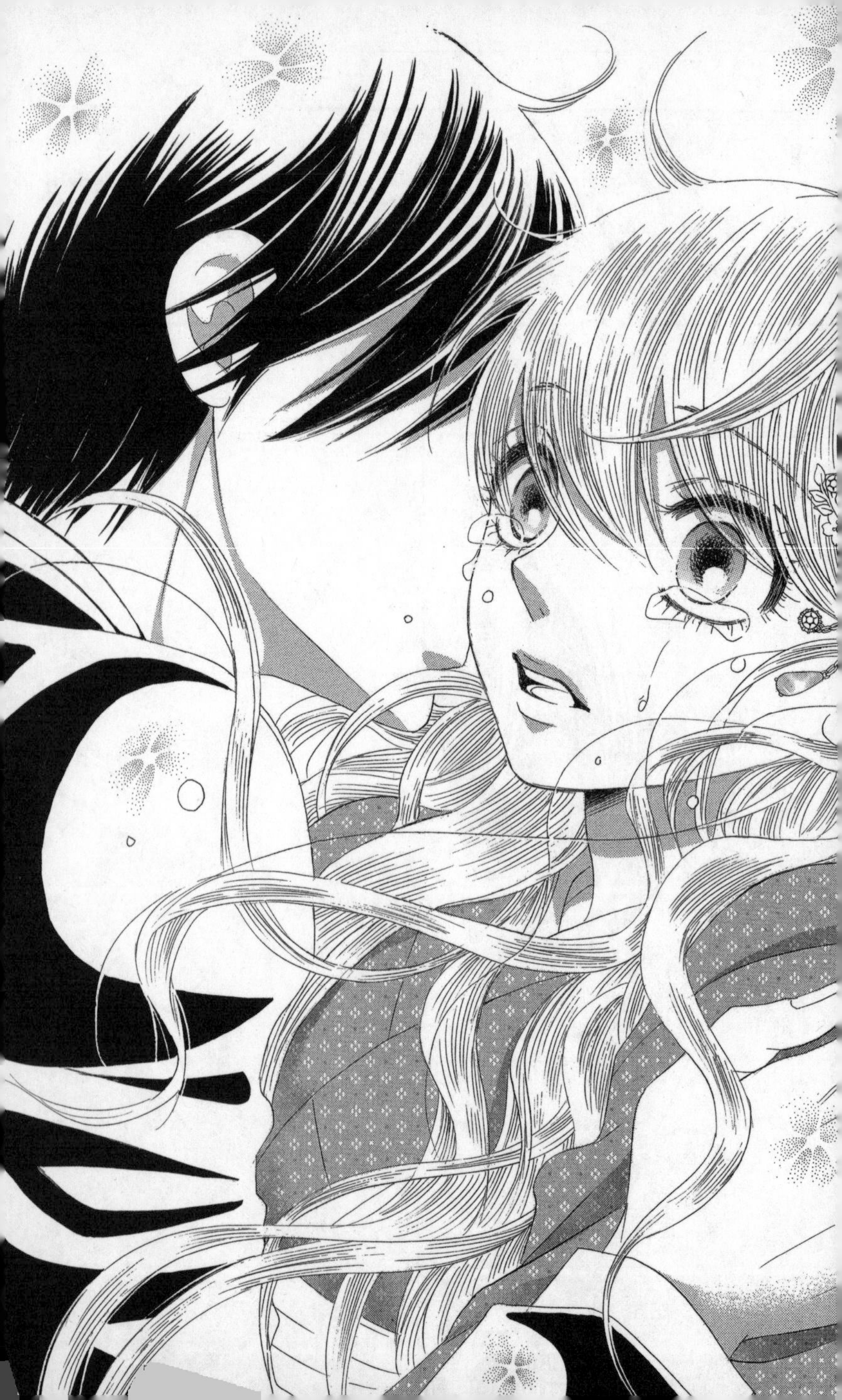

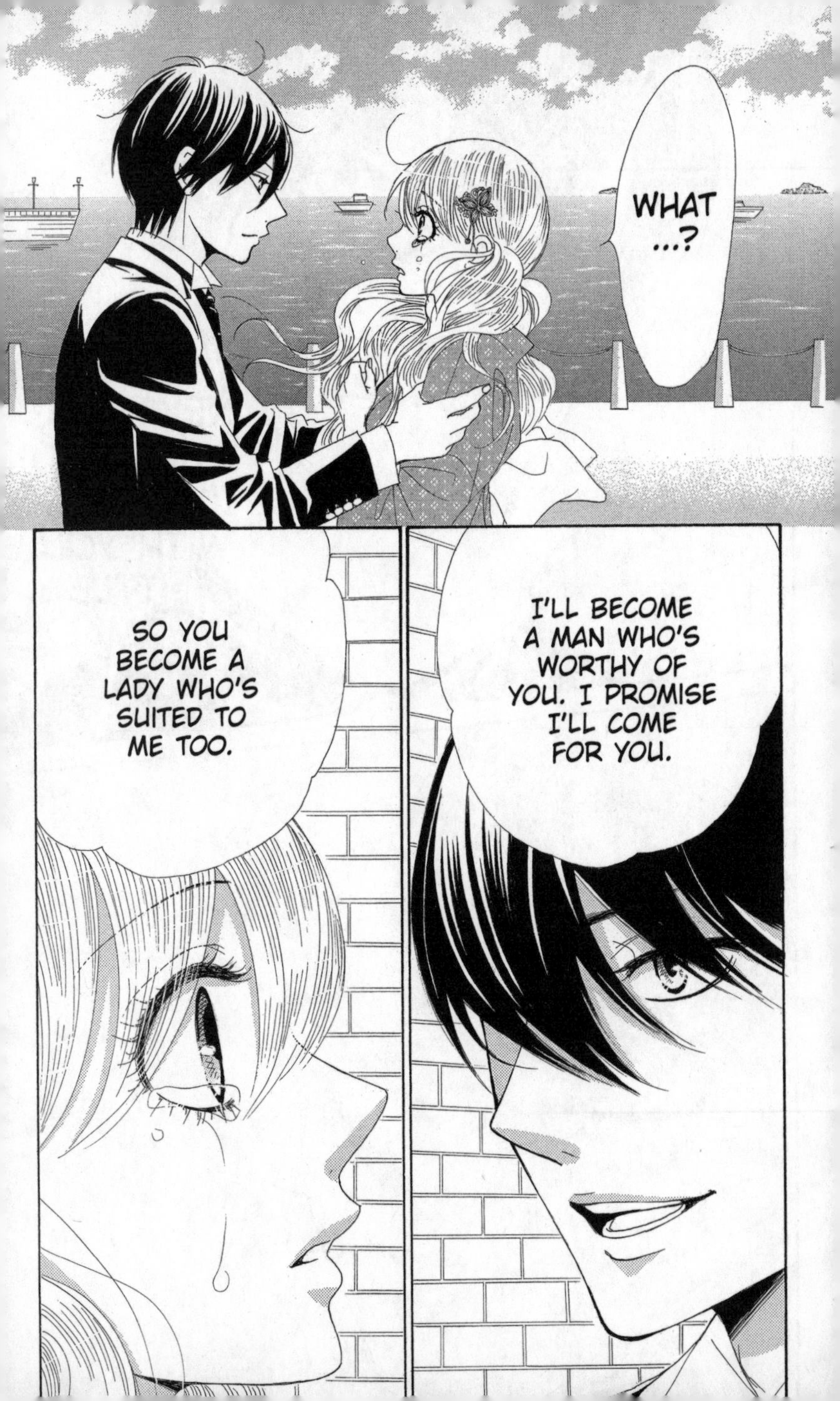
WHAT ...?
I'LL BECOME A MAN WHO'S WORTHY OF YOU. I PROMISE I'LL COME FOR YOU.
SO YOU BECOME A LADY WHO'S SUITED TO ME TOO.

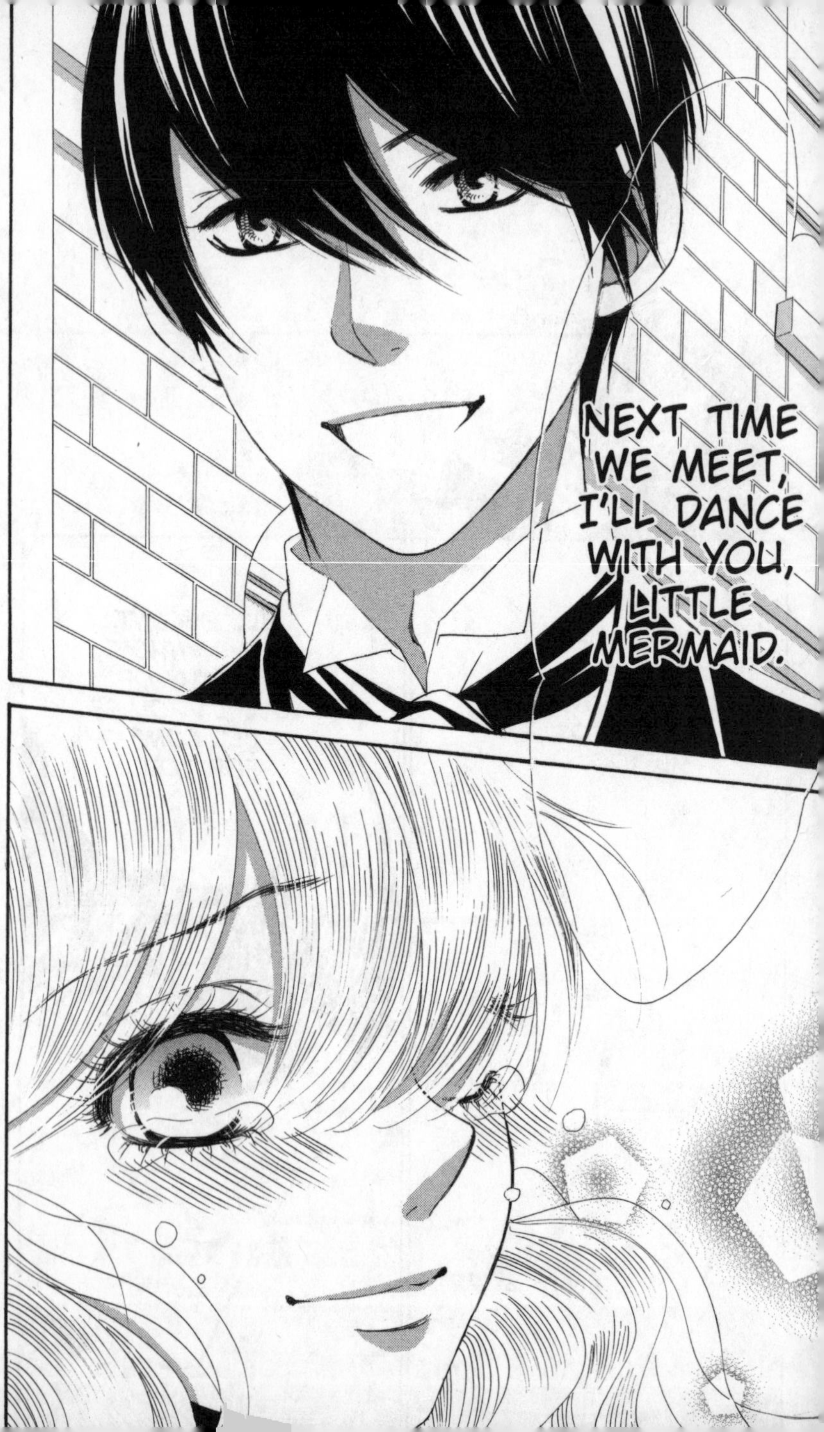
NEXT TIME WE MEET, I'LL DANCE WITH YOU, LITTLE MERMAID.

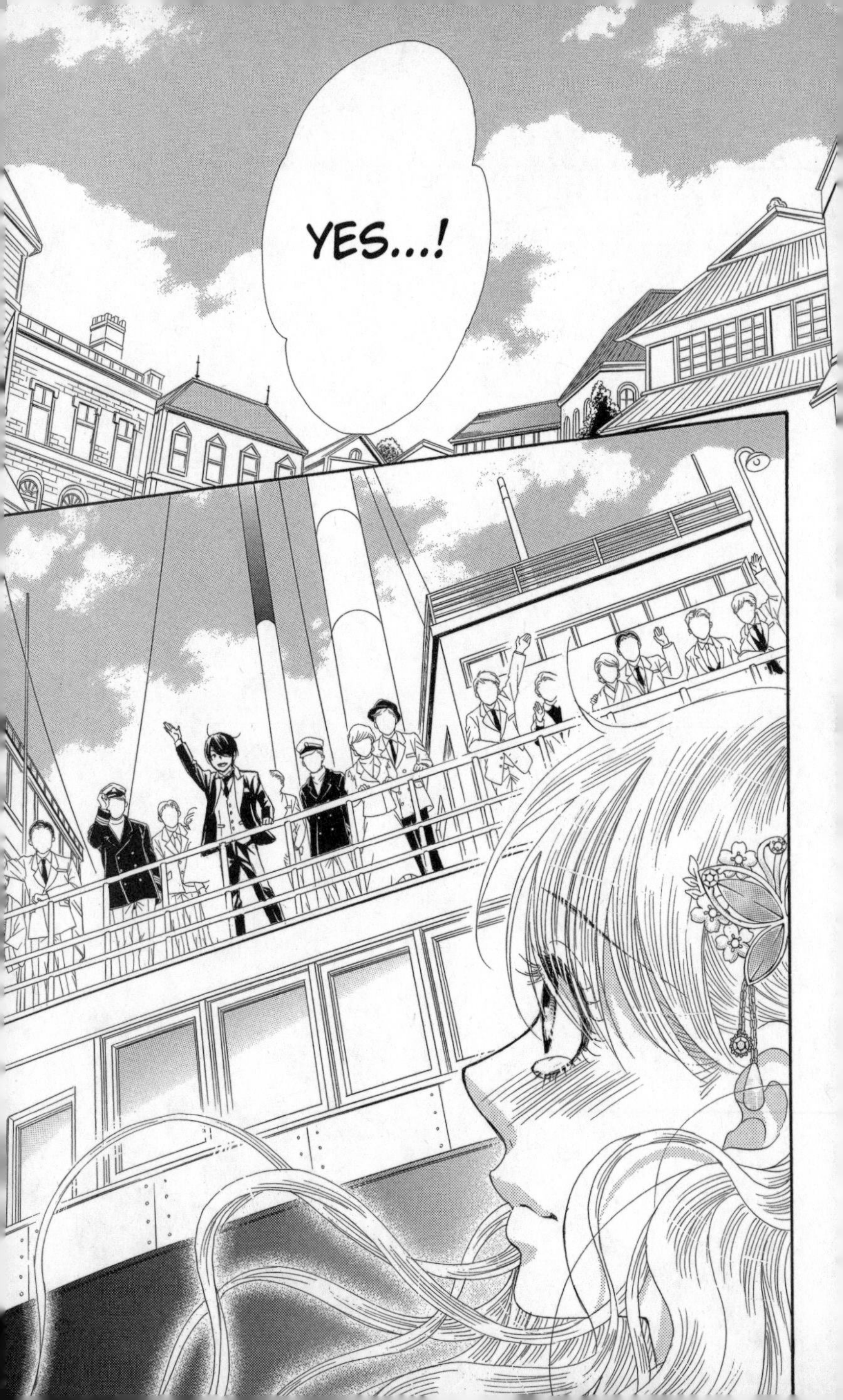
YES...!

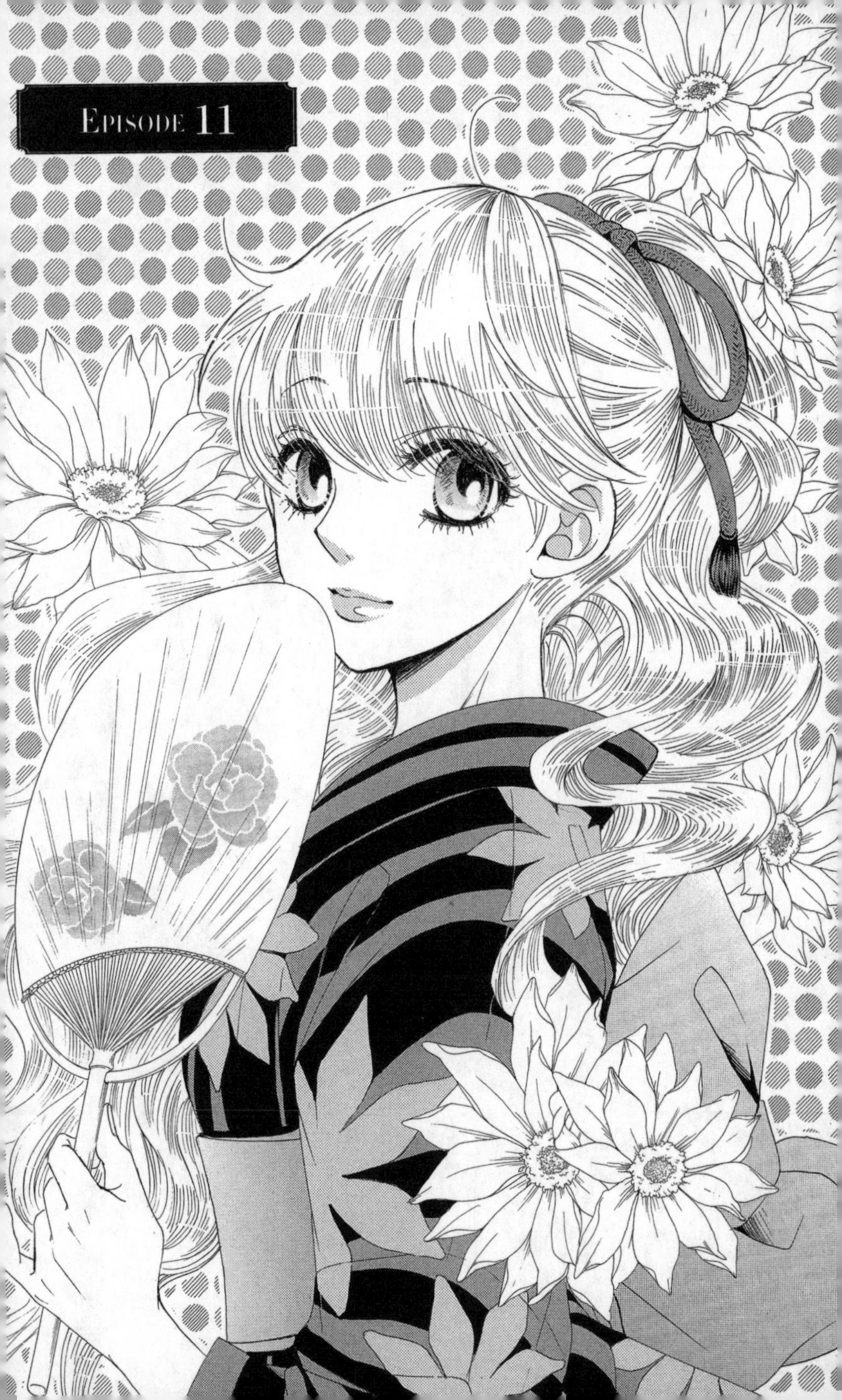
Episode 11

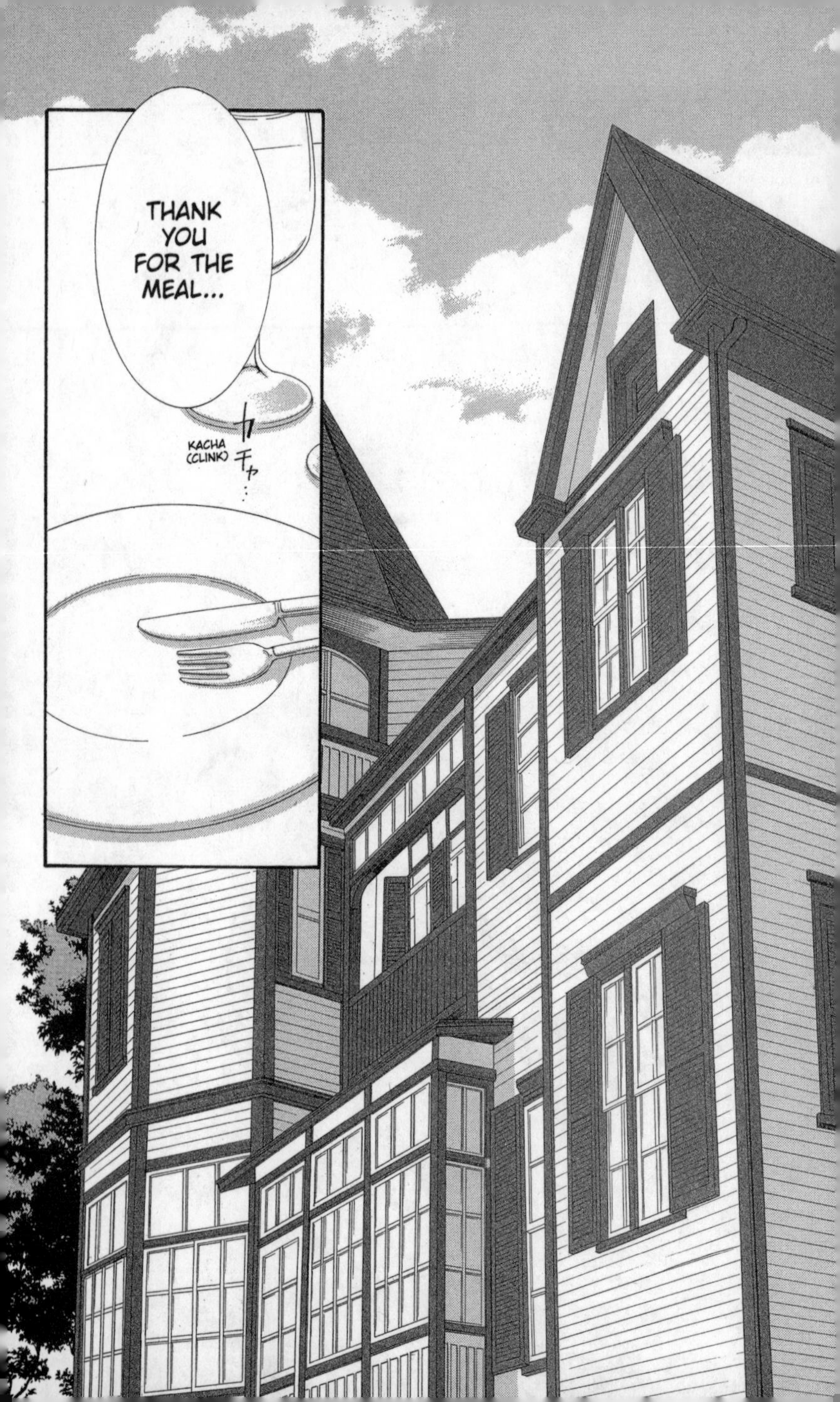
THANK YOU FOR THE MEAL...
カチャ…
KACHA (CLINK)

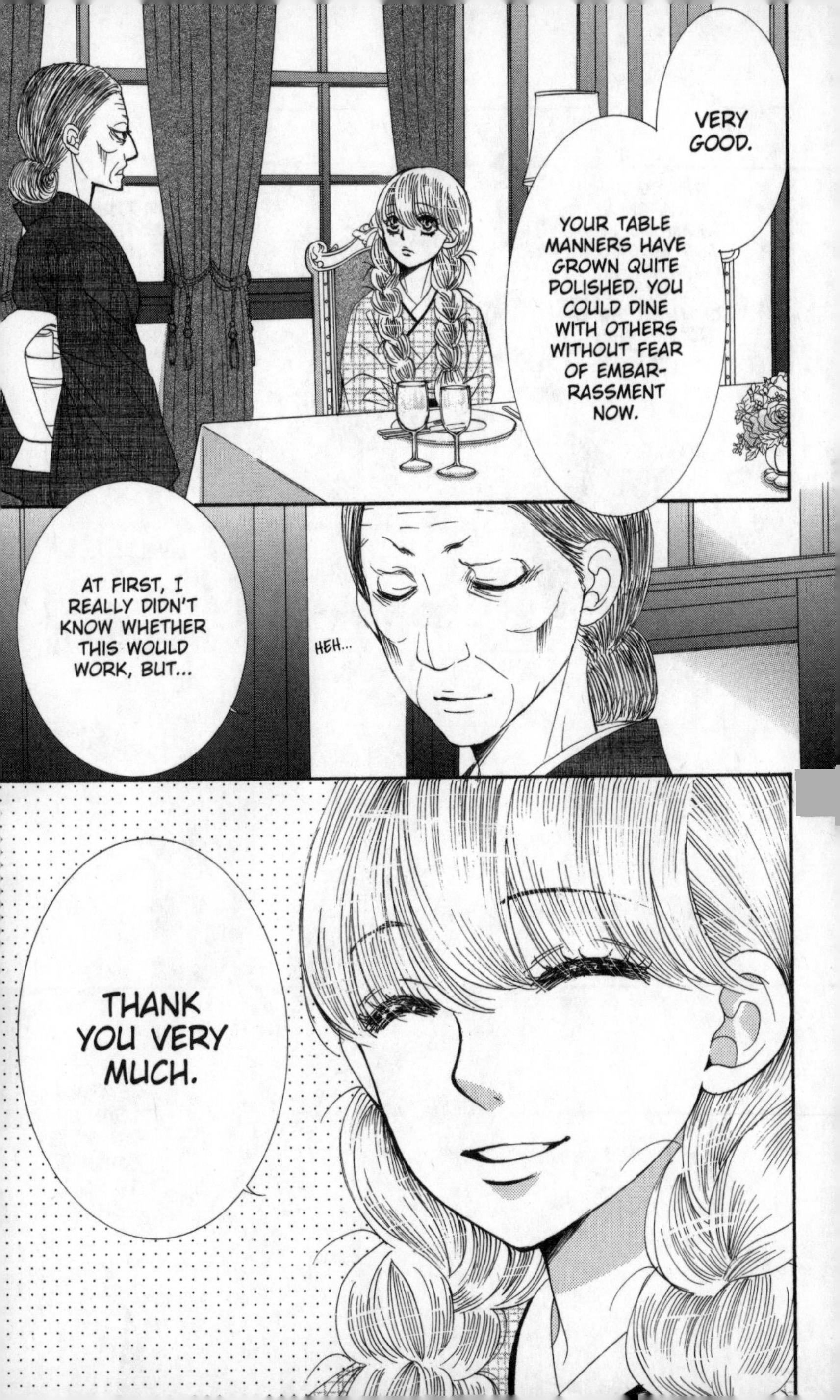
VERY GOOD.
YOUR TABLE MANNERS HAVE GROWN QUITE POLISHED. YOU COULD DINE WITH OTHERS WITHOUT FEAR OF EMBAR-RASSMENT NOW.
HEH...
AT FIRST, I REALLY DIDN'T KNOW WHETHER THIS WOULD WORK, BUT...
THANK YOU VERY MUCH.

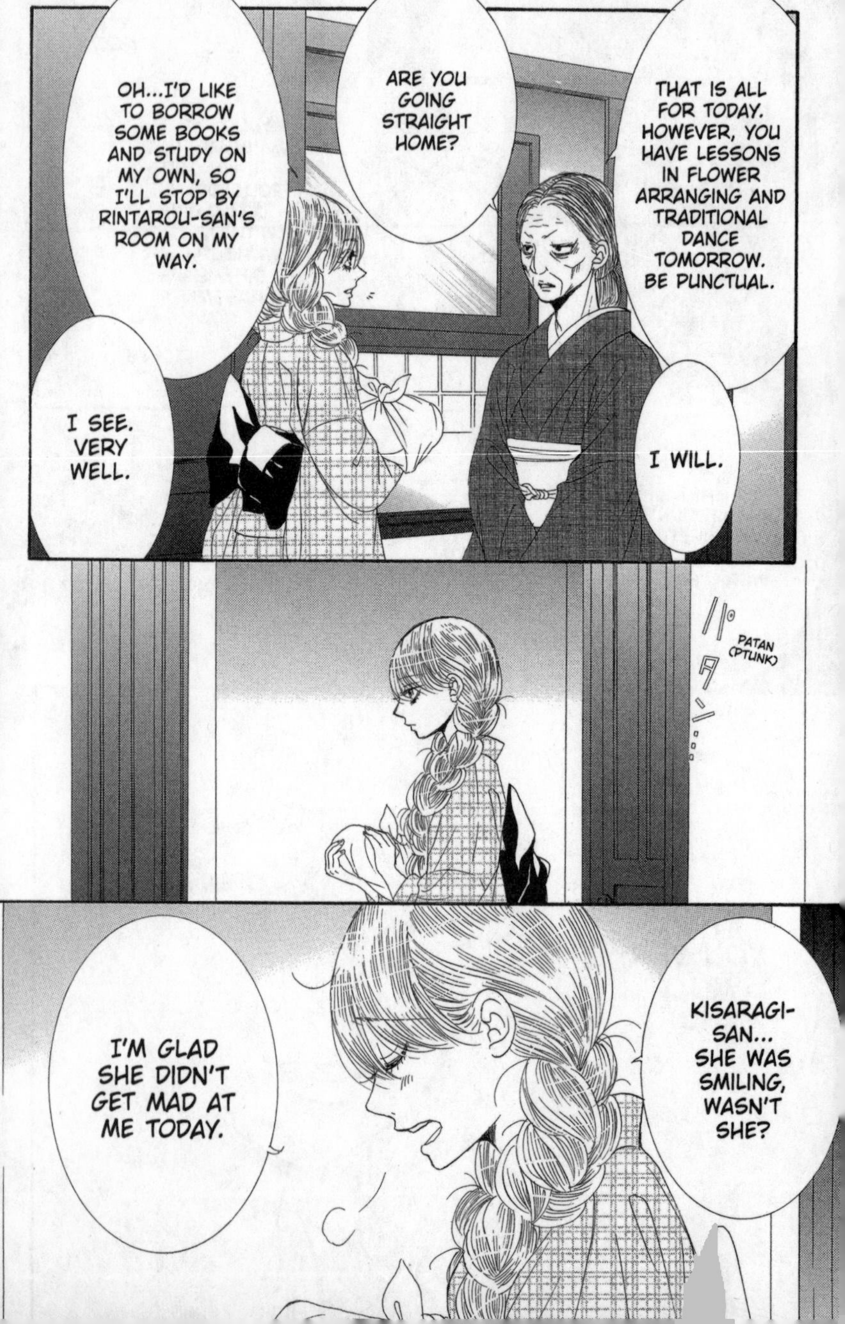
THAT IS ALL FOR TODAY. HOWEVER, YOU HAVE LESSONS IN FLOWER ARRANGING AND TRADITIONAL DANCE TOMORROW. BE PUNCTUAL.
I WILL.
ARE YOU GOING STRAIGHT HOME?
OH...I'D LIKE TO BORROW SOME BOOKS AND STUDY ON MY OWN, SO I'LL STOP BY RINTAROU-SAN'S ROOM ON MY WAY.
I SEE. VERY WELL.
パタン
PATAN (PTUNK)
KISARAGI-SAN... SHE WAS SMILING, WASN'T SHE?
I'M GLAD SHE DIDN'T GET MAD AT ME TODAY.

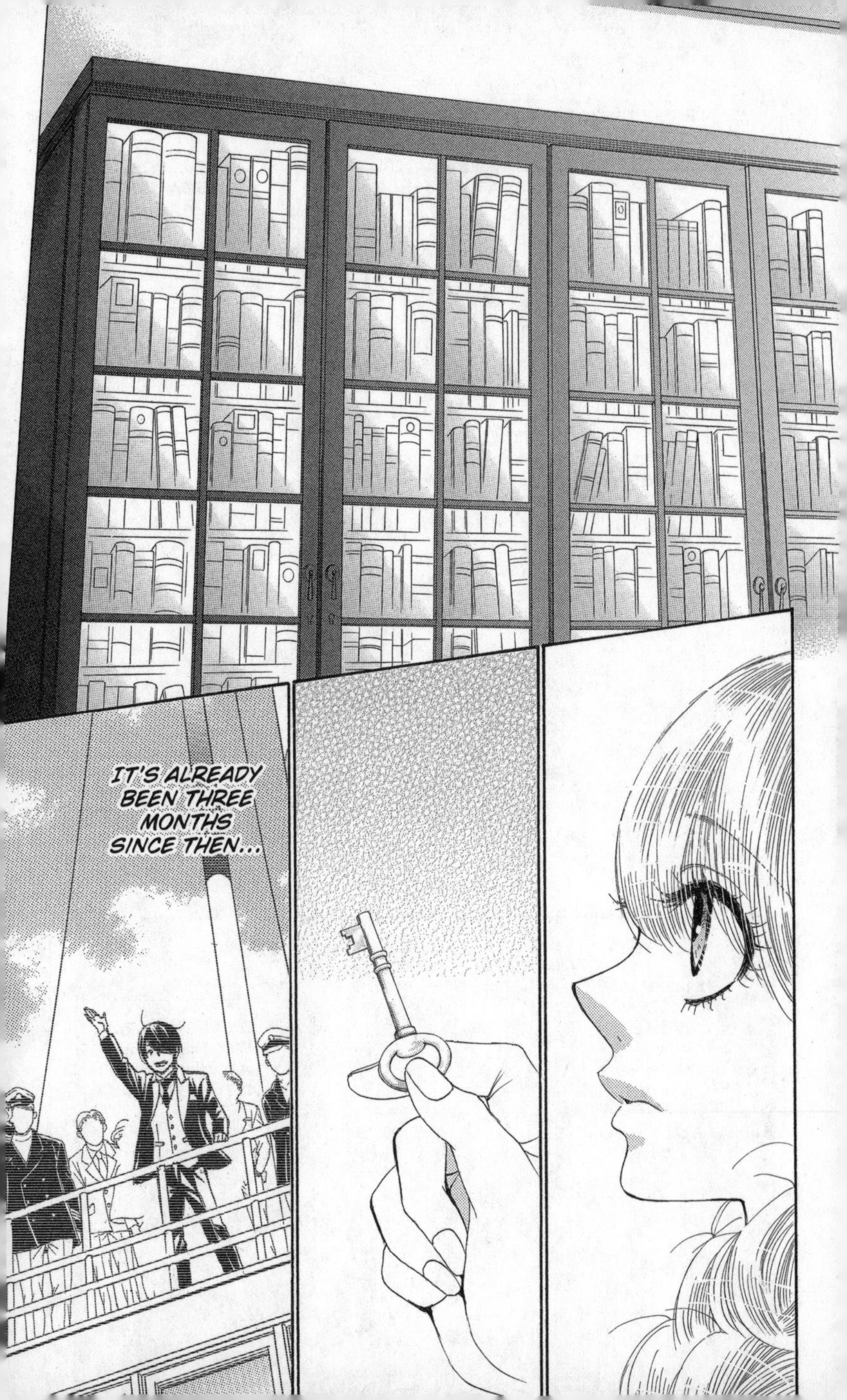
IT'S ALREADY BEEN THREE MONTHS SINCE THEN...

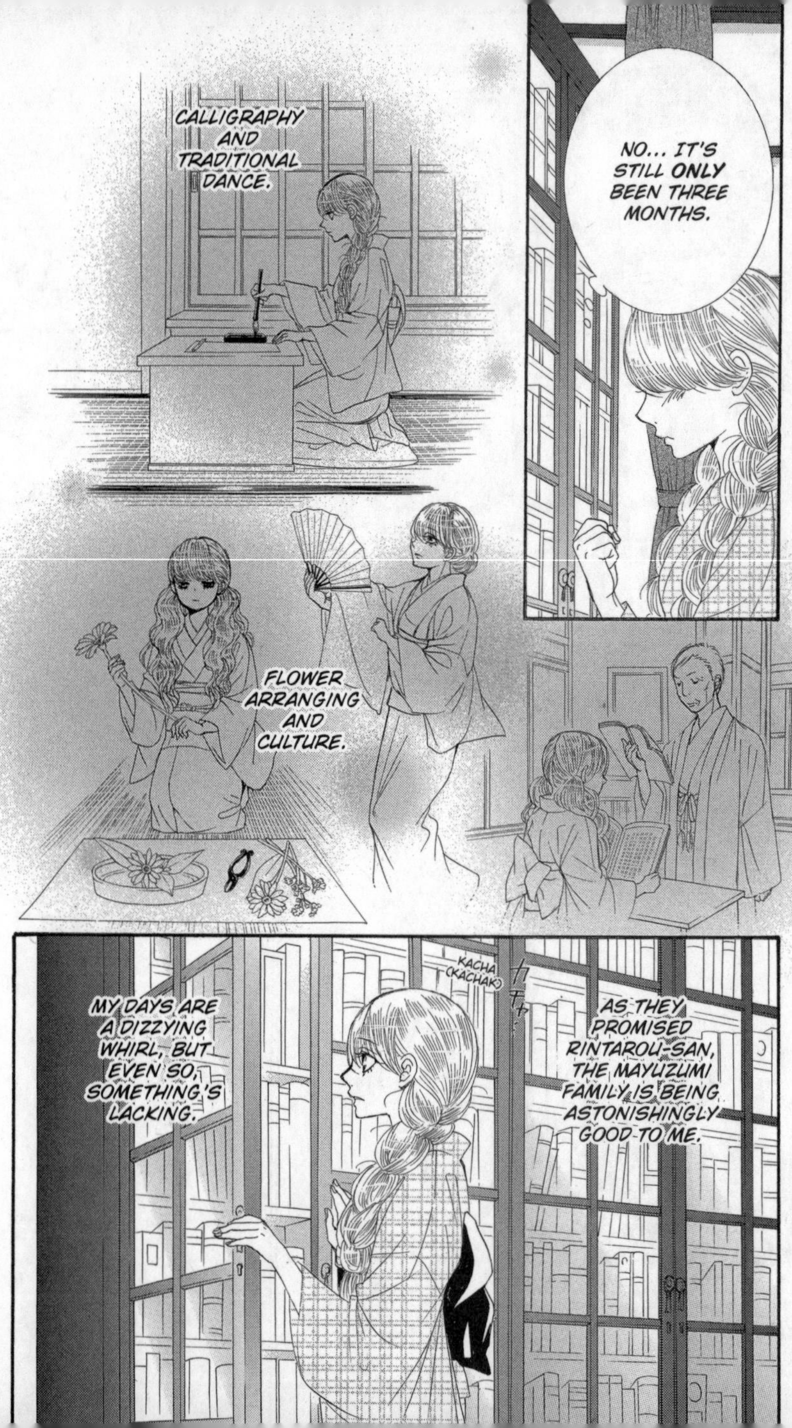
NO... IT'S STILL ONLY BEEN THREE MONTHS.
CALLIGRAPHY AND TRADITIONAL DANCE.
FLOWER ARRANGING AND CULTURE.
AS THEY PROMISED RINTAROU-SAN, THE MAYUZUMI FAMILY IS BEING ASTONISHINGLY GOOD TO ME.
KACHA (KACHAK)
MY DAYS ARE A DIZZYING WHIRL, BUT EVEN SO, SOMETHING'S LACKING.

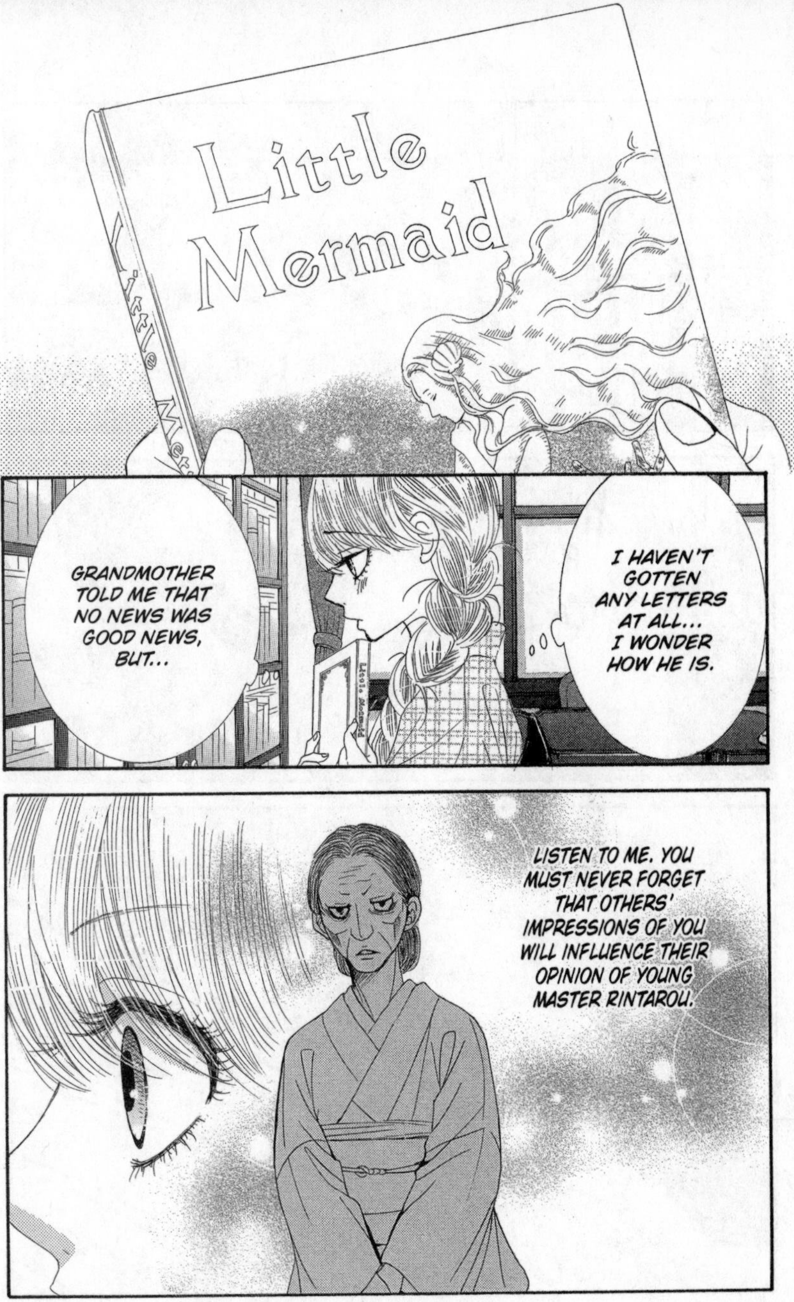
Little Mermaid
I HAVEN'T GOTTEN ANY LETTERS AT ALL... I WONDER HOW HE IS.
GRANDMOTHER TOLD ME THAT NO NEWS WAS GOOD NEWS, BUT...
LISTEN TO ME. YOU MUST NEVER FORGET THAT OTHERS' IMPRESSIONS OF YOU WILL INFLUENCE THEIR OPINION OF YOUNG MASTER RINTAROU.

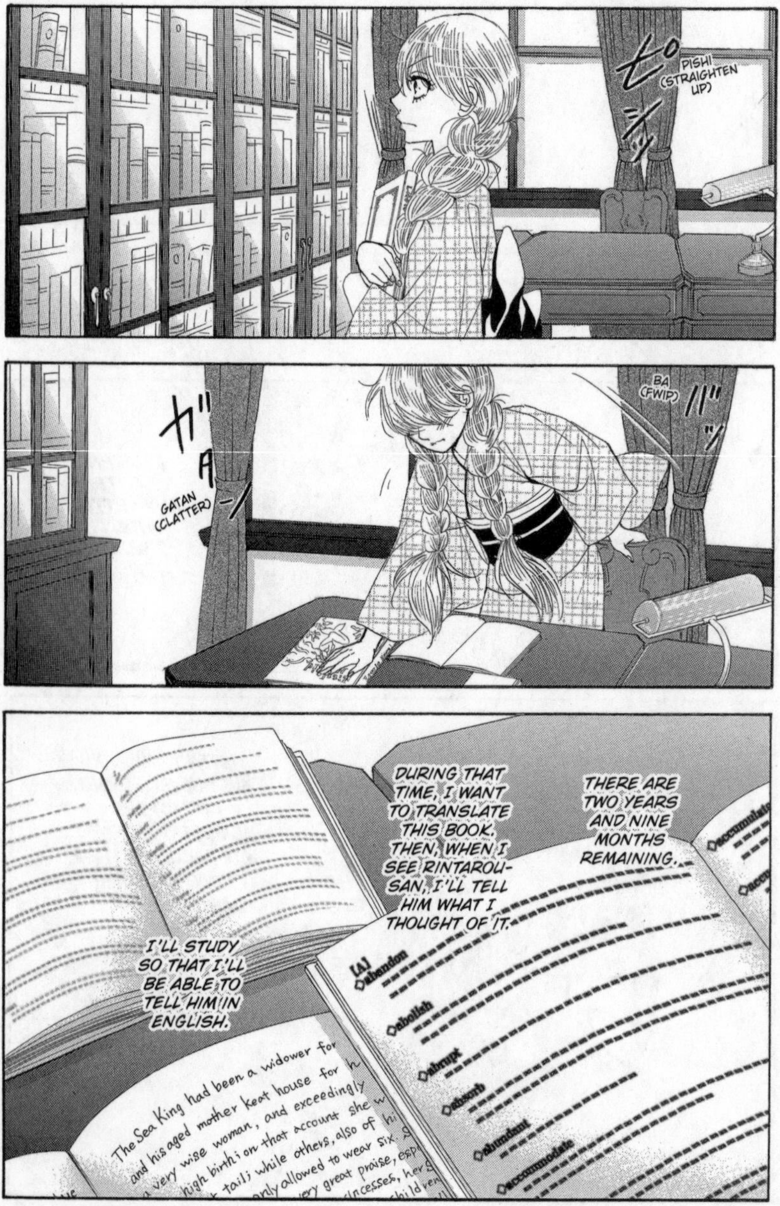
PISHI (STRAIGHTEN UP)
BA (FWIP)
GATAN (CLATTER)
THERE ARE TWO YEARS AND NINE MONTHS REMAINING.
DURING THAT TIME, I WANT TO TRANSLATE THIS BOOK. THEN, WHEN I SEE RINTAROU-SAN, I'LL TELL HIM WHAT I THOUGHT OF IT.
I'LL STUDY SO THAT I'LL BE ABLE TO TELL HIM IN ENGLISH.
[A]
abandon
abolish
abrupt
absorb
abundant
accommodate
The Sea King had been a widower for
and his aged mother keat house for
very wise woman, and exceedingly
high birth; on that account she
tail; while others, also of
allowed to wear six.
very great praise,

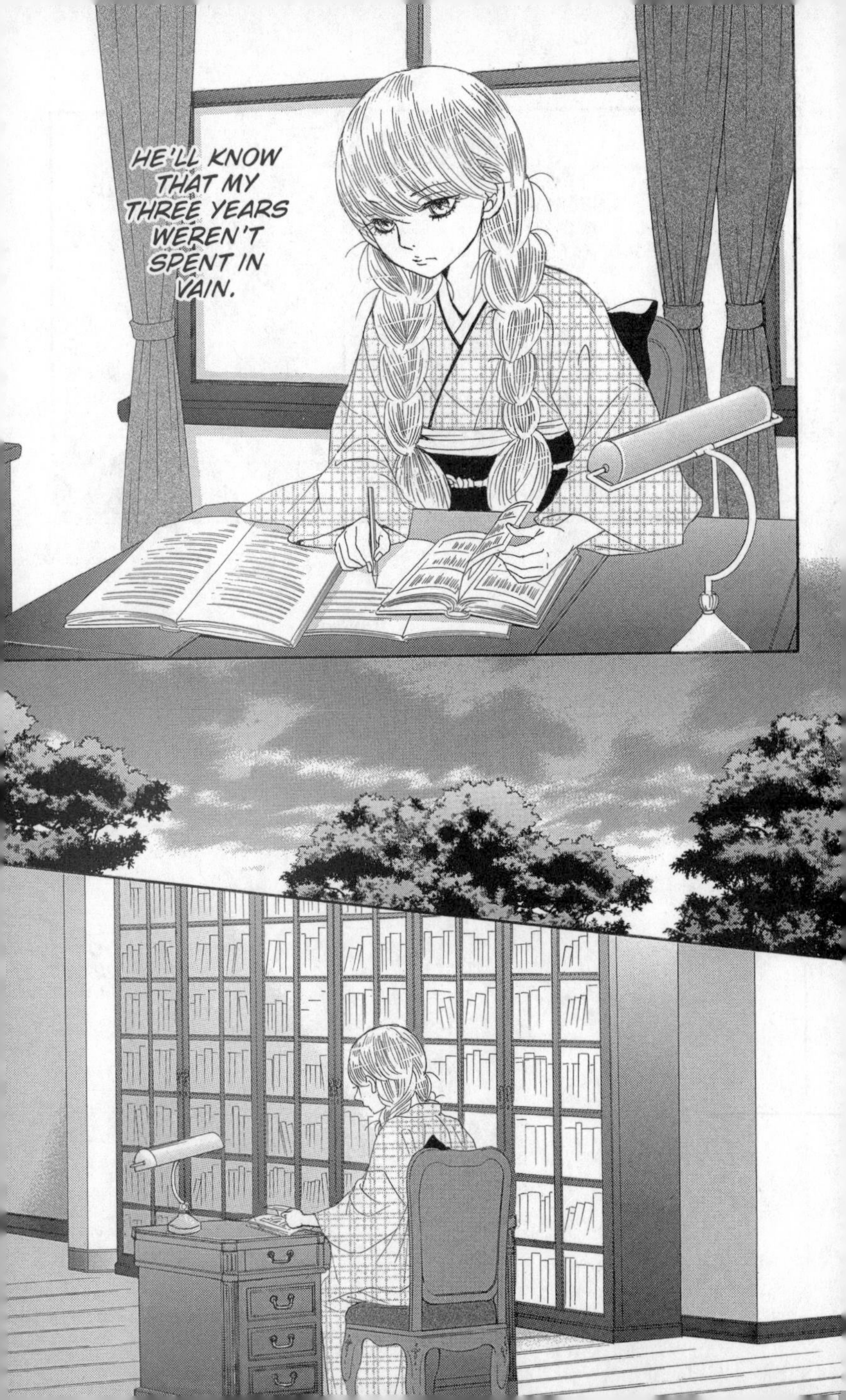
HE'LL KNOW THAT MY THREE YEARS WEREN'T SPENT IN VAIN.

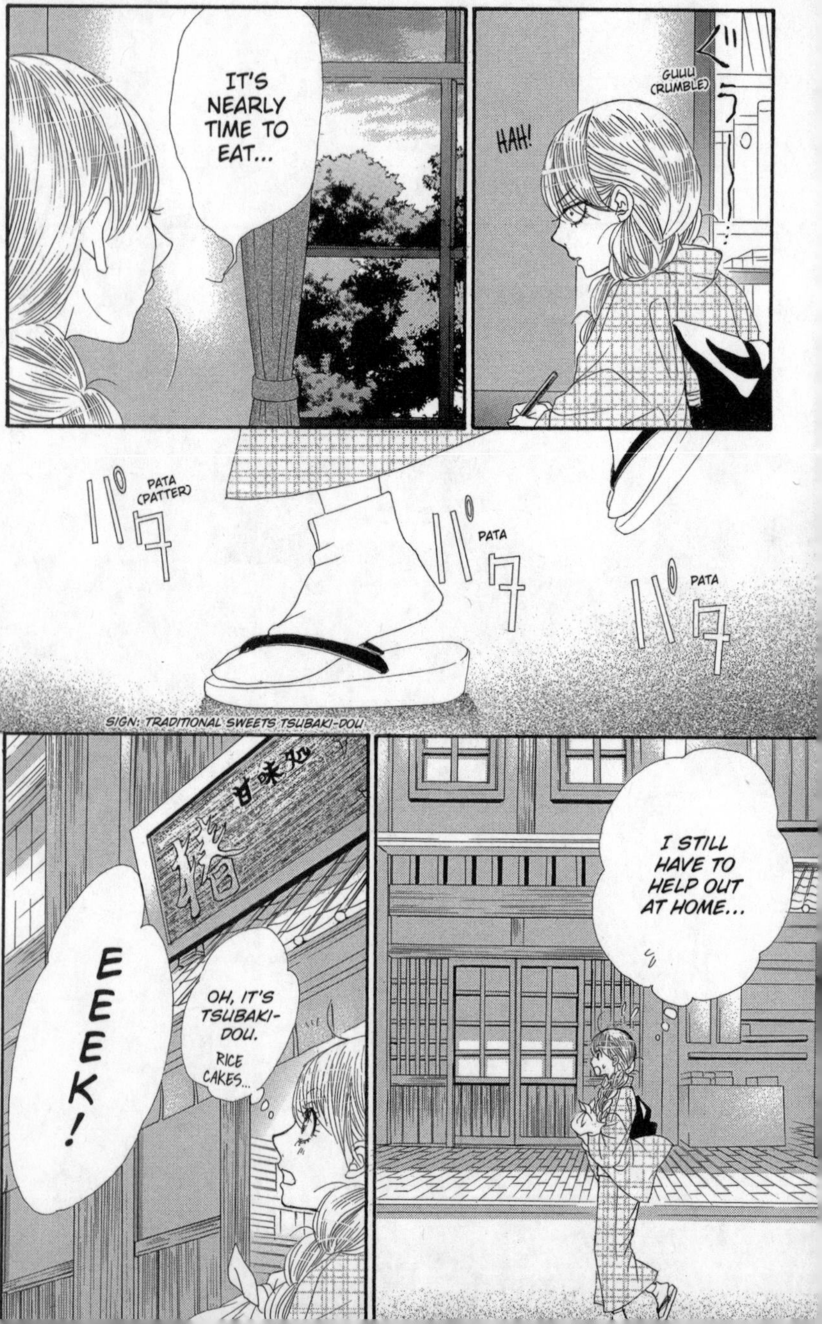
GUUU (RUMBLE)
HAH!
IT'S NEARLY TIME TO EAT...
PATA
PATA
PATA (PATTER)
I STILL HAVE TO HELP OUT AT HOME...
SIGN: TRADITIONAL SWEETS TSUBAKI-DOU
OH, IT'S TSUBAKI-DOU.
RICE CAKES...
EEEEK!

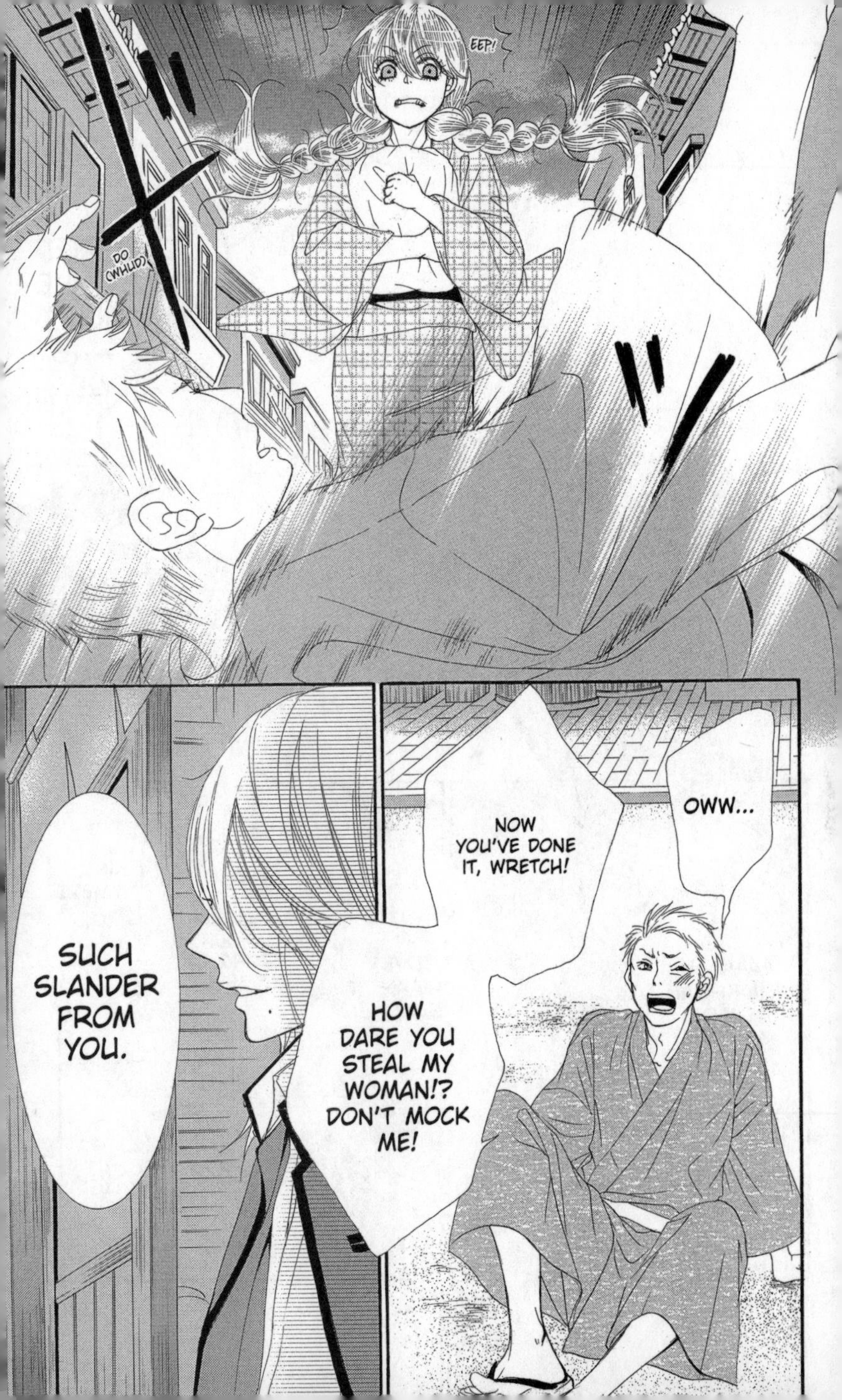
EEP!
DO (WHUD)
OWW...
NOW YOU'VE DONE IT, WRETCH!
HOW DARE YOU STEAL MY WOMAN!? DON'T MOCK ME!
SUCH SLANDER FROM YOU.

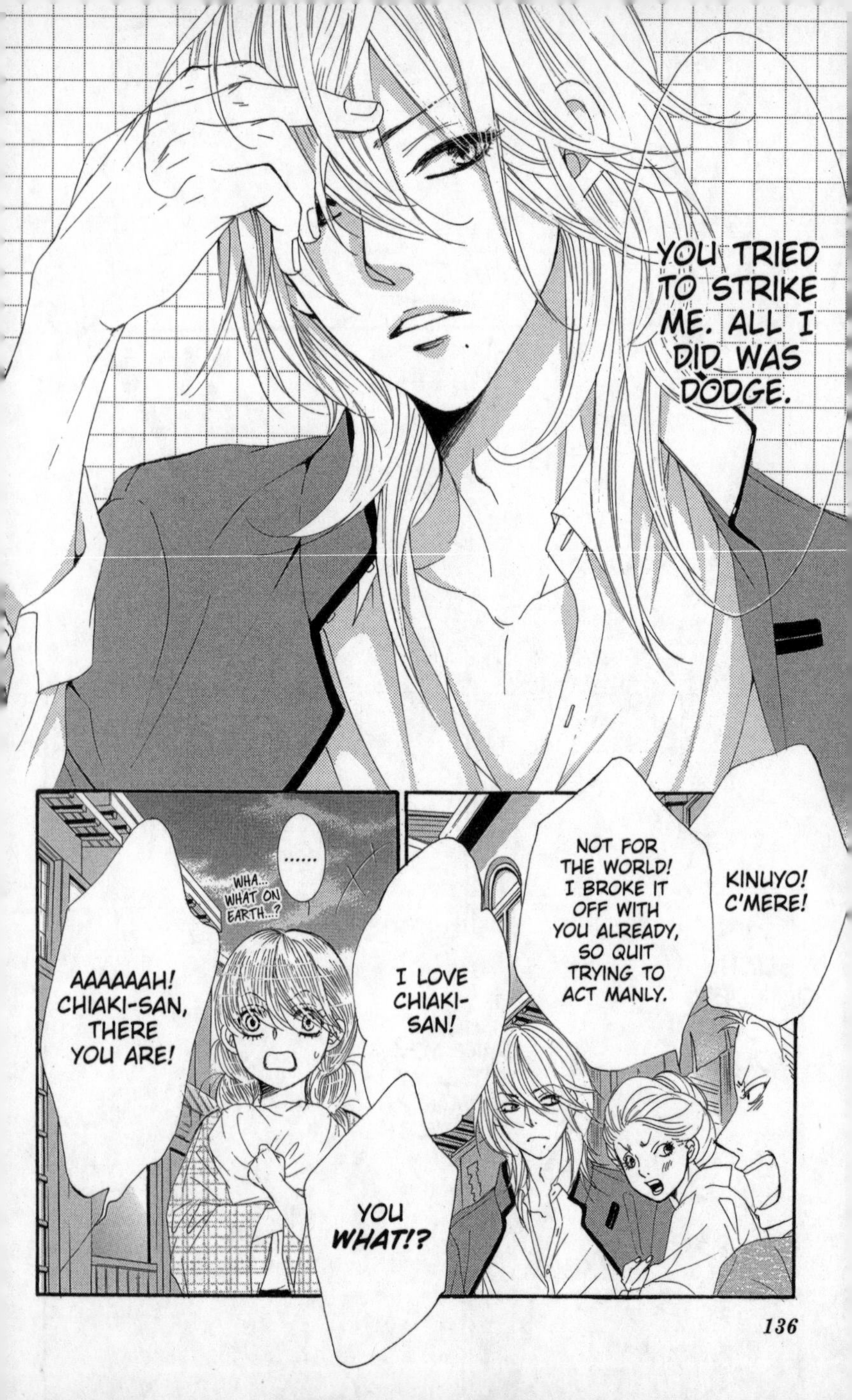
YOU TRIED TO STRIKE ME. ALL I DID WAS DODGE.
KINUYO! C'MERE!
NOT FOR THE WORLD! I BROKE IT OFF WITH YOU ALREADY, SO QUIT TRYING TO ACT MANLY.
AAAAAAH! CHIAKI-SAN, THERE YOU ARE!
I LOVE CHIAKI-SAN!
......
WHA... WHAT ON EARTH...?
YOU *WHAT!?*

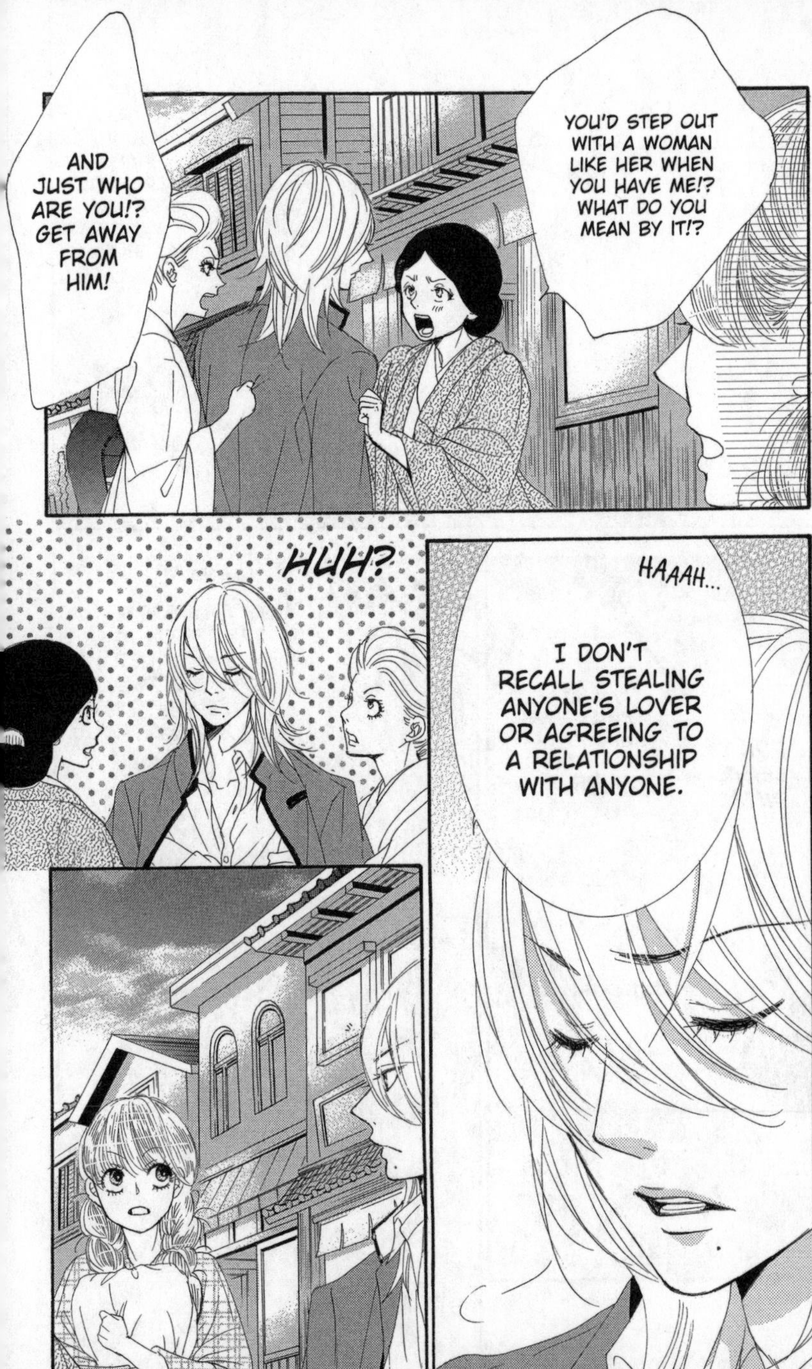
YOU'D STEP OUT WITH A WOMAN LIKE HER WHEN YOU HAVE ME!? WHAT DO YOU MEAN BY IT!?
AND JUST WHO ARE YOU!? GET AWAY FROM HIM!
HAAAH...
I DON'T RECALL STEALING ANYONE'S LOVER OR AGREEING TO A RELATIONSHIP WITH ANYONE.
HUH?

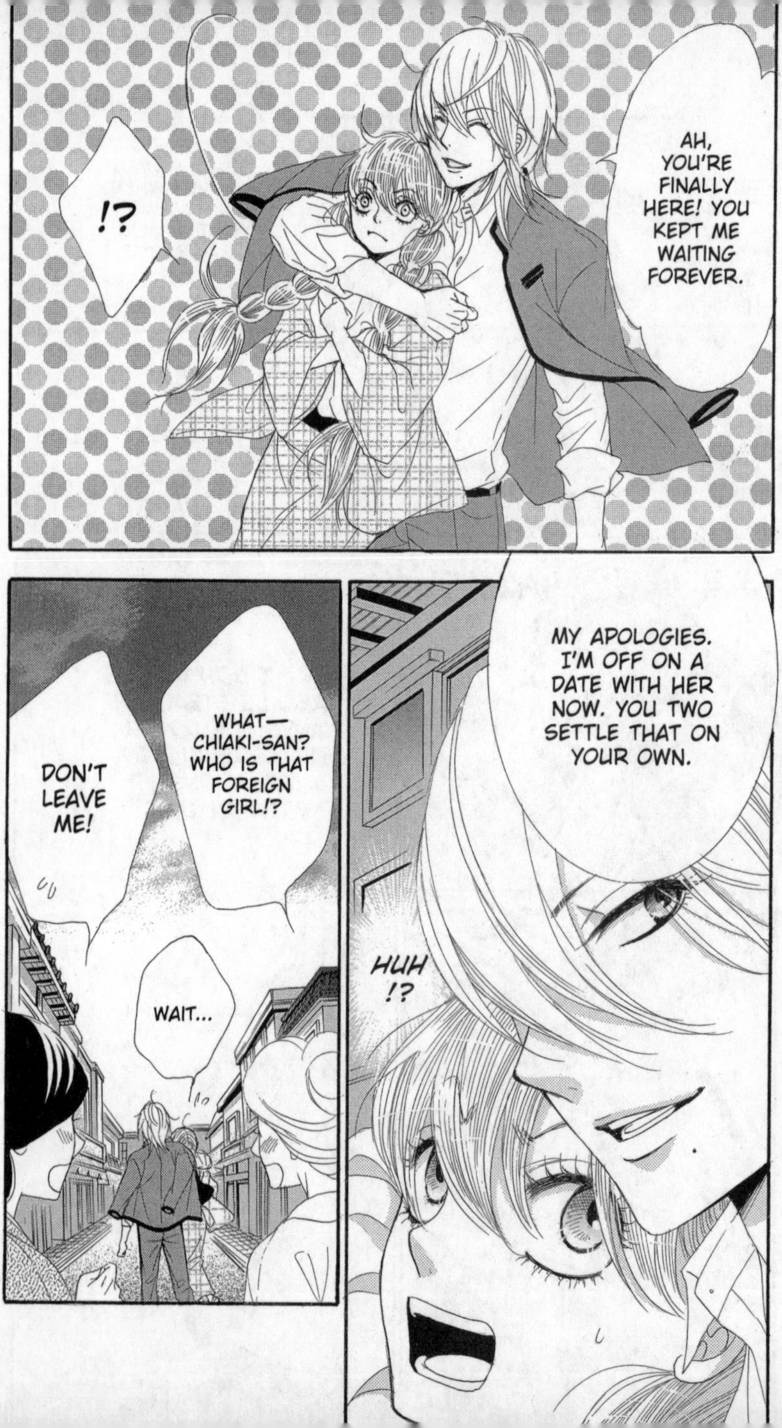
AH, YOU'RE FINALLY HERE! YOU KEPT ME WAITING FOREVER.
!?
MY APOLOGIES. I'M OFF ON A DATE WITH HER NOW. YOU TWO SETTLE THAT ON YOUR OWN.
HUH !?
WHAT— CHIAKI-SAN? WHO IS THAT FOREIGN GIRL!?
DON'T LEAVE ME!
WAIT...

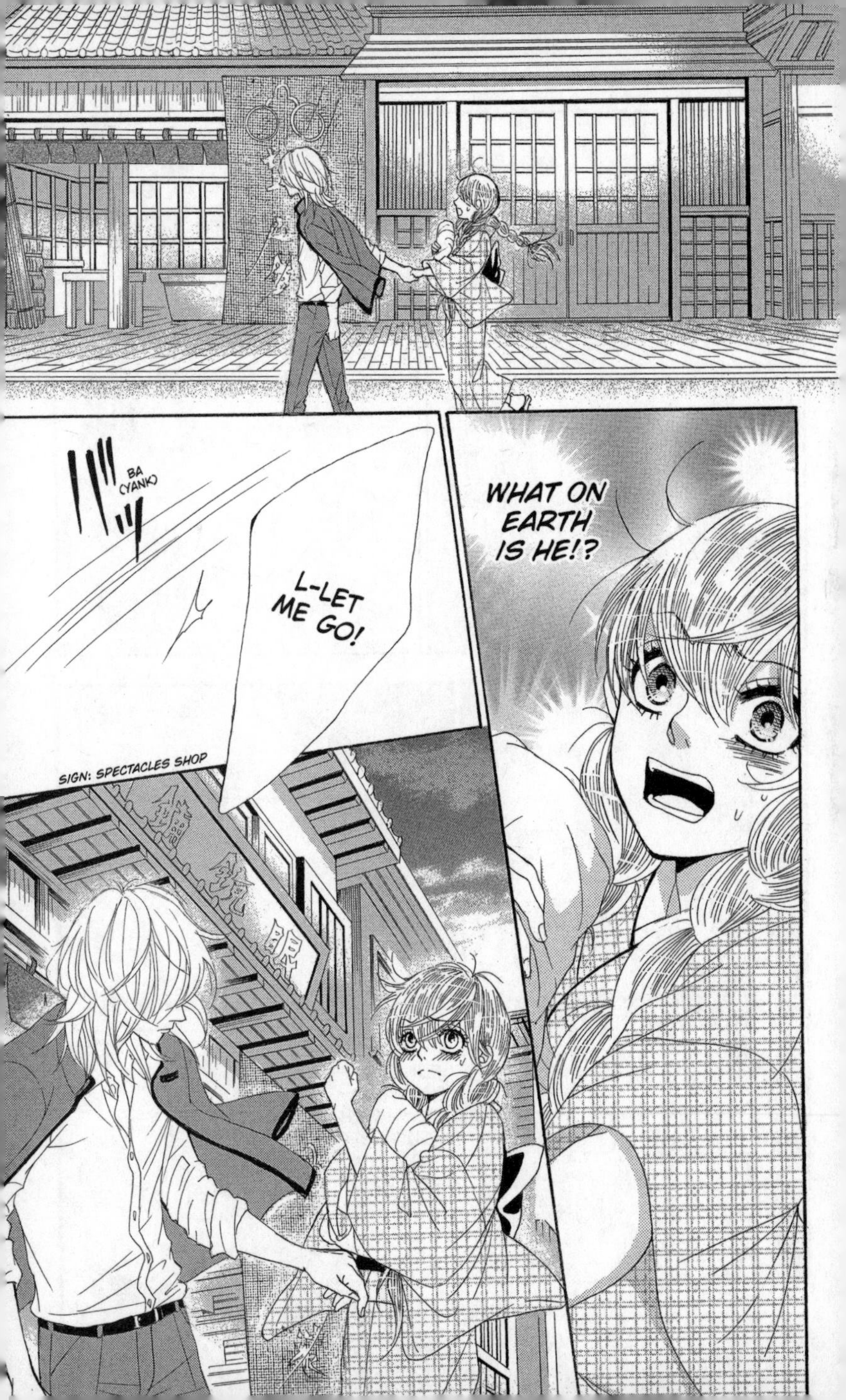
WHAT ON EARTH IS HE!?
L-LET ME GO!
BA (YANK)
SIGN: SPECTACLES SHOP

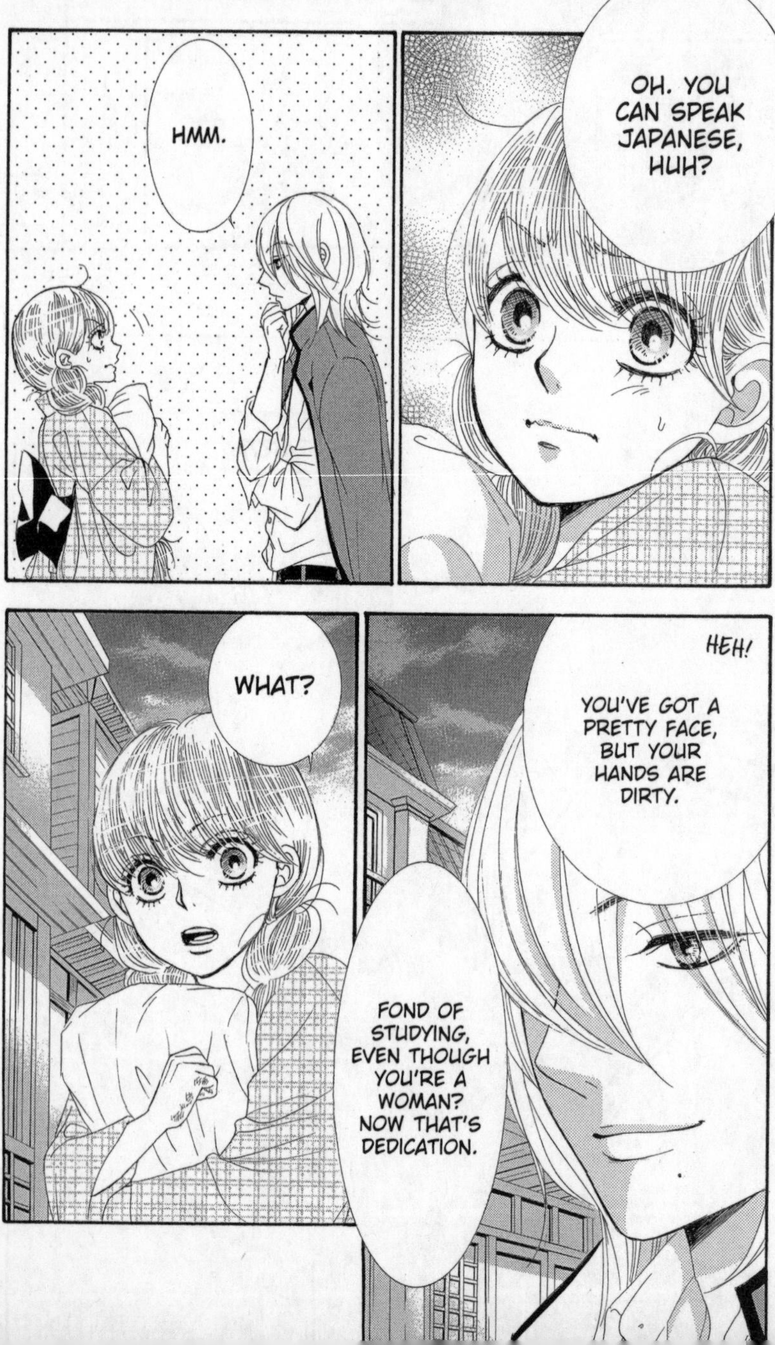
OH. YOU CAN SPEAK JAPANESE, HUH?
HMM.
HEH!
YOU'VE GOT A PRETTY FACE, BUT YOUR HANDS ARE DIRTY.
FOND OF STUDYING, EVEN THOUGH YOU'RE A WOMAN? NOW THAT'S DEDICATION.
WHAT?

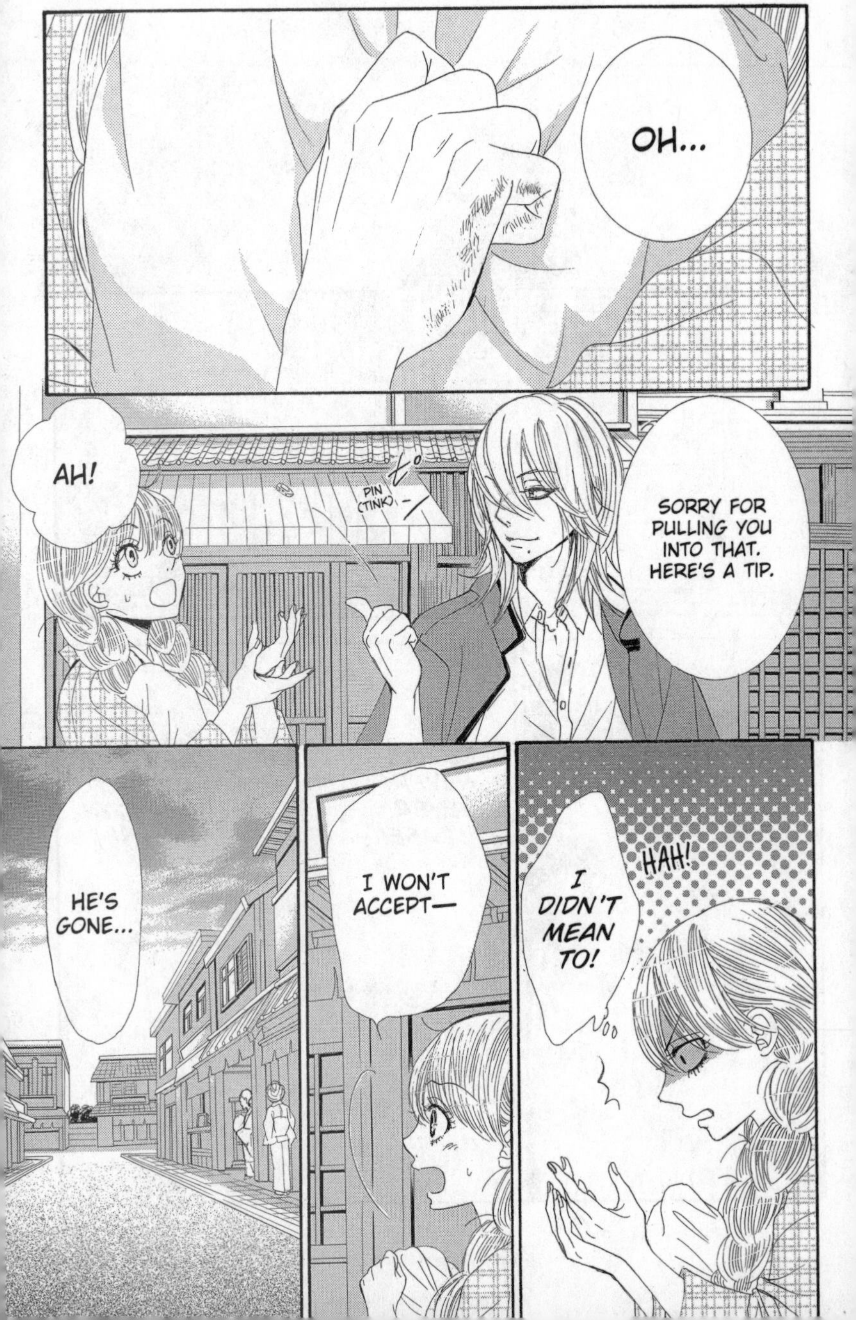
OH...
SORRY FOR PULLING YOU INTO THAT. HERE'S A TIP.
PIN (TINK)
AH!
HAH!
I DIDN'T MEAN TO!
I WON'T ACCEPT—
HE'S GONE...

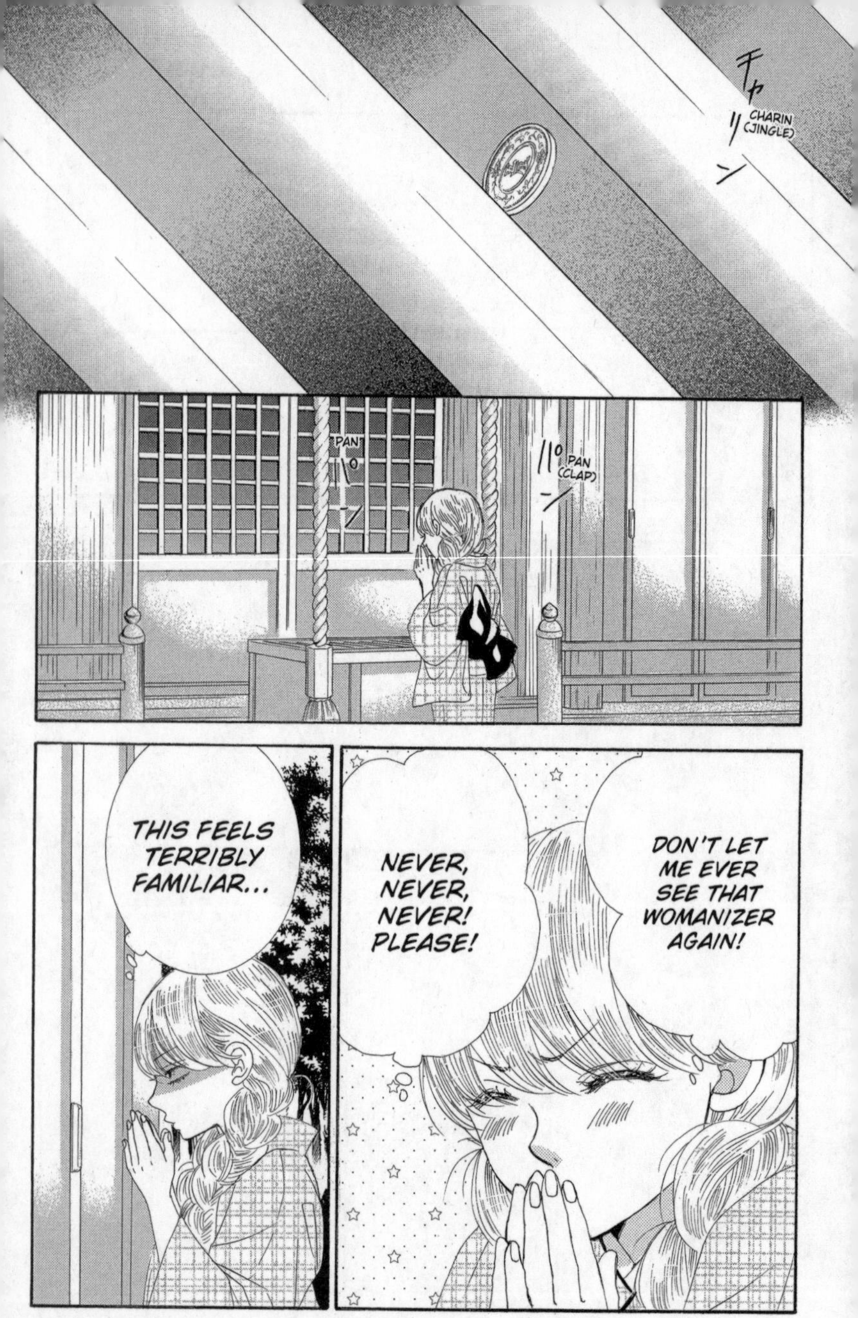
チャリーン
CHARIN (JINGLE)
PAN (CLAP)
PAN
DON'T LET ME EVER SEE THAT WOMANIZER AGAIN!
NEVER, NEVER, NEVER! PLEASE!
THIS FEELS TERRIBLY FAMILIAR...

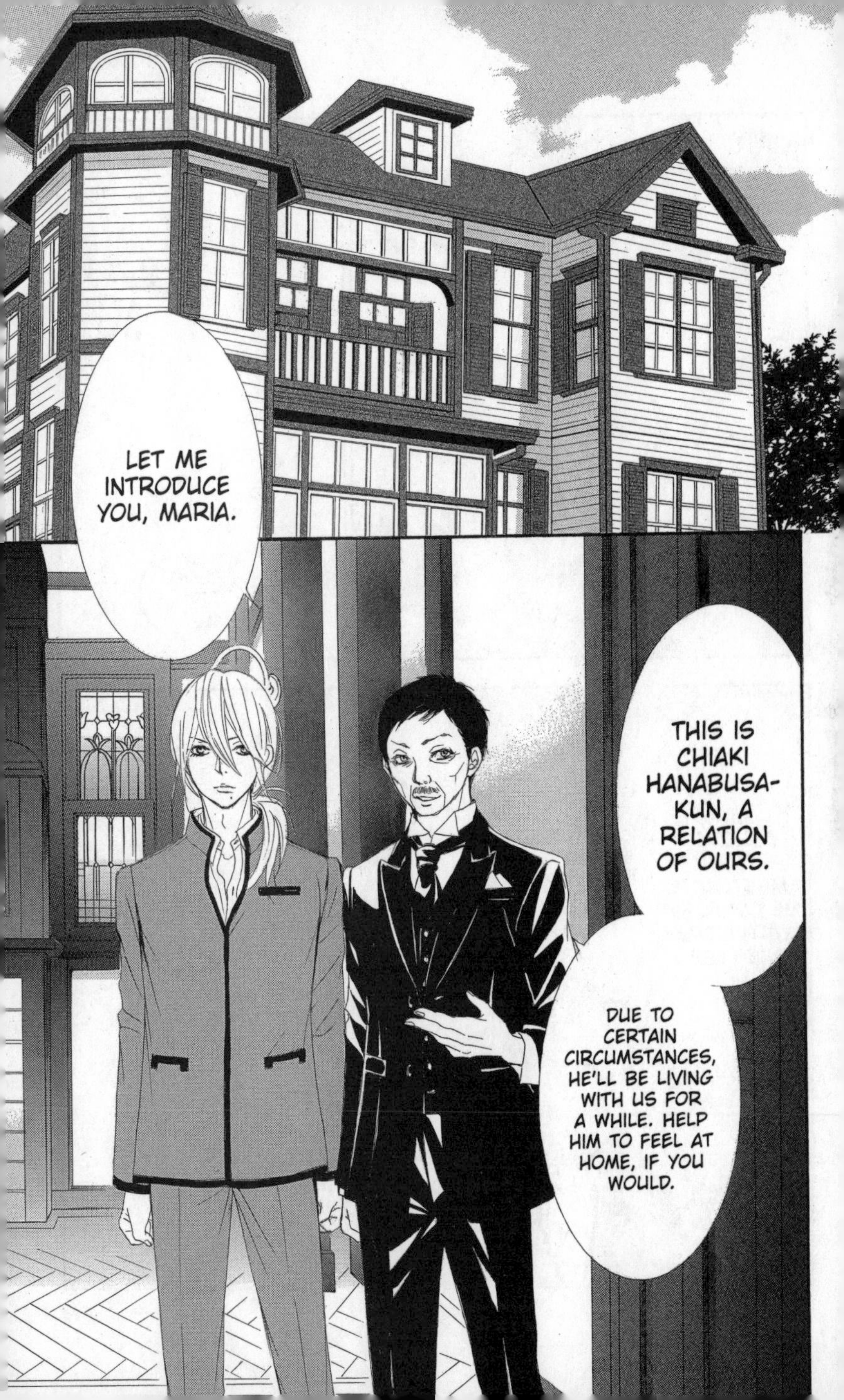
LET ME INTRODUCE YOU, MARIA.
THIS IS CHIAKI HANABUSA-KUN, A RELATION OF OURS.
DUE TO CERTAIN CIRCUMSTANCES, HE'LL BE LIVING WITH US FOR A WHILE. HELP HIM TO FEEL AT HOME, IF YOU WOULD.

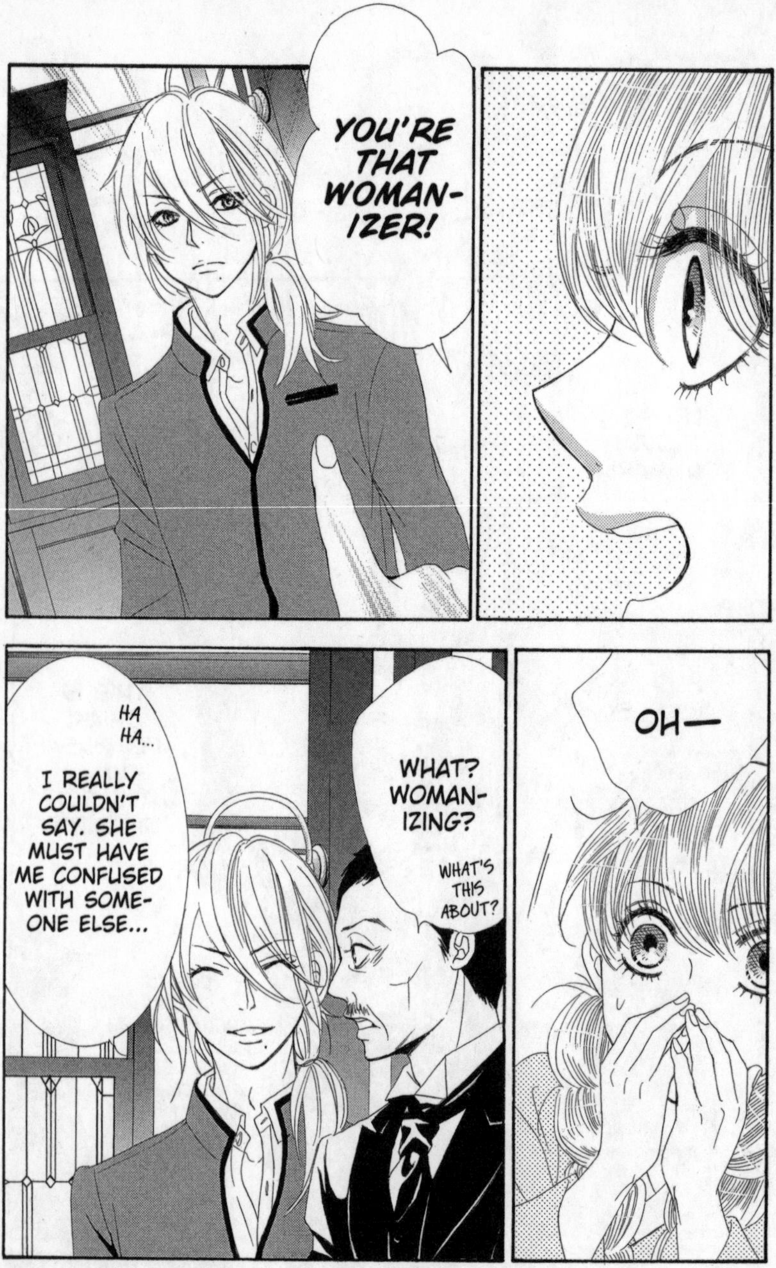
YOU'RE THAT WOMAN-IZER!
OH—
WHAT? WOMAN-IZING?
WHAT'S THIS ABOUT?
HA HA...
I REALLY COULDN'T SAY. SHE MUST HAVE ME CONFUSED WITH SOME-ONE ELSE...

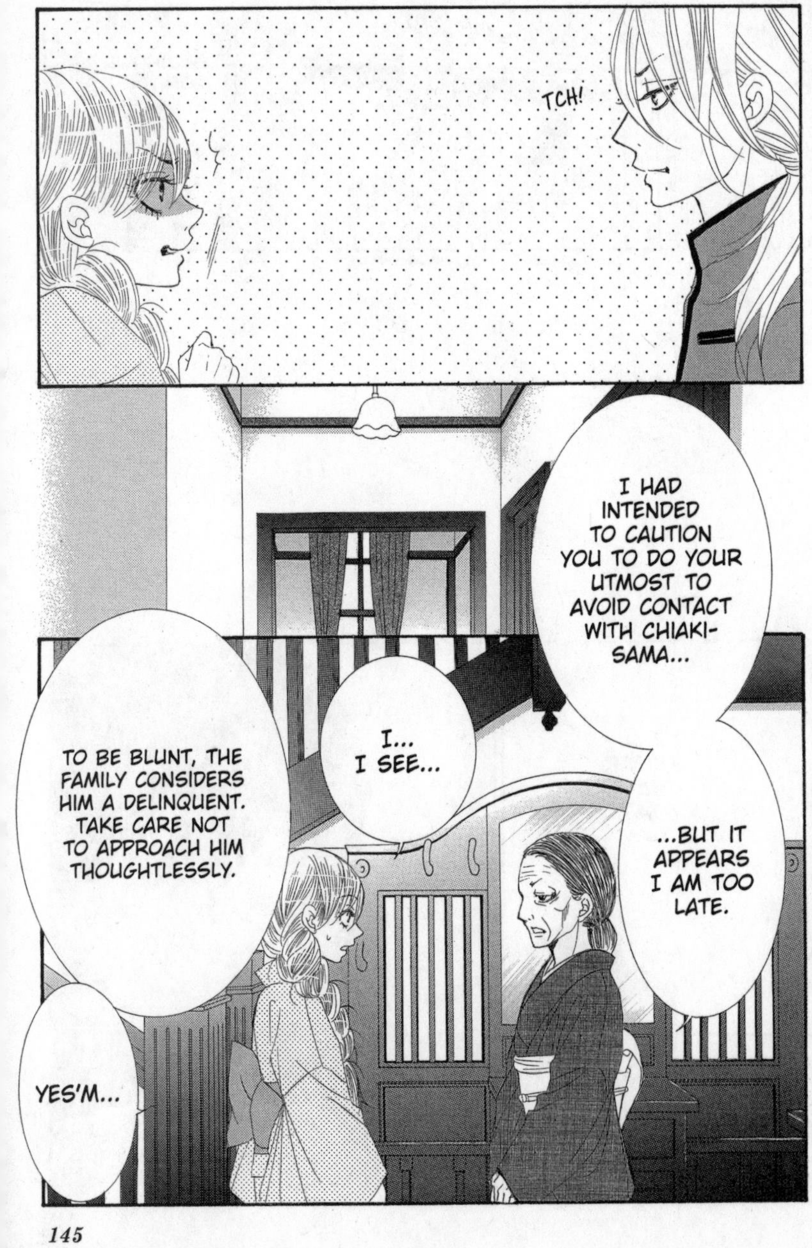
TCH!
I HAD INTENDED TO CAUTION YOU TO DO YOUR UTMOST TO AVOID CONTACT WITH CHIAKI-SAMA...
...BUT IT APPEARS I AM TOO LATE.
I... I SEE...
TO BE BLUNT, THE FAMILY CONSIDERS HIM A DELINQUENT. TAKE CARE NOT TO APPROACH HIM THOUGHTLESSLY.
YES'M...

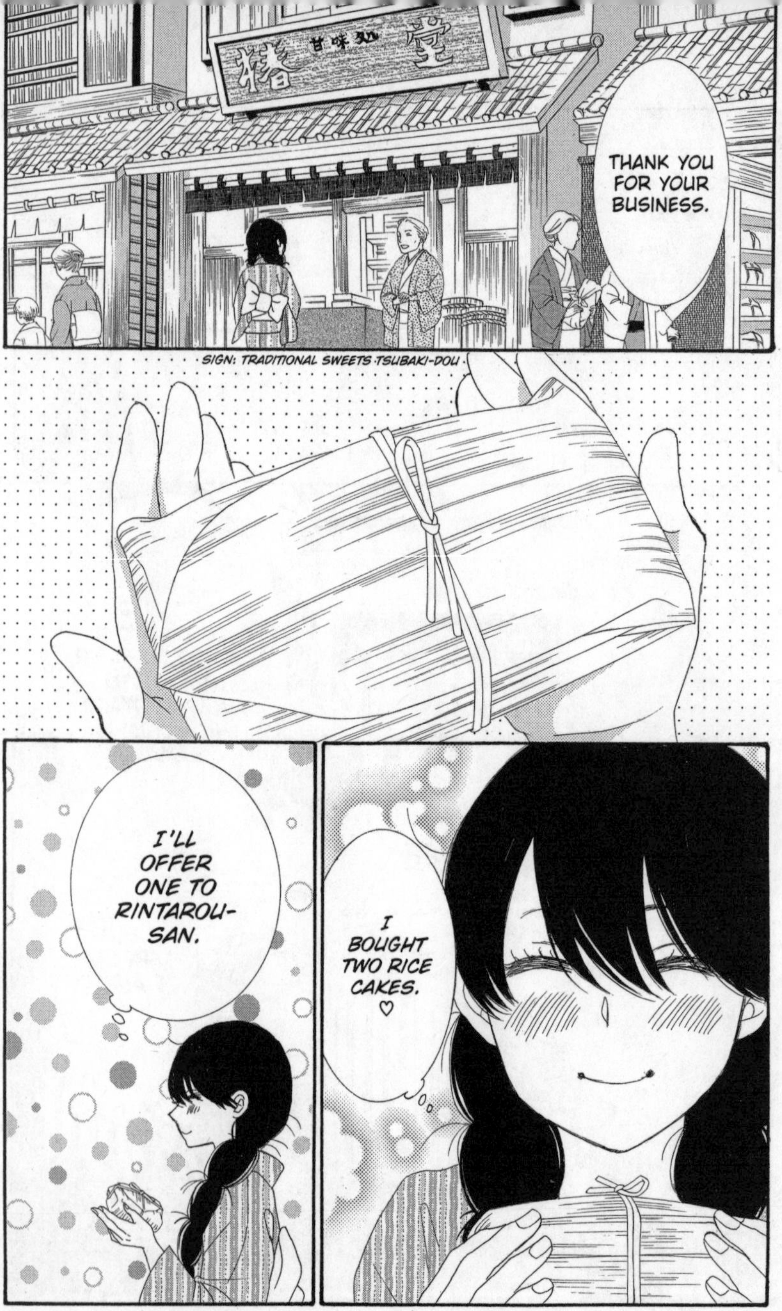
THANK YOU FOR YOUR BUSINESS.
SIGN: TRADITIONAL SWEETS TSUBAKI-DOU
I BOUGHT TWO RICE CAKES. ♡
I'LL OFFER ONE TO RINTAROU-SAN.

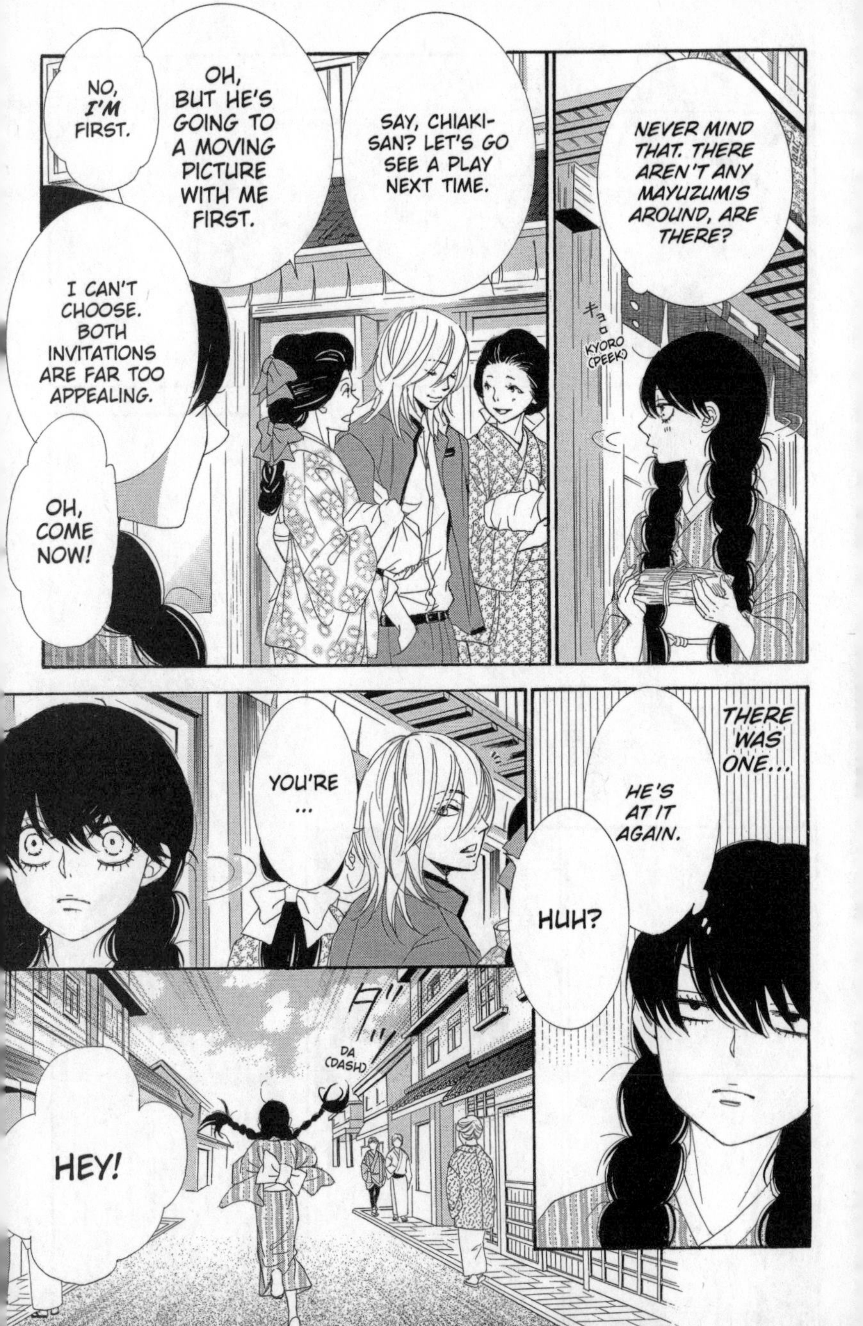
NEVER MIND THAT. THERE AREN'T ANY MAYUZUMIS AROUND, ARE THERE?
キョロ
KYORO (PEEK)
SAY, CHIAKI-SAN? LET'S GO SEE A PLAY NEXT TIME.
OH, BUT HE'S GOING TO A MOVING PICTURE WITH ME FIRST.
NO, *I'M* FIRST.
I CAN'T CHOOSE. BOTH INVITATIONS ARE FAR TOO APPEALING.
OH, COME NOW!
THERE WAS ONE...
HE'S AT IT AGAIN.
HUH?
YOU'RE ...
DA (DASH)
HEY!

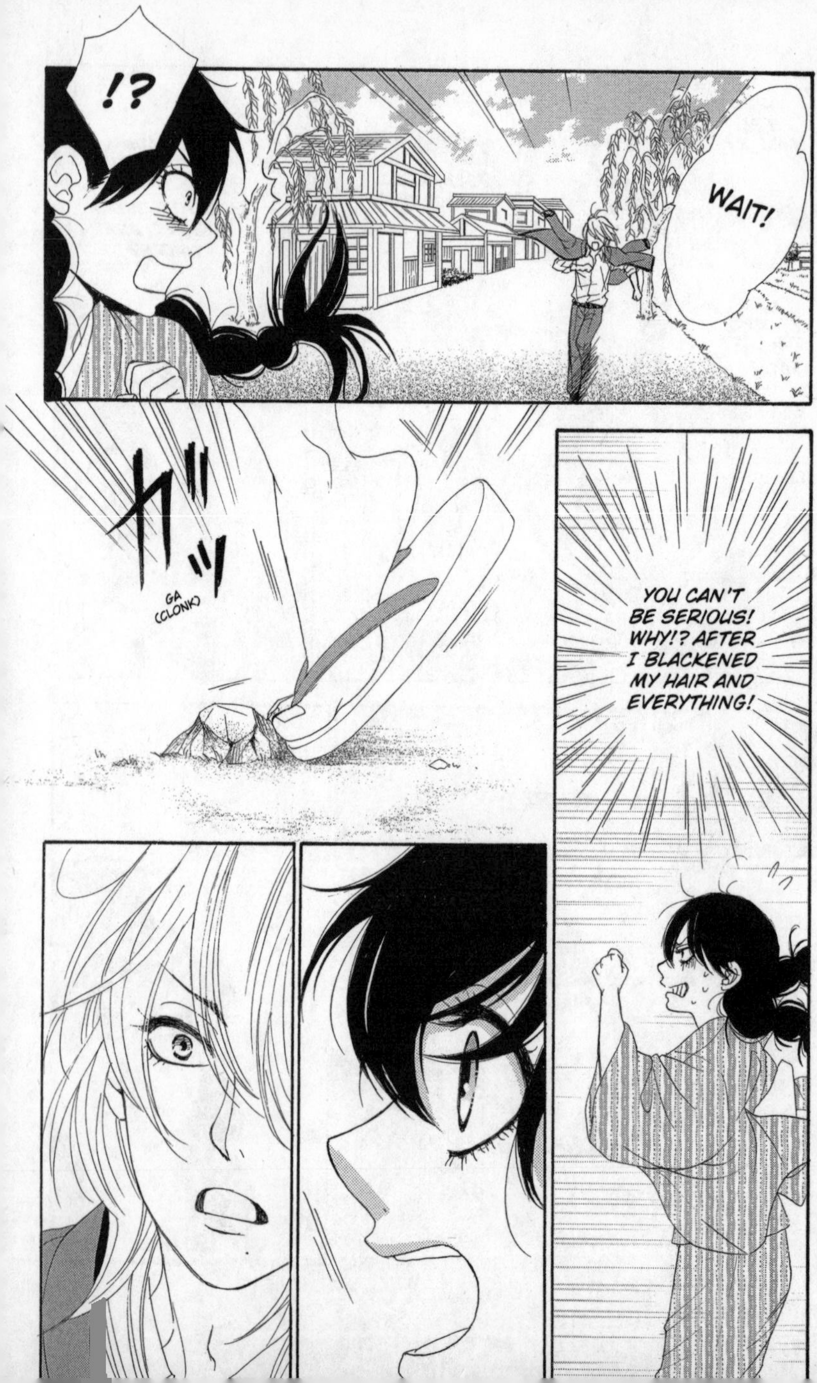
WAIT!
!?
YOU CAN'T BE SERIOUS! WHY!? AFTER I BLACKENED MY HAIR AND EVERYTHING!
ガッ
GA (CLONK)

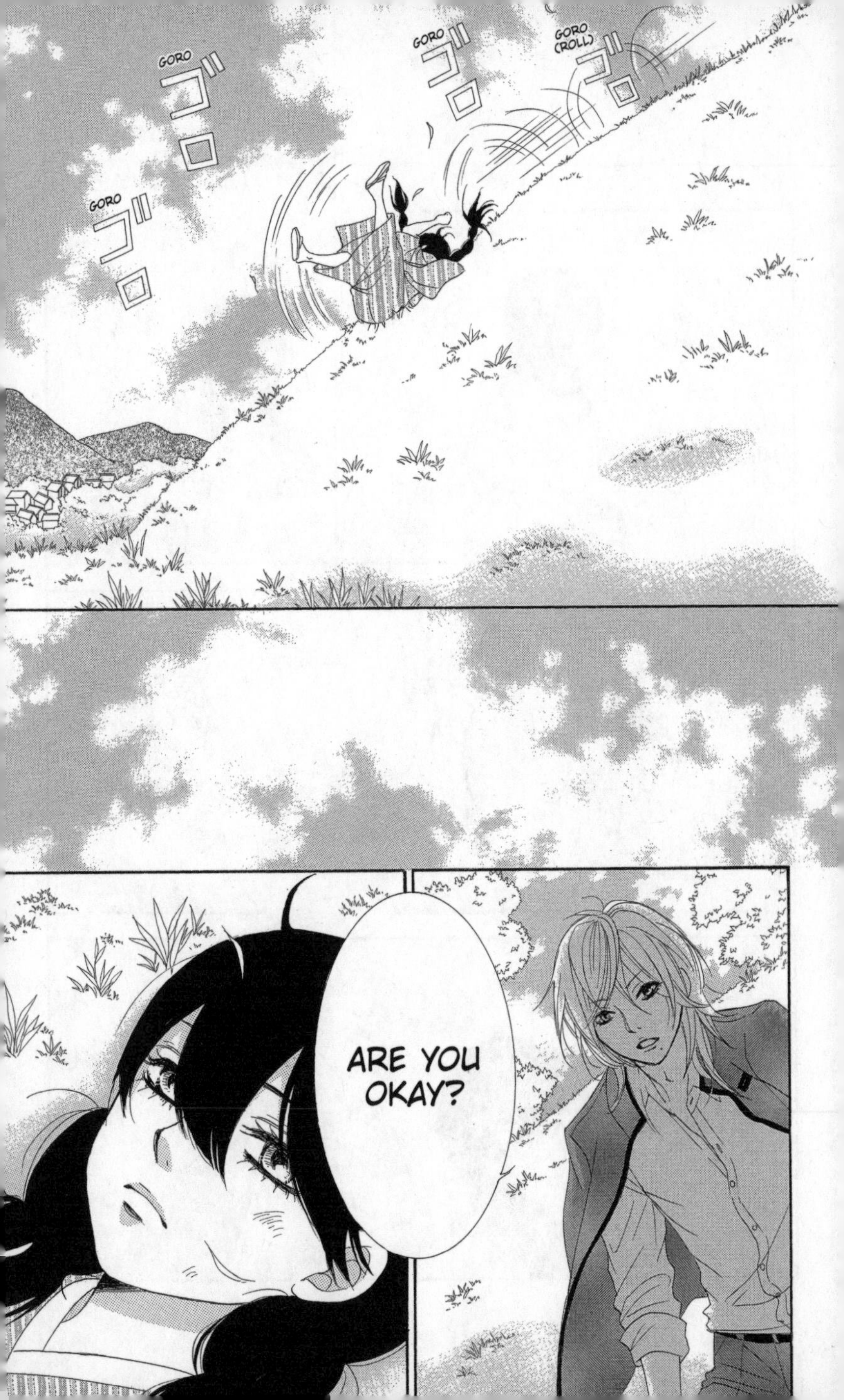
ゴロ
GORO (ROLL)
ゴロ
GORO
ゴロ
GORO
ゴロ
GORO
ARE YOU OKAY?

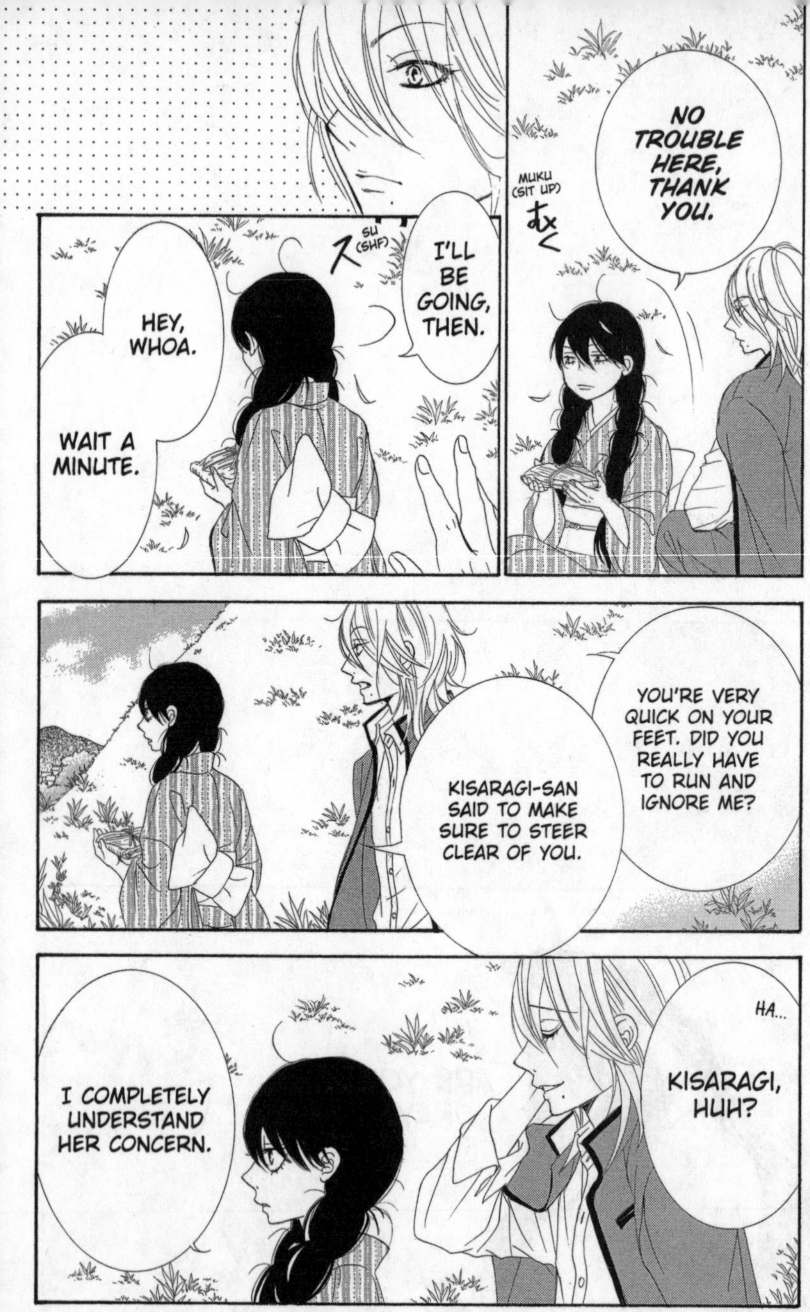
NO TROUBLE HERE, THANK YOU.
MUKU (SIT UP)
むく
I'LL BE GOING, THEN.
SU (SHF)
ス
HEY, WHOA.
WAIT A MINUTE.
YOU'RE VERY QUICK ON YOUR FEET. DID YOU REALLY HAVE TO RUN AND IGNORE ME?
KISARAGI-SAN SAID TO MAKE SURE TO STEER CLEAR OF YOU.
HA...
KISARAGI, HUH?
I COMPLETELY UNDERSTAND HER CONCERN.

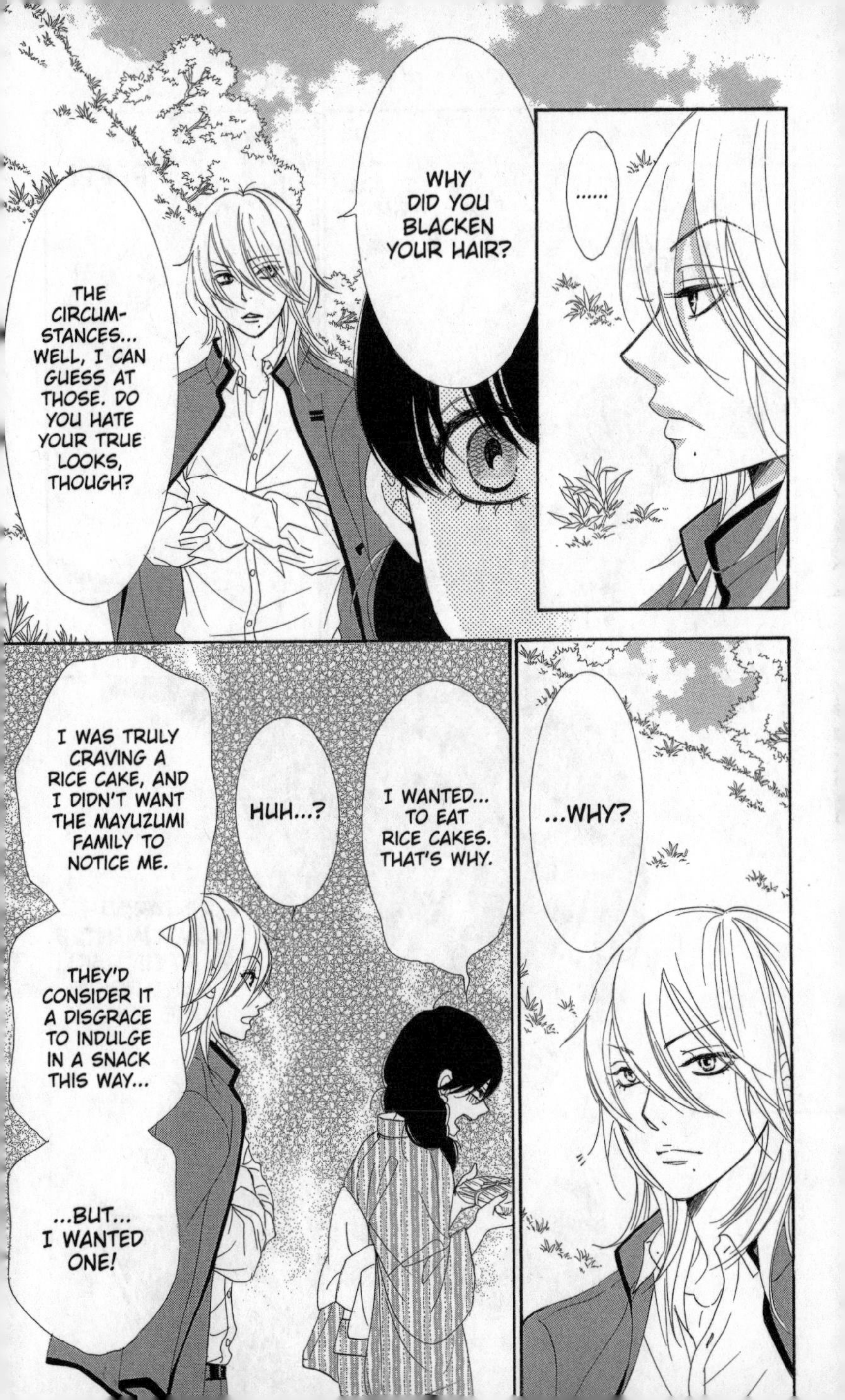
......
WHY DID YOU BLACKEN YOUR HAIR?
THE CIRCUM-STANCES... WELL, I CAN GUESS AT THOSE. DO YOU HATE YOUR TRUE LOOKS, THOUGH?
...WHY?
I WANTED... TO EAT RICE CAKES. THAT'S WHY.
HUH...?
I WAS TRULY CRAVING A RICE CAKE, AND I DIDN'T WANT THE MAYUZUMI FAMILY TO NOTICE ME.
THEY'D CONSIDER IT A DISGRACE TO INDULGE IN A SNACK THIS WAY...
...BUT... I WANTED ONE!

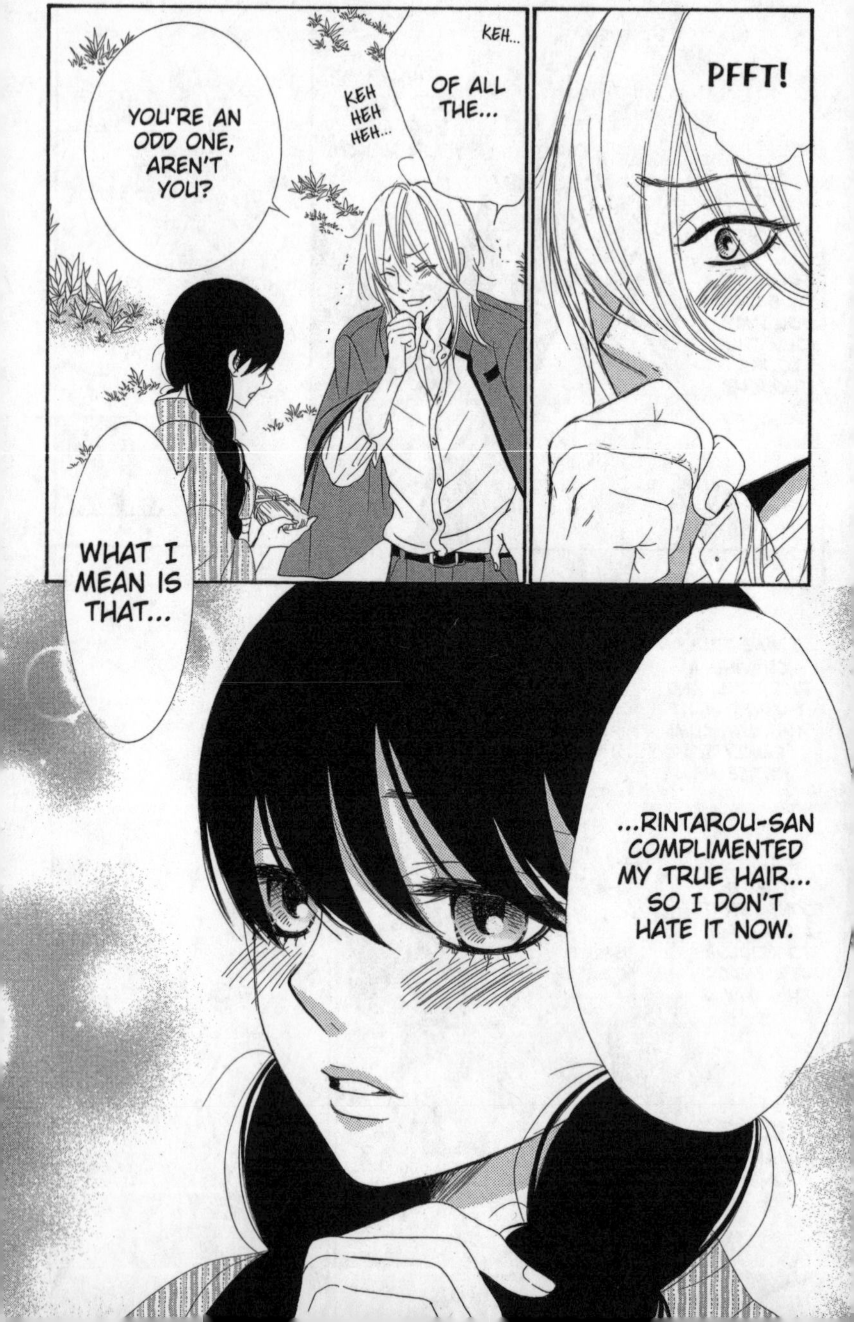
PFFT!
KEH...
OF ALL THE...
KEH HEH HEH...
YOU'RE AN ODD ONE, AREN'T YOU?
WHAT I MEAN IS THAT...
...RINTAROU-SAN COMPLIMENTED MY TRUE HAIR... SO I DON'T HATE IT NOW.

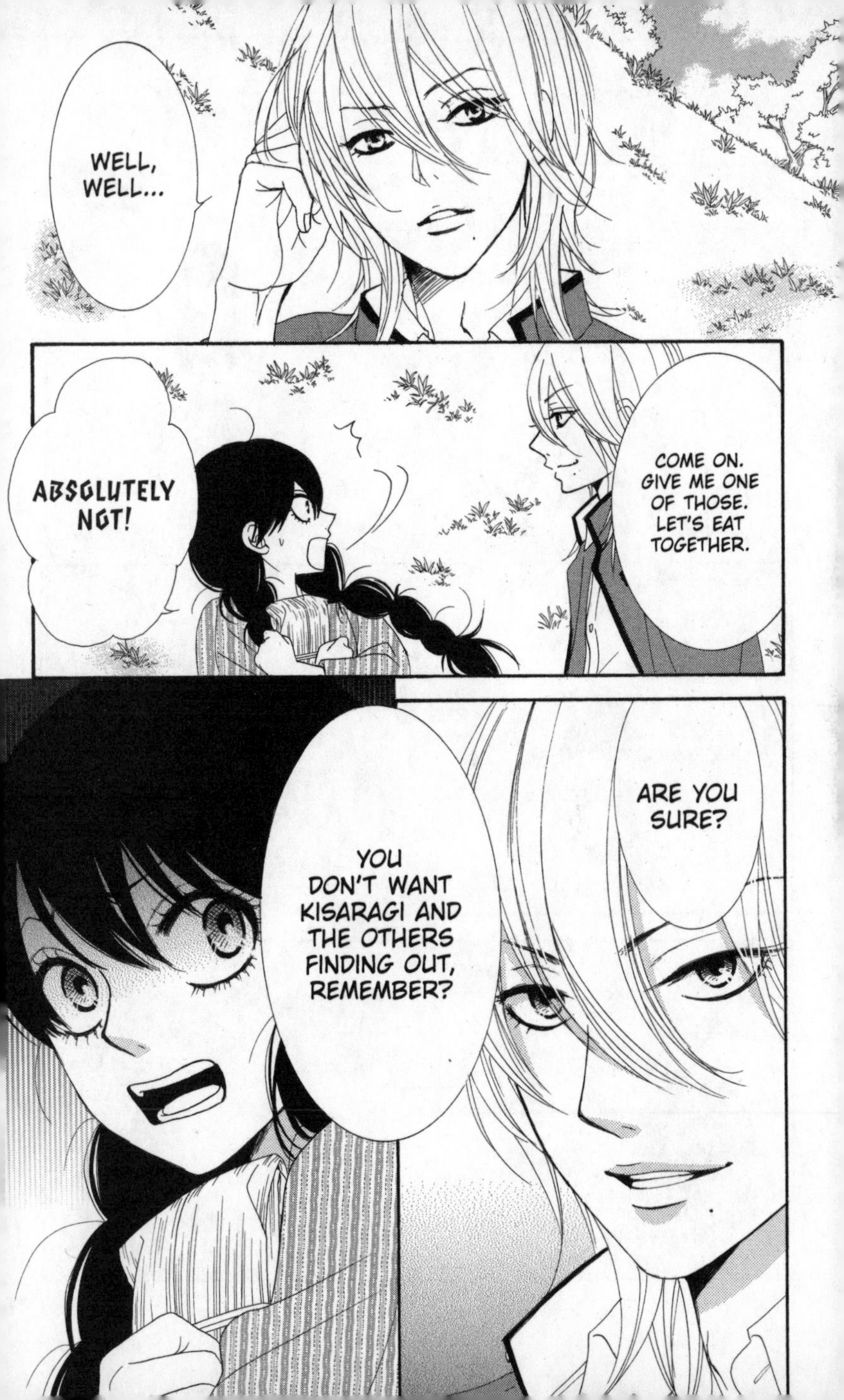
WELL, WELL...
COME ON. GIVE ME ONE OF THOSE. LET'S EAT TOGETHER.
ABSOLUTELY NOT!
ARE YOU SURE?
YOU DON'T WANT KISARAGI AND THE OTHERS FINDING OUT, REMEMBER?

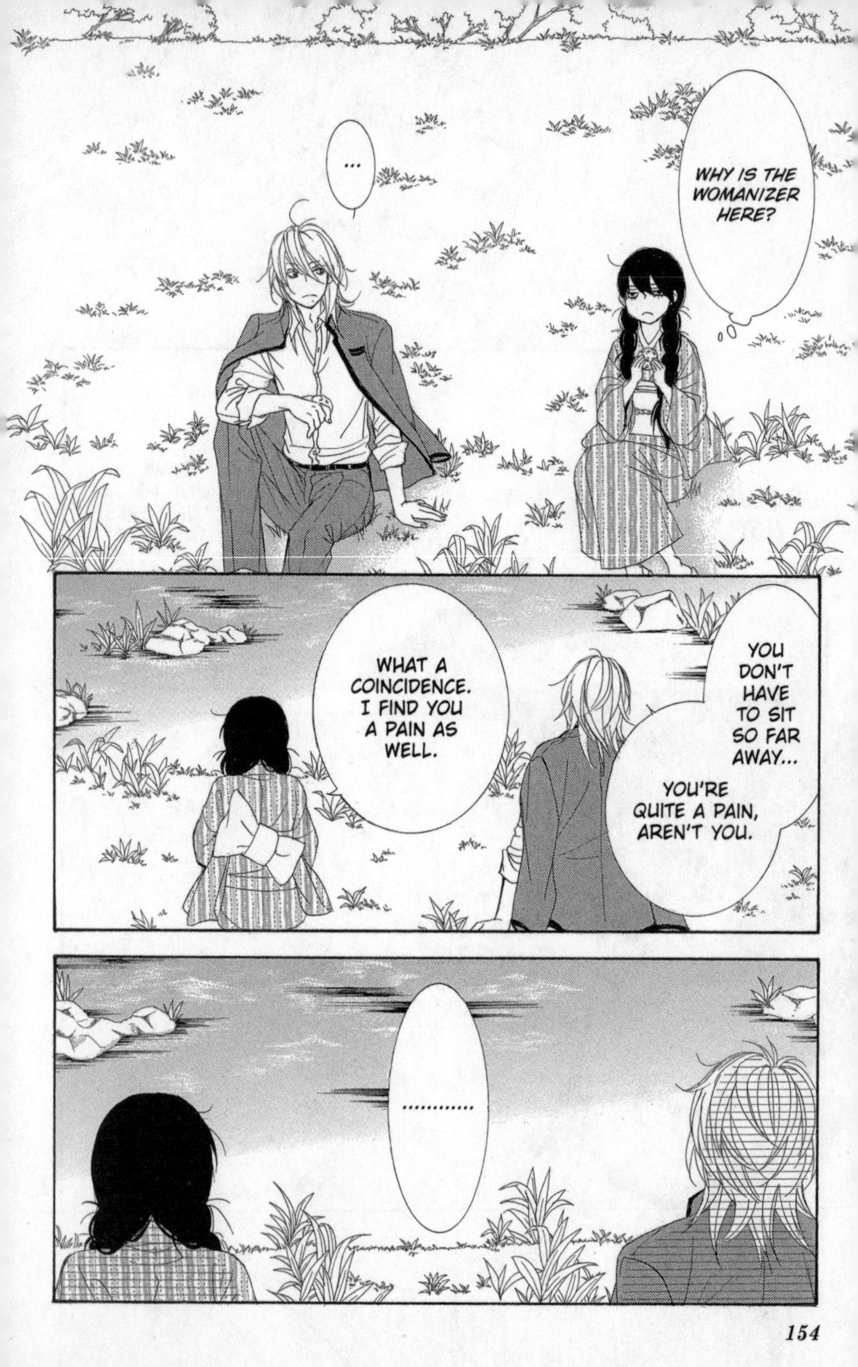
WHY IS THE WOMANIZER HERE?
...
YOU DON'T HAVE TO SIT SO FAR AWAY...
YOU'RE QUITE A PAIN, AREN'T YOU.
WHAT A COINCIDENCE. I FIND YOU A PAIN AS WELL.
....

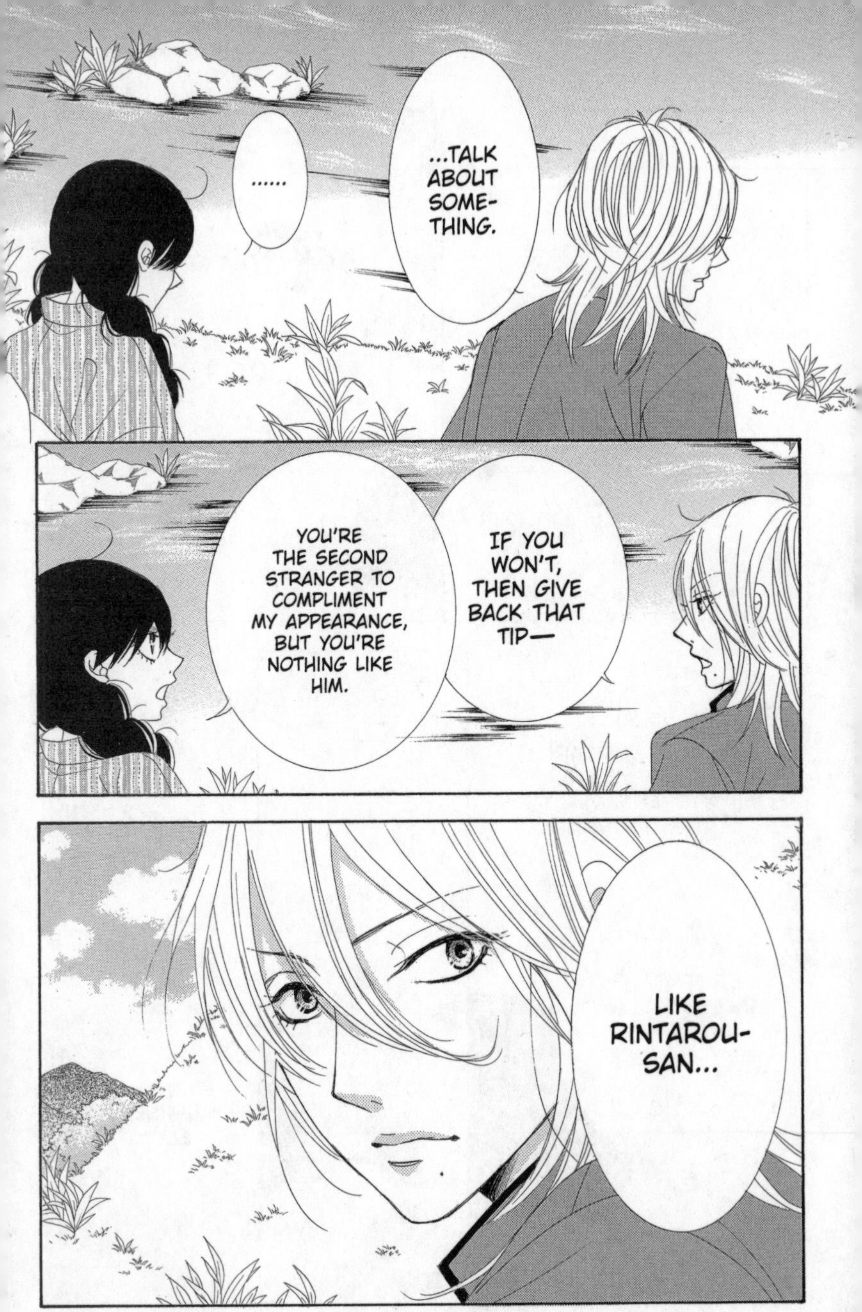
...TALK ABOUT SOMETHING.
......
IF YOU WON'T, THEN GIVE BACK THAT TIP—
YOU'RE THE SECOND STRANGER TO COMPLIMENT MY APPEARANCE, BUT YOU'RE NOTHING LIKE HIM.
LIKE RINTAROU-SAN...

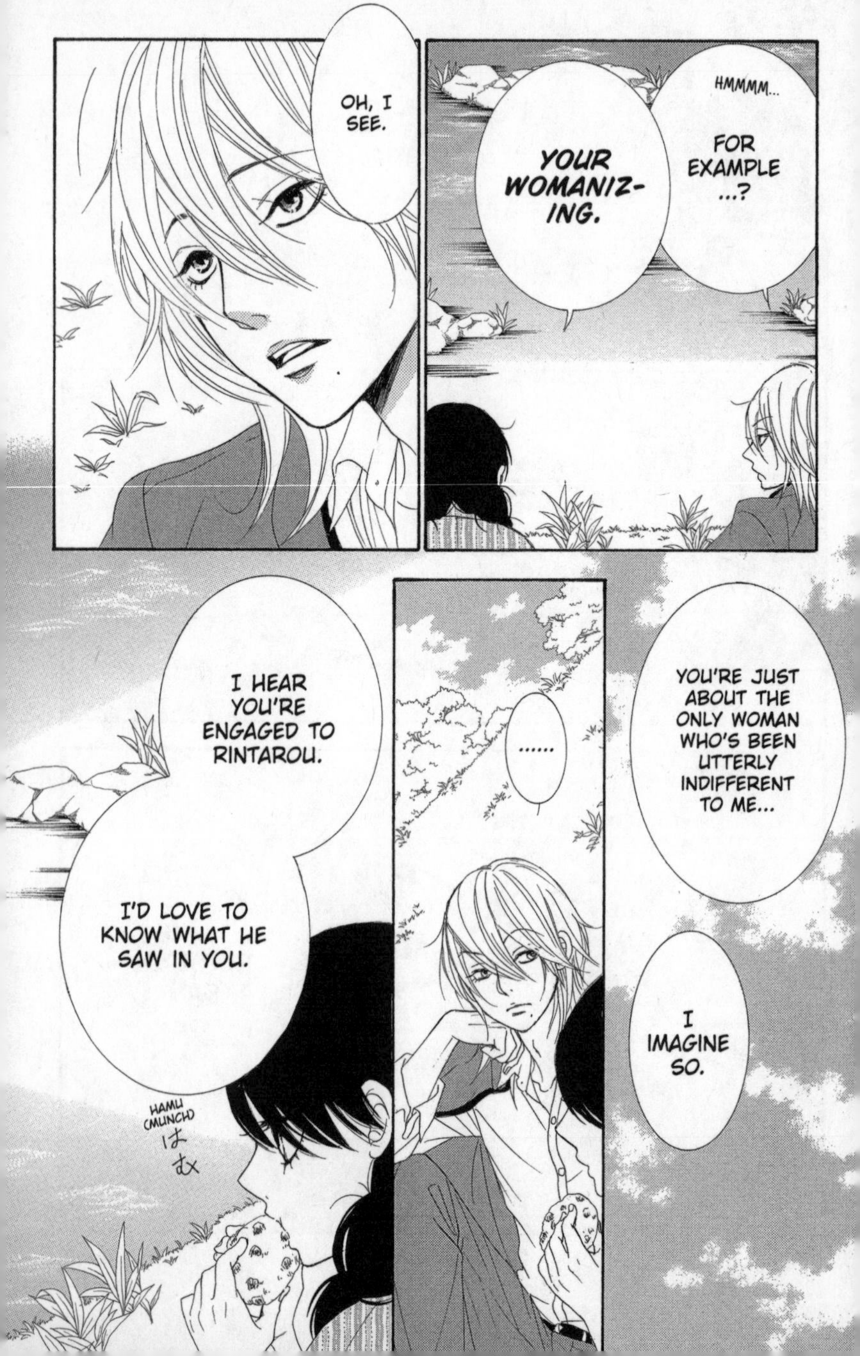
HMMMM...
FOR EXAMPLE ...?
YOUR WOMANIZ-ING.
OH, I SEE.
YOU'RE JUST ABOUT THE ONLY WOMAN WHO'S BEEN UTTERLY INDIFFERENT TO ME...
I IMAGINE SO.
......
I HEAR YOU'RE ENGAGED TO RINTAROU.
I'D LOVE TO KNOW WHAT HE SAW IN YOU.
HAMU (MUNCH)
はむ

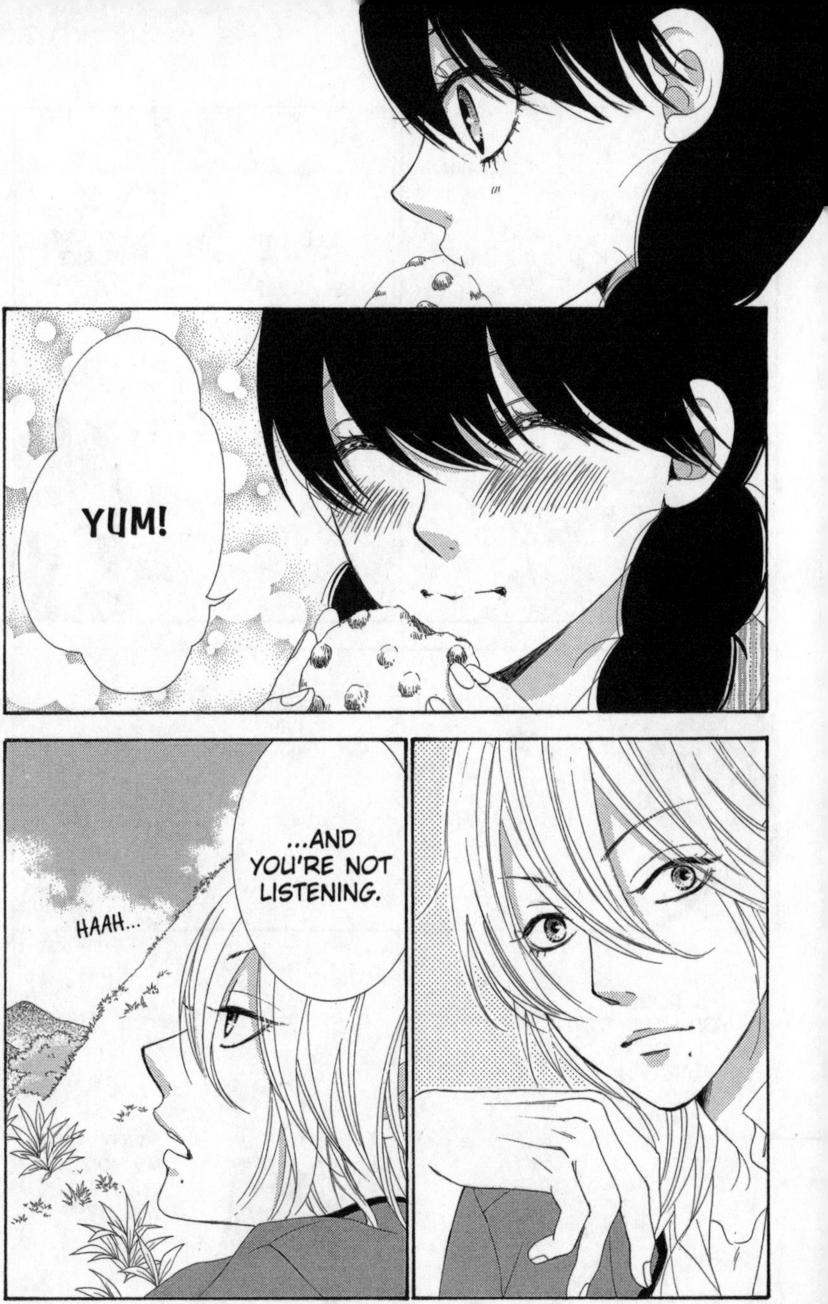
YUM!
...AND YOU'RE NOT LISTENING.
HAAH...

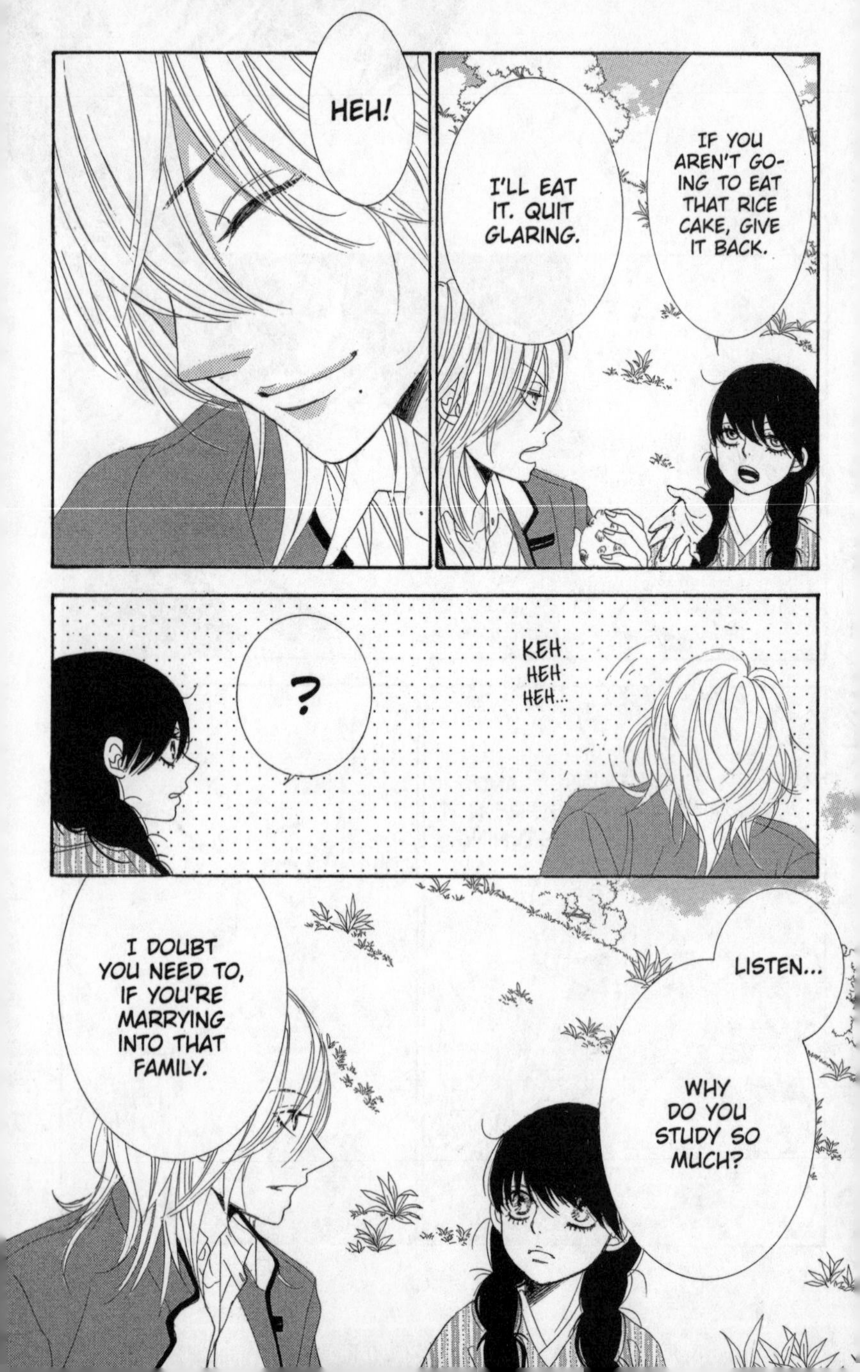
IF YOU AREN'T GO-ING TO EAT THAT RICE CAKE, GIVE IT BACK.
I'LL EAT IT. QUIT GLARING.
HEH!
KEH HEH HEH...
?
LISTEN...
WHY DO YOU STUDY SO MUCH?
I DOUBT YOU NEED TO, IF YOU'RE MARRYING INTO THAT FAMILY.

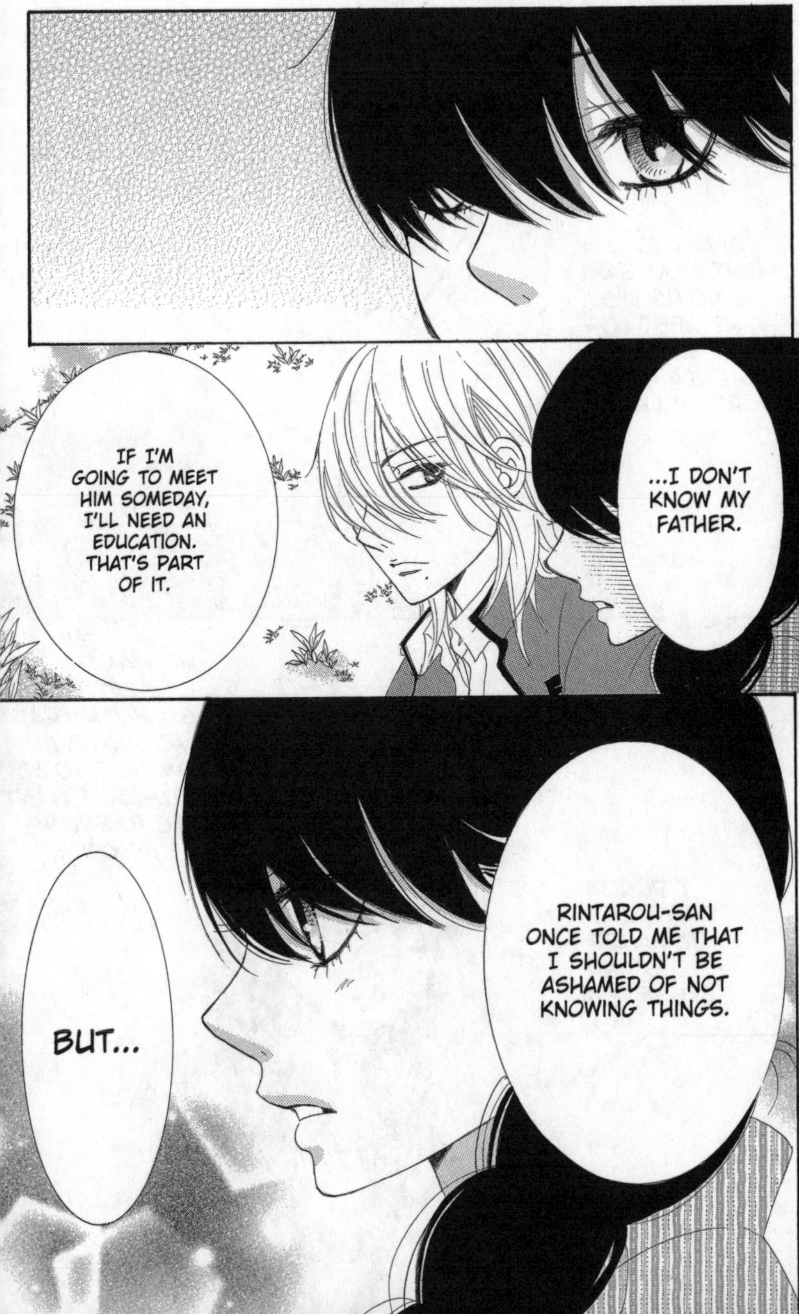
...I DON'T KNOW MY FATHER.
IF I'M GOING TO MEET HIM SOMEDAY, I'LL NEED AN EDUCATION. THAT'S PART OF IT.
RINTAROU-SAN ONCE TOLD ME THAT I SHOULDN'T BE ASHAMED OF NOT KNOWING THINGS.
BUT...

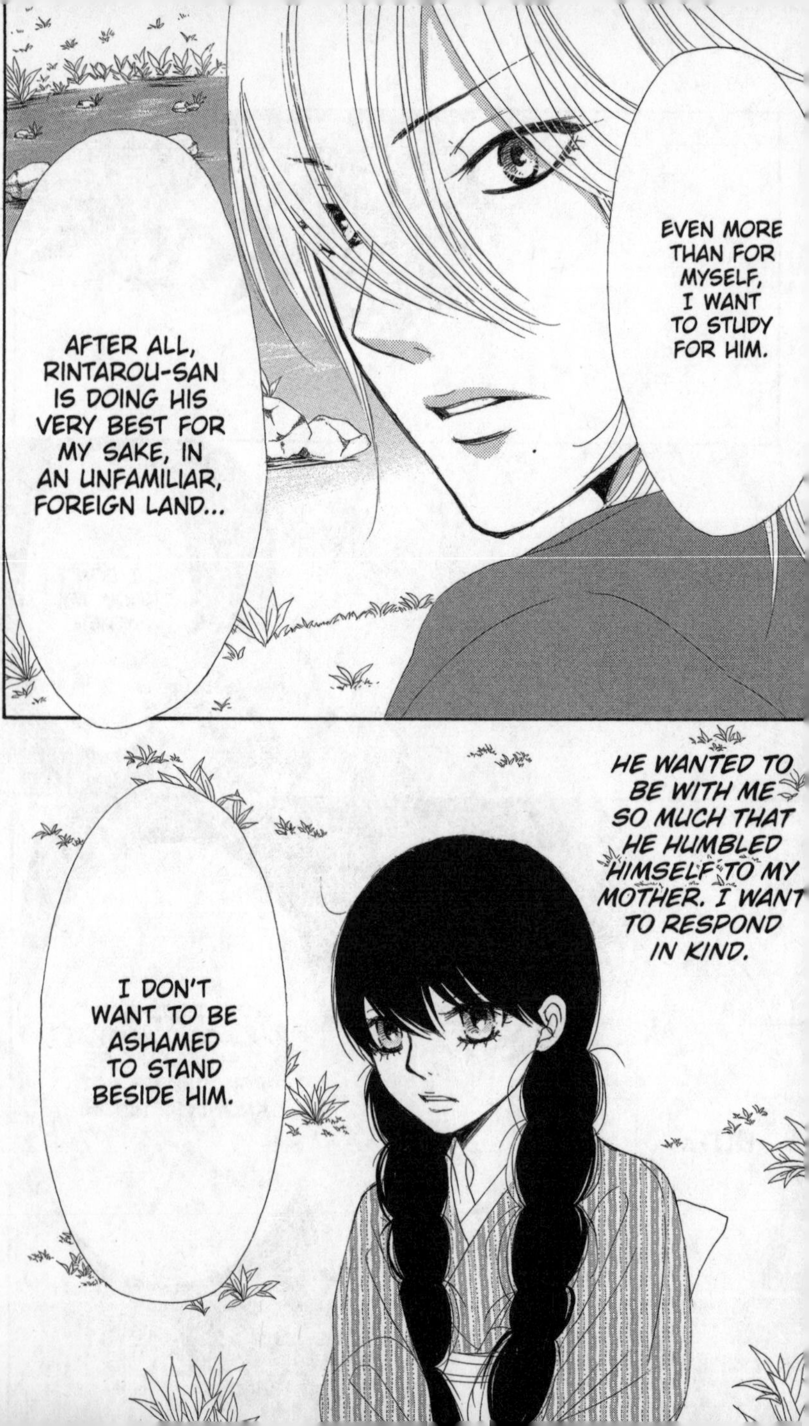
EVEN MORE THAN FOR MYSELF, I WANT TO STUDY FOR HIM.
AFTER ALL, RINTAROU-SAN IS DOING HIS VERY BEST FOR MY SAKE, IN AN UNFAMILIAR, FOREIGN LAND...
HE WANTED TO BE WITH ME SO MUCH THAT HE HUMBLED HIMSELF TO MY MOTHER. I WANT TO RESPOND IN KIND.
I DON'T WANT TO BE ASHAMED TO STAND BESIDE HIM.

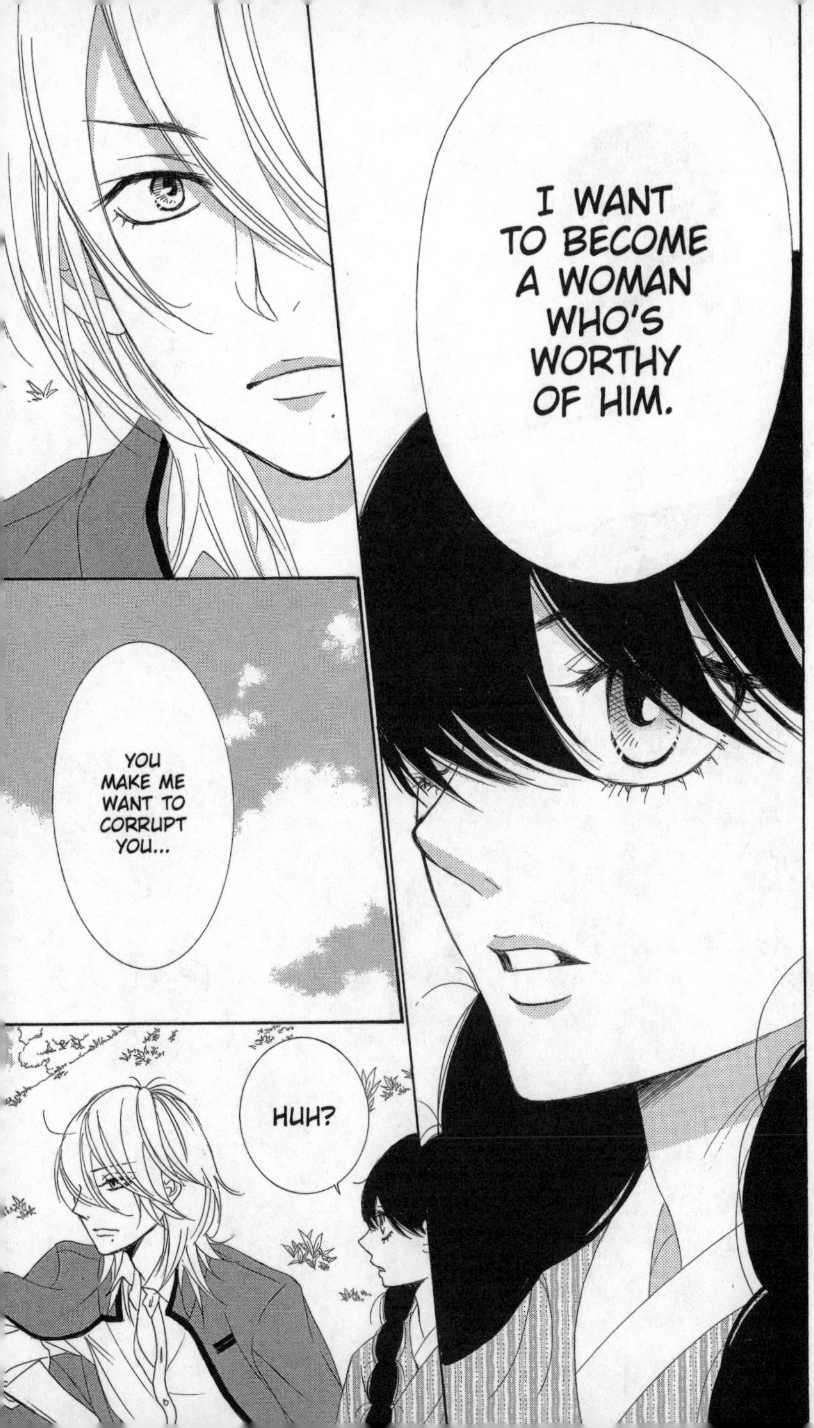
I WANT TO BECOME A WOMAN WHO'S WORTHY OF HIM.
YOU MAKE ME WANT TO CORRUPT YOU...
HUH?

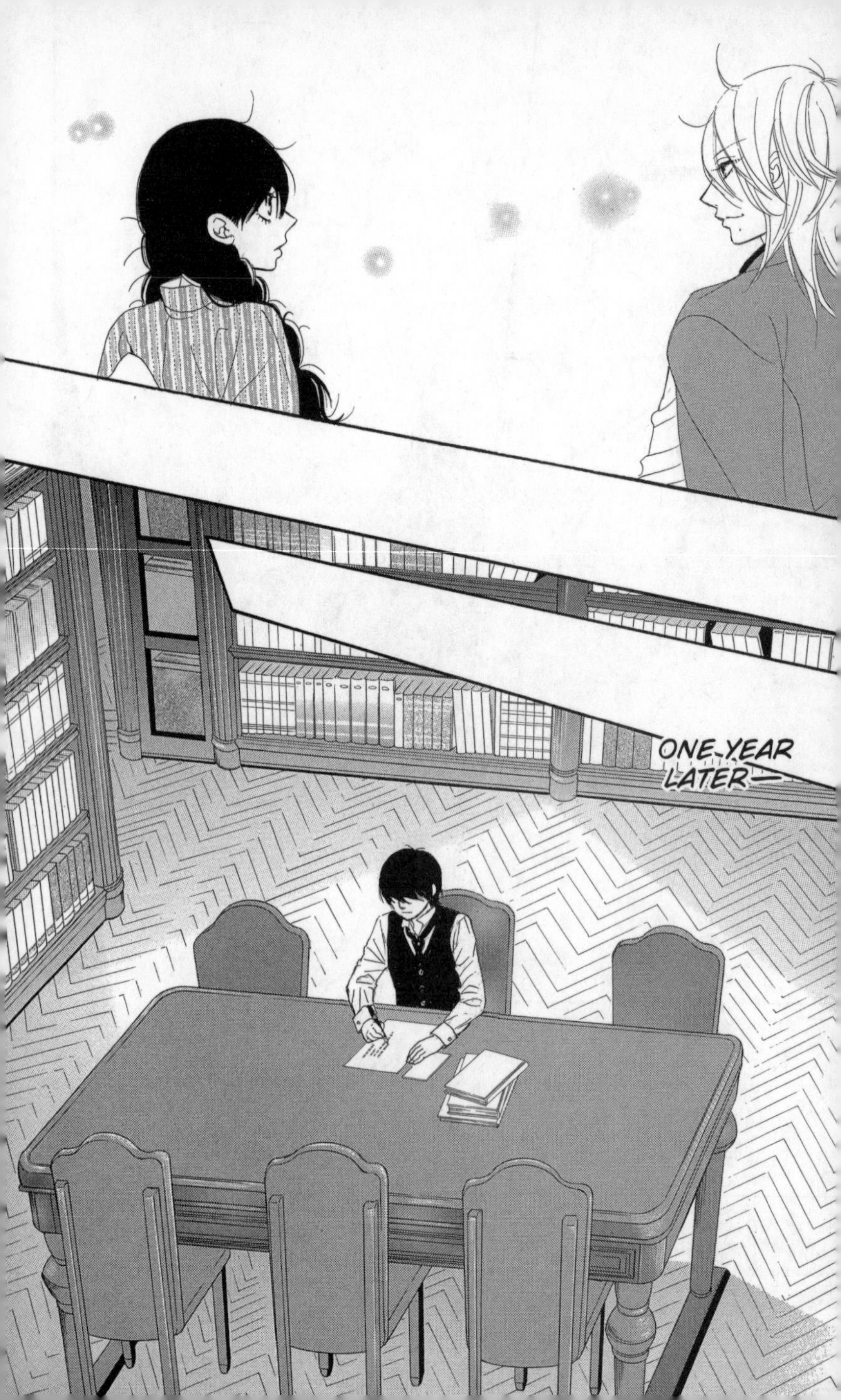
ONE YEAR
LATER—

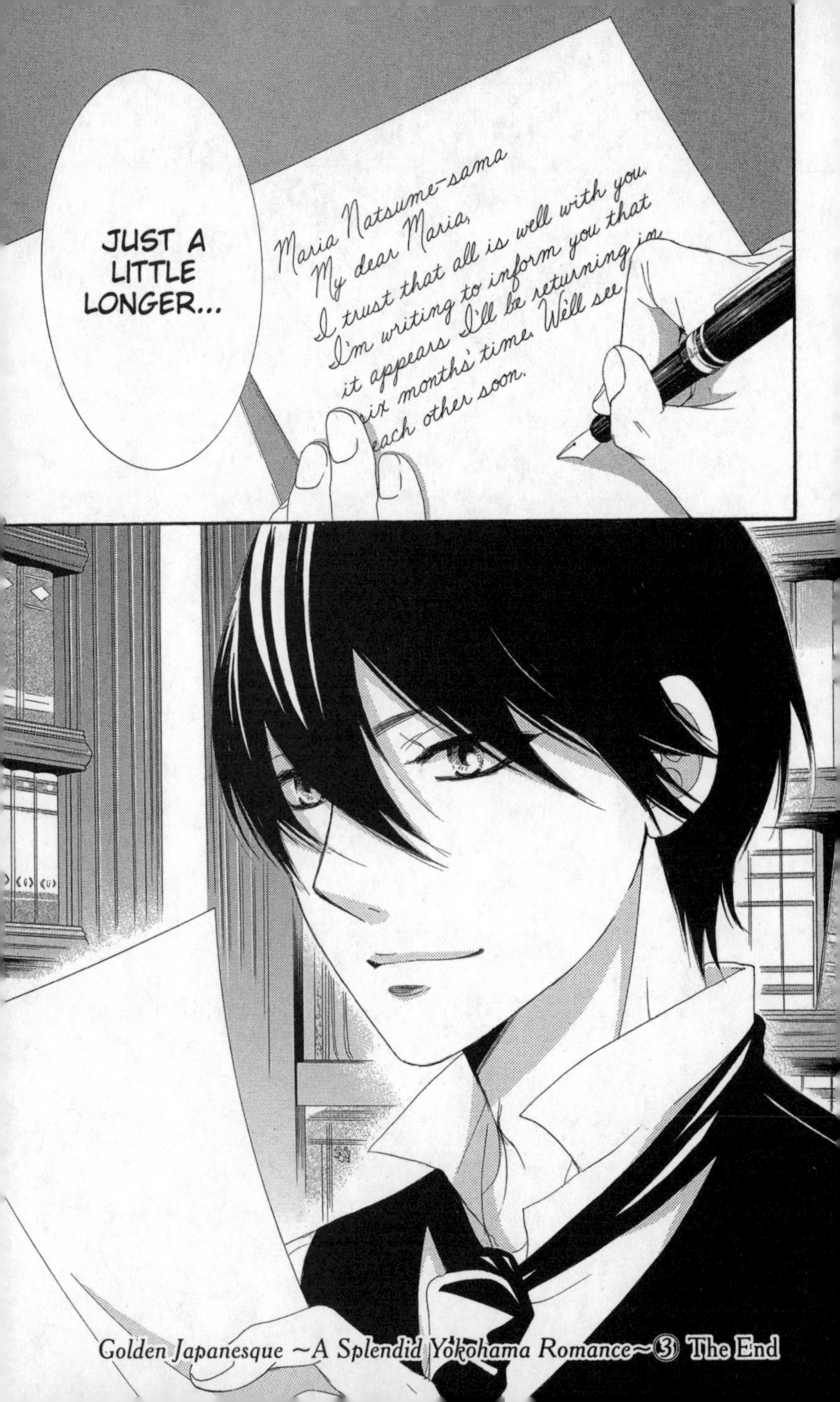
Maria Natsume-sama
My dear Maria,
I trust that all is well with you.
I'm writing to inform you that
it appears I'll be returning in
six months' time. We'll see
each other soon.
JUST A LITTLE LONGER...

Golden Japanesque ~A Splendid Yokohama Romance~ ③ The End

＊Special Thanks＊

■Assistants■

Alice Tsukada
Nozomi Hirama
Ikuko Shiroya
Yuri Sato
T. Sato
R. Nishida

■Editor■
Sanae Morihara

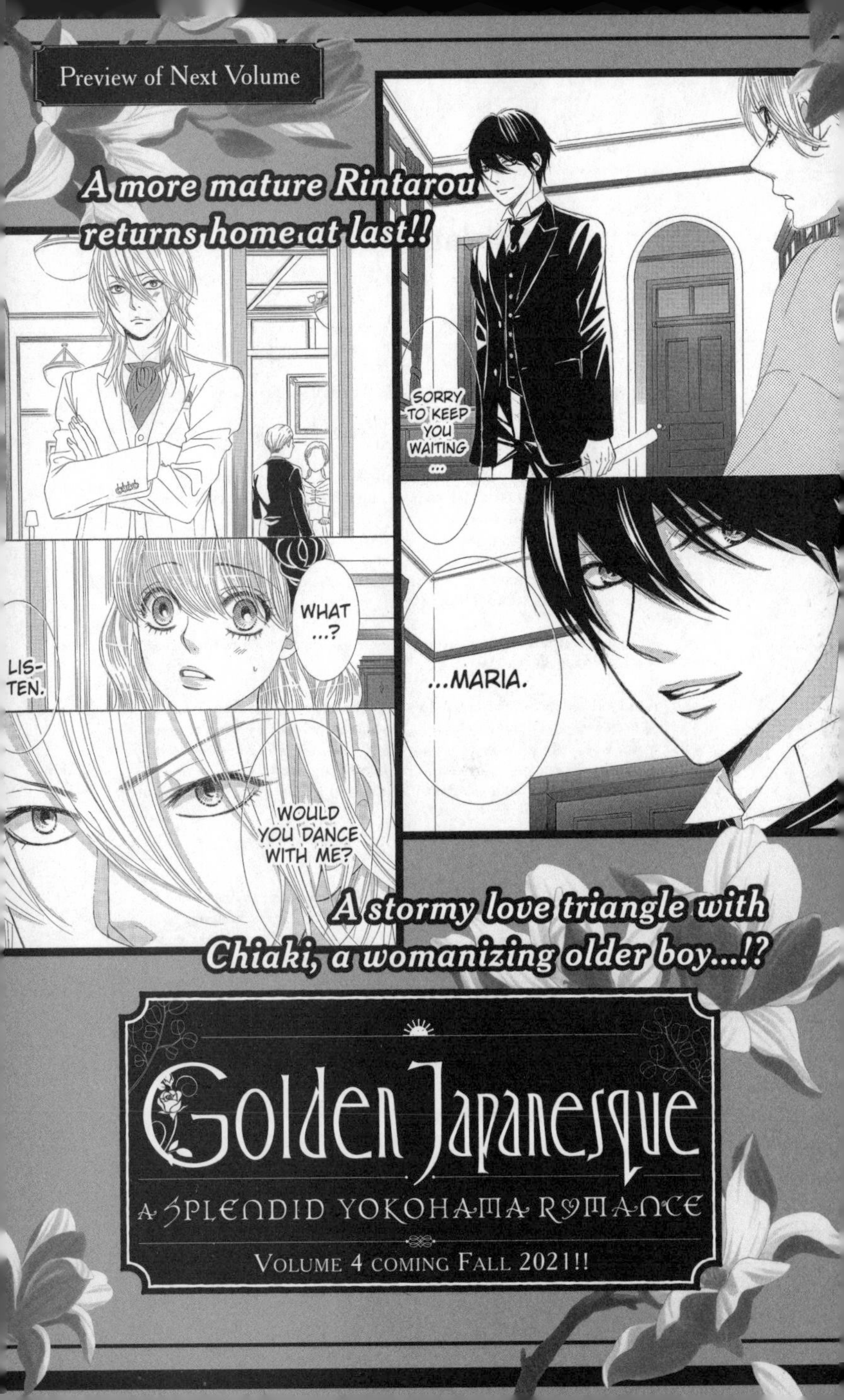
Preview of Next Volume
A more mature Rintarou returns home at last!!
SORRY TO KEEP YOU WAITING ...
...MARIA.
WHAT ...?
LIS-TEN.
WOULD YOU DANCE WITH ME?
A stormy love triangle with Chiaki, a womanizing older boy...!?
Golden Japanesque
A SPLENDID YOKOHAMA ROMANCE
VOLUME 4 COMING FALL 2021!!

Translation Notes

GENERAL

no honorific: Indicates familiarity or closeness; if used without permission or reason, addressing someone in this manner would constitute an insult.

-san: The Japanese equivalent of Mr./Mrs./Miss. If a situation calls for politeness, this is the fail-safe honorific.

-sama: Conveys great respect; may also indicate that the social status of the speaker is lower than that of the addressee.

-shi: An impersonal honorific used in formal speech or writing, e.g., legal documents.

-dono: Roughly equivalent to "master" or "milord."

-kun: Used most often when referring to boys, this indicates affection or familiarity. Occasionally used by older men among their peers, but it may also be used by anyone referring to a person of lower standing.

-chan: An affectionate honorific indicating familiarity used mostly in reference to girls; also used in reference to cute persons or animals of either gender.

-(o)nii/(o)nee: Meaning "big brother"/ "big sister," it can also refer to those older but relatively close in age to the speaker. It can be combined with other honorifics, such as *-san*, *-chan*, or *-sama*.

-senpai: An honorific for describing someone with more immediate seniority, such as an upperclassman or senior club member.

Golden Japanesque is set in the Meiji era, which lasted from 1868 to 1912 and is known as a time of great Western influence in Japan. The era is named after the Meiji emperor, and it coincides with his reign. Referring to a given year in terms of an emperor's reign is typical in Japan—for example, Meiji Year 1 refers to 1868. The Meiji era is followed by Taisho (1912 to 1926), Showa (1926 to 1989), Heisei (1989 to 2019), and Reiwa (2019 to present).

Yokohama Port was opened to foreign trade in 1859.

The Japanese language uses three different sets of characters in writing: *hiragana* and *katakana* (which are akin to alphabets) and *kanji* (Chinese characters). Achieving full literacy in Japanese requires mastering all three, with *kanji* being by far the most complex and difficult. However, it was even more challenging in the Meiji era, as that's when attempts to simplify and formalize the written language had only begun to take place. Prior to then, written and spoken Japanese could also be incredibly different from each other.

PAGE 022

Rice cakes, or *daifuku*, are a bun made of sweet red bean paste wrapped in sweetened mochi (cakes made from rice flour). In this particular variety, the mochi is studded with salted beans.

PAGE 024

Mixed jelly, or *anmitsu*, is a dessert made with small cubes of white agar jelly, sweet red bean paste, soft mochi, and slices of fruits such as peaches, tangerines, pineapples, or cherries, with a sweet brown-sugar syrup poured over the top just before serving.

PAGE 026

Sweet rice dumplings, or *mitarashi dango*, are a snack served on a skewer and coated with a sweetened soy sauce glaze. "*Mitarashi*" technically refers to the glaze.

Kudzu cakes, or *kuzumochi*, are made of kudzu starch, sugar, and water. The texture is about halfway between mochi and gelatin, and they're usually served in squares topped with toasted soy flour (*kinako*) and molasses.

PAGE 106

These are older forms of **kanji** which are still in use, but have been simplified over the years. From right to left, the current forms and translations are: 駅 (train station), 厳 (rock, crag), 芸 (performance), 号 (counter for numbers or editions), 顕 (clarity), 数 (number), 弥 (second character in the Buddha's name), and 炉 (hearth).

PAGE 146

Maria's planning to **"offer"** the rice cake to Rintarou in the same way she'd offer it on the altar of a deceased relative. Rintarou's certainly not dead, and you wouldn't normally do a thing like that for someone who wasn't; however, since she can't physically get the rice cake to him, it may seem like the best method available to her.

A Loner's Worst Nightmare: Human Interaction!

Volumes 1–11 on sale now!

MY YOUTH R♥MANTIC COMEDY iS WRØNG, AS I EXPECTED

Hachiman Hikigaya is a cynic. He believes "youth" is a crock—a sucker's game, an illusion woven from failure and hypocrisy. But when he turns in an essay for a school assignment espousing this view, he's sentenced to work in the Service Club, an organization dedicated to helping students with problems! Worse, the only other member of the club is the haughty Yukino Yukinoshita, a girl with beauty, brains, and the personality of a garbage fire. How will Hachiman the Cynic cope with a job that requires—*gasp!*—social skills?

Check out the manga too!

Light Novel © 2011 Wataru WATARI / SHOGAKUKAN, Illustrations by PONKAN⑧
Manga ©2013 Wataru WATARI, Naomichi IO, Ponkan⑧/SHOGAKUKAN

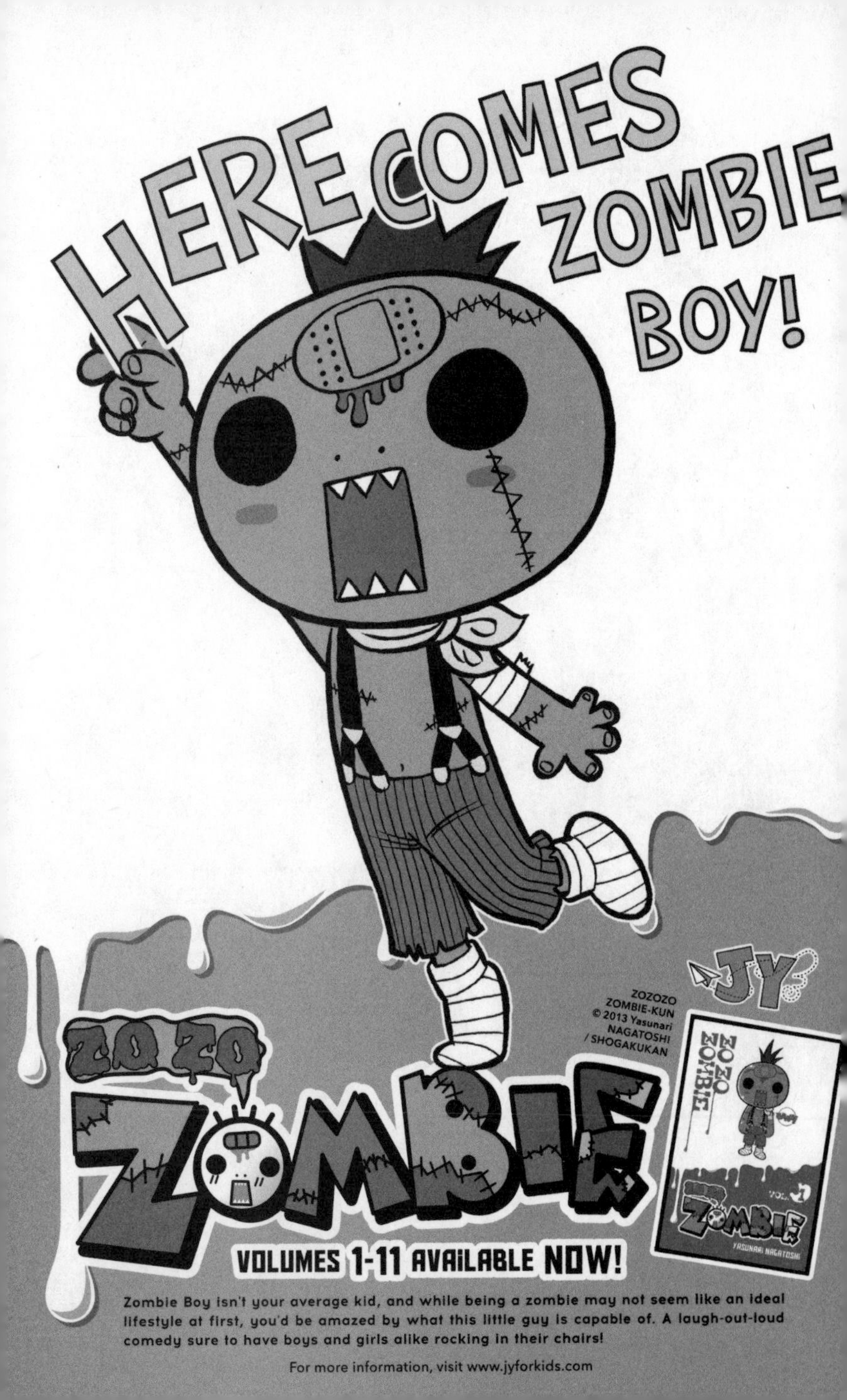
HERE COMES ZOMBIE BOY!
ZOZOZO ZOMBIE-KUN © 2013 Yasunari NAGATOSHI / SHOGAKUKAN
JY
ZO ZO ZOMBIE
VOLUMES 1-11 AVAILABLE NOW!
Zombie Boy isn't your average kid, and while being a zombie may not seem like an ideal lifestyle at first, you'd be amazed by what this little guy is capable of. A laugh-out-loud comedy sure to have boys and girls alike rocking in their chairs!
For more information, visit www.jyforkids.com

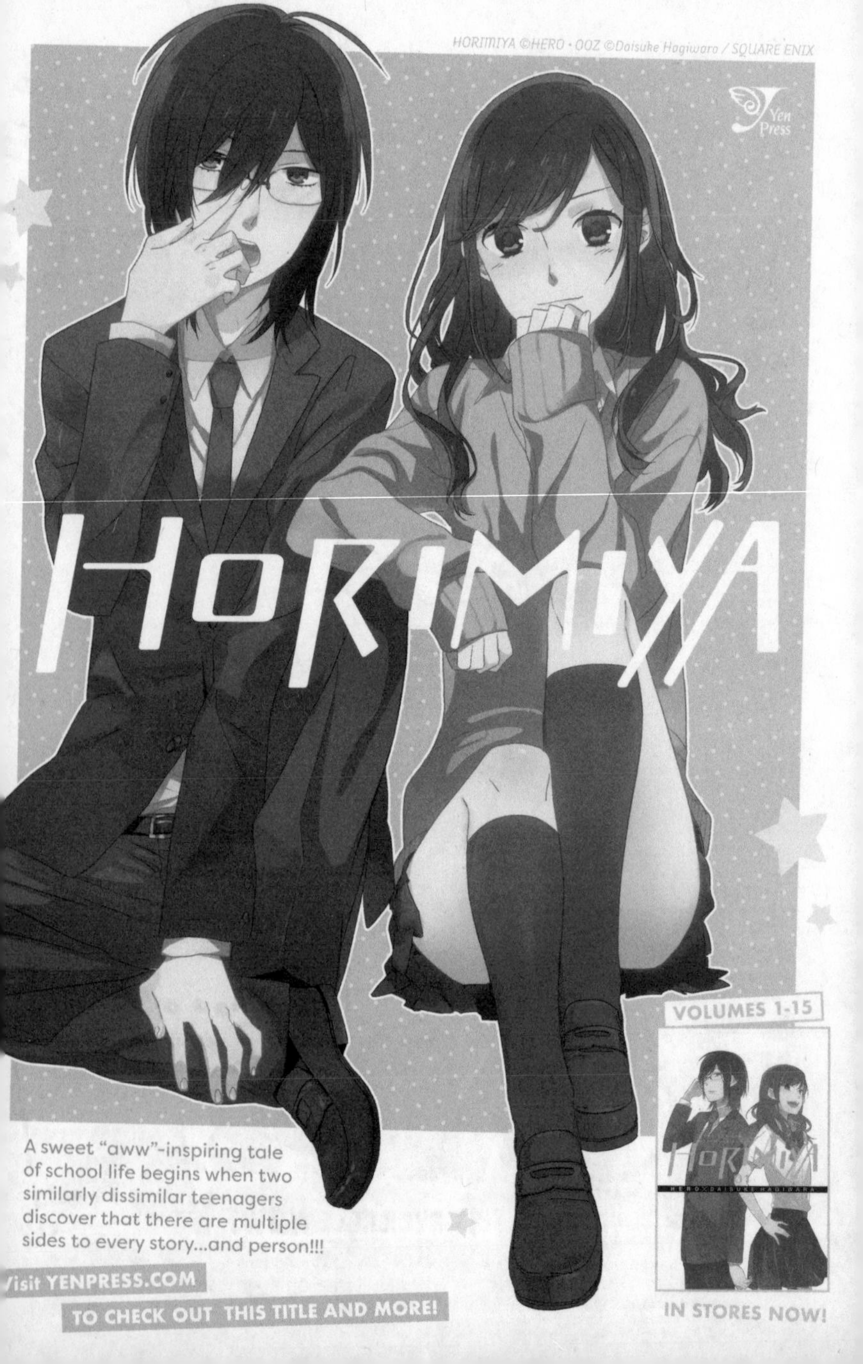

©Aidalro/SQUARE ENIX

Toilet-bound Hanako-Kun

At Kamome Academy, rumors abound about the school's Seven Mysteries, one of which is Hanako-san. Said to occupy the third stall of the third floor girls' bathroom in the old school building, Hanako-san grants any wish when summoned. Nene Yashiro, an occult-loving high school girl who dreams of romance, ventures into this haunted bathroom...but the Hanako-san she meets there is nothing like she imagined! Kamome Academy's Hanako-san...is a boy!

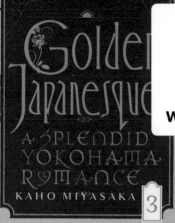

Golden
Japanesque
A SPLENDID
YOKOHAMA·
ROMANCE

KAHO MIYASAKA

3

Translation:
TAYLOR ENGEL

Lettering:
LYS BLAKESLEE

Original Japanese edition published by SHOGAKUKAN.
English translation rights in the United States of America,
Canada, the United Kingdom, Ireland, Australia and
New Zealand arranged with SHOGAKUKAN through
Tuttle-Mori Agency, Inc.

English translation © 2021 by Yen Press, LLC

Yen Press
150 West 30th Street, 19th Floor
New York, NY 10001

Visit us at yenpress.com 🌸
        facebook.com/yenpress 🌸
        twitter.com/yenpress 🌸
        yenpress.tumblr.com 🌸
        instagram.com/yenpress 🌸

First Yen Press Edition: July 2021

Yen Press is an imprint of Yen Press, LLC.
The Yen Press name and logo are trademarks
of Yen Press, LLC.

The publisher is not responsible for websites (or their
content) that are not owned by the publisher.

Library of Congress Control Number:
2020948881

ISBNs: 978-1-9753-1979-3 (print)
       978-1-9753-2415-5 (ebook)

10 9 8 7 6 5 4 3 2 1

BVG

Printed in the United States of America